ASKING ANGELA MACNAMARA

An Intimate History of Irish Lives

Paul Ryan

IRISH ACADEMIC PRESS
DUBLIN • PORTLAND, OR

First published in 2012 by Irish Academic Press

2 Brookside,
Dundrum Road,
Dublin 14, Ireland

920 NE 58th Avenue, Suite 300
Portland, Oregon,
97213-3786, USA

© Paul Ryan 2012

www.iap.ie

British Library Cataloguing in Publication Data
An entry can be found on request

ISBN 978 0 7165 3038 1 (cloth)
ISBN 978 0 7165 3039 8 (paper)

Library of Congress Cataloging-in-Publication Data
An entry can be found on request

Printed by Good News Digital Books, Ongar, Essex

In memory of my grandmother, Margaret O'Grady

Contents

Acknowledgements

This book was completed while I was an Irish Research Council for the Humanities and Social Science (IRCHSS) postdoctoral research fellow in the Department of Sociology at NUI Maynooth (NUIM). I would like to express my gratitude to the IRCHSS for their support. I would like to thank my colleagues in the Department of Sociology, particularly Sean Ó'Riain and Jane Gray, and the National Institute for Regional Spatial Analysis (NIRSA) who provided administrative support during the fellowship.

I am grateful to the staff at the National Library; to Teresa Whitington and Peter Costello at the Catholic Central Library for their assistance; and to Hugh Ryan and Mary Kenny for talking with me. To the men who agreed to be interviewed and whose stories are so central to this book I am very grateful.

Earlier versions of two chapters have been published elsewhere. Chapter 4 is an expanded and modified version of 'Love, Lust and the Irish: Exploring Intimate Lives through Angela Macnamara's Problem Page' which was published in *Sexualities*, 14, 2 (2011), pp.218–34. Chapter 7 is a revised version of 'Asking Angela: Discourses about Sexuality in an Irish Problem Page, 1963–80', which appeared in the *Journal of the History of Sexuality*, 19, 2 (2010), pp.317–39.

I would like to thank Lisa Hyde and the staff at Irish Academic Press for their encouragement and support for the book at every stage of the process. I would also like to thank those who read chapters and provided detailed comments – Tom Inglis, Rebecca King Ó'Riain, Betty Hilliard, Angela Macnamara, Aileen O'Carroll, Katie Baird and Vern Power. Finally, I would like to thank those closest to me – my family, my friends and my partner.

This book is dedicated to the memory of an extraordinary woman, my grandmother Margaret O'Grady.

Paul Ryan
Dublin

CHAPTER ONE

The Informalization of Emotional Life

I was diagnosed with bowel cancer in April 2009. In the following days it quickly became apparent that I would have great difficulty in communicating my diagnosis to those closest to me. The problem, if that is what it was, saw me unable to retell my story – of a tumour being found and the chemotherapy that would follow – without crying. It necessitated a Herculean effort on my part to remain calm, rational and focused on the challenge ahead whilst denying the rising wave of fear and anxiety that was sweeping through me. I was praised for my calmness and my optimism. The decision to keep that door as tightly closed as possible was, I thought, in my best interest and certainly in the best interests of those around me. When I had time to prepare and compose I told the story with a stoic optimism, highlighting the early diagnosis and the almost routine nature of the treatment. Other times, when caught off guard by a phone call or a chance encounter, I would invariably break down. I even resorted to cowardly emailing a friend with the news to avoid *that* conversation. I was embarrassed by my public displays of emotion and the response it invoked in others. Furthermore, I was baffled by my own embarrassment and wondered whether I was missing some crucial piece of emotional DNA. Marie Reck, writing of her diagnosis of breast cancer in *The Irish Times* health supplement, described how she 'went home, sat in the garden and cried with all my family around me'.[1] It would seem the appropriate response. I wasn't the only one that behaved oddly. Some responded to the news of my illness with a deathly silence or a torrent of good cheer under which I was left struggling to communicate the real fear of treatment, of recurrence, of death. Some were steadfast in their support while other more casual acquaintances faded away. This book isn't a story about cancer. It *is* a story about how we communicate the most intimate part of our lives to those we hold closest.

While pondering my own inability to express emotion in the face of my diagnosis, I remained intrigued at the ease with which others spoke emotionally or spontaneously broke down in tears. While receiving chemotherapy treatment and often too tired to leave the sofa, I would indulge in numerous downloaded episodes of 'Australian MasterChef', where grown men would regularly break down when their soufflés didn't rise or when they eventually failed a culinary task and were asked to leave the show. Even when the contestants were successful, more tears would flow. The situation may not be very different in Ireland. In September 2008 the publication of *The Irish Times*/Behaviour and Attitudes survey revealed that a majority of men (58 per cent) think it is now acceptable for men to cry in public.[2] Whether there was an appropriate social context for this emotion remained unclear.

I was writing this book at the time of my diagnosis and treatment. I set out to explore how a dominant narrative of Irish masculinity had contributed to an understanding of Irish men as unemotional, unromantic and lacking intimacy within society. This view of Irish men was most clearly articulated through the letters that women sent to Angela Macnamara's problem page in *The Sunday Press* newspaper over a seventeen-year period. The women wrote movingly of relationships defined by sex rather than sexual intimacy, and of emotional coldness rather than self-disclosure. I was conducting life history interviews with men who spoke about their experiences of a transformation in the world of dating, marriage and sexuality in a rapidly changing Ireland. Used in conjunction with the analysis of the letters, a more complete picture of this time could be constructed. The assumption, though I was challenging it, was that older Irish men would have great difficulty in talking openly about the emotional dimension of their lives. I was motivated by my belief that although the stories of men's public lives had been told in Ireland, there was a missing piece to the story. While men were slow in coming forward to participate in the study, those who did spoke openly about the difficulties in navigating an intimate world where the expectations of men were changing. These men, the oldest being 75 years old, struggled to become proficient in a new language of intimacy and self-disclosure but their stories, used throughout this book, reveal men who were simultaneously romantic yet emotionally austere.

I firmly believed, however, that I was proficient in this language of intimacy. As a sociologist I had taught and researched issues such as sexuality and masculinity. I had written journal articles that argued for an increased role for intellectual autobiography within research practice.[3] I had thought that I epitomized a more modern male – more open, affectionate, tactile and emotional. My experiences of my own illness revealed I was comfortable with everybody's emotions bar my own. It was a revelation that would find voice again throughout the writing of the book. The possession of a language in which to speak proficiently in the art of emotion did not make one more likely to use it, or illustrate any greater emancipation in the field of intimacy. Similarly, a life lived in the 1960s did not necessarily bestow greater or lesser emotional prowess than a life lived in earlier decades. While I am not suggesting that the manner in which people speak about their intimate lives is divorced from their social and historical contexts – it certainly is – I am arguing that great limitations exist in how this era of twentieth-century Irish history is divided up and labelled as 'traditional' or 'modern'.

PUBLIC AND PRIVATE MORALITIES

This book maps a change in how Irish men and women conducted their intimate lives. The manner in which dating couples interacted with each other in the dancehall, in the darkness of the cinema or down country lanes began to change in the 1960s. The manner in which married couples communicated their need for love, affection and sex changed also. Irish people slowly turned away from understanding their intimate lives through the framework of Catholic social teaching and started listening to new voices on the radio, on television and in newspapers. These voices told a different story. They spoke of the importance of sex, equality and emotional self-disclosure in married life. They encouraged independence and self-development, particularly amongst women. The transition provoked anxiety for conservative Catholics who struggled to see their bodies less as conduits of sin and more as instruments of pleasure.

These people turned for advice to one of their own: a young, devout Catholic mother called Angela Macnamara who had been advising people since 1960 on how to negotiate themselves around the changing range of intimacies now deemed permissible between dating couples. Her career as an agony aunt began when, aged 32, she wrote a series of articles to *The Sunday Press* on teenage dating. Such was the response that she was invited by the editor to reply. In 1963 she began writing a weekly column. Angela Macnamara's column received 4,000 letters a year in *The Sunday Press* newspaper.[4] She published a handful of replies in her column each week but wrote privately to hundreds of other correspondents every month. With a peak circulation of 400,000 copies a week, *The Sunday Press* was the most popular Sunday newspaper in the country. It was launched in 1949 and was critical of the growing popularity of British Sunday newspapers that were believed to be alien to the Irish character.[5] It was part of the Irish Press Group, first published in 1931, and had closely allied itself to the cause of Irish nationalism, the promotion of the Irish language and coverage of Gaelic games which had received scant coverage by other competing newspaper groups. It promoted a vision of Ireland built on a romantic notion of the respective roles of men and women in Irish society, enshrined in the constitution and articulated most cogently in de Valera's 1943 St Patrick's Day broadcast – 'The Ireland we dreamed of where "sturdy children" and "happy maidens" inhabited the countryside'.[6] It was an Ireland that now bore little resemblance to the reality of people's everyday lives.

Angela Macnamara adjudicated over moral quandaries, often where the letter writer was torn between an internalized sense of guilt about sexual experimentation and the desire to experiment, encouraged by boyfriends, peers and wider media messages (Chapter 3). She often advised confession or alternative reparation that would return the person to more traditional moral boundaries. Married couples wrote too, anxious to benefit from a more relaxed intimate culture that could transform their sex lives from the procreative duty that they had become to a source of mutual pleasure which strengthened their relationship (Chapter 4). Parents wrote anxiously, fearing that a new climate of increased wealth and opportunity had overindulged their children, contributing to a perception that they had become disobedient – defying their parents' authority on matters of religion, morality and career choice (Chapter 5). Parents were challenged on whether corporal punishment remained an appropriate form of discipline for children, often as old as 19 years of age. This new open and informal culture allowed other Catholics who had been marginalized and condemned by their Church to speak out. Gay men and their families wrote to Angela Macnamara, often confused and anxious about the sinfulness of their sexuality and seeking solutions so that they might be reconciled with their faith (Chapter 6). Other gay men had already questioned the Church's authority over their private intimate lives and sought no such approval or reconciliation.

Those who wrote to or read the column were representative of a specific constituency of readers who believed and followed the teachings of the Catholic Church. Cas Wouters argues that within processes of emancipation of sexuality there are different groups, and different tempos at which it occurs. He identifies more conservative groups – for example, the readers of the Macnamara column – as 'trend followers'.[7] Compared to radicals or moderates who are open to greater levels of sexual experimentation, for trend followers there is little exploration of sexuality, where a desire for stability, predictability and observing the sexual 'do's and don'ts' remain paramount. The discussion of a wider spectrum of sexual desire encourages not emancipation but great anxiety among trend followers or traditionalists, who remain slow to adapt to a new sexual culture but who eventually do adapt. Although *The Sunday Press* was read throughout the country, Macnamara recognizes that the majority of her letters were from people living in rural areas, suggesting that there 'was more openness in the cities and more in the way of magazines ... in the cities that people bought and learned from'. These rural readers were also the most forthright in their criticism of the column if, as Macnamara describes, she was perceived as 'stepping away from my responsibility if I didn't take that [view] exclusively'.

Angela Macnamara carved a unique niche for herself as an expert in the field of love, dating and marriage. She was part of the new openness with which intimate relationships were discussed on the airwaves and in newspapers. She advocated a more open discussion about sexuality. It was not a discussion that was welcomed by all. The elevation of a lay woman to such a prominent position and the subject material of the column were initially viewed with suspicion by the Catholic Church and by some readers. Talking about sexuality was seen to be dangerous. Angela Macnamara believed that by giving sexual education within an appropriate moral context – rather than destroying the innocence of children, of which she was accused – would enable young people to make the right and appropriate choices in their intimate lives. In contrast, others, including the Catholic Church, believed that it was the cloak of secrecy, ignorance and fear that contributed to the unwillingness of young people to engage in sexual experimentation. Readers were already availing themselves of a wider range of expert literature on sexuality and relationships, most of which was contrary to the Catholic Church's position. Angela Macnamara struggled to refute alternative explanations of moral issues such as contraception, masturbation and homosexuality and to restate the Church's position. This became increasingly difficult after the publication in 1968 of *Humanae Vitae*, which confirmed the Church's opposition to contraception and, in the process, alienated moderate Catholics who now questioned this jurisdiction over their sexual lives. Macnamara brought an even wider discussion of terminology into the public sphere. Talking about sex and intimacy had come out of the darkness of the confessional and into the living rooms of Irish families. By attempting to solve personal problems, people were also reconstructing the social context of those problems. Or, in the words of C. Wright Mills, these intimate problems now became 'public issues'.[8]

This book is based upon the analysis of 645 letters and replies published in the Angela Macnamara column. The letters, like all documents, reveal only a partial analysis of a social phenomenon. The letters were subject to an editorial censorship that excluded letters about intimate sexual problems and homosexuality, especially during the early 1960s. The column reflected the conservatism of the newspaper's owners and ethos. Letters were also edited by Macnamara to fill the available space in the column. I was sensitive to what extent documents such as the problem page claimed an authoritative status, and to the implications of this on the relationship between their production (authorship) and consumption (readership).[9] When questioned, Macnamara often declared, after consultation with 'experts' (usually religious), that her reply was simply the 'truth'. The publication of letters that revealed sexual ignorance or supported the Catholic Church's social teaching on contraception, divorce and especially sex before marriage sparked some speculation amongst Dublin's liberal elite about the authenticity of the letters. This book does not rely exclusively on the letters. The column is located within a body of literature that advised Catholics, including Macnamara herself, on dating and marriage. The columns are compared and contrasted with other articles in *The Sunday Press* and other problem pages of the era and are understood and analyzed in the light of interviews with Macnamara. The letters are also analyzed in conjunction with a series of life history interviews that I conducted with men who read the Angela Macnamara column. These interviews are central to the overall understanding of intimate life in the book. While the letters were predominantly by women and speak of their difficulties in managing intimate relationships with men, the interviews provide a valuable and all too infrequent means for men to explain how they understood themselves to be romantic and emotional within relationships. These men were from both urban and rural areas of Ireland and contacted me through a series of newspaper advertisements which I posted, seeking men who had read Macnamara's column to participate in the research.

The advice column or problem page is not a recent historical phenomenon. It is attributed to Englishman John Dunton, editor of the *Athenian Gazette* in 1691. It marked the emergence of a unique form of audience participation in publications that addressed lofty concerns such as slavery and the mystery of creation. Robin Kent argues that subsequent publications like *The British Apollo* and *The Review* moved the focus of the advice column into the area of personal morality where agony aunts became advocates of Victorian moral values opposing premarital sex, sex after menopause and divorce.[10] By the mid-eighteenth century, after the success of columnists such as Mrs Eliza Haywood, the reading public had come to expect a woman to hold the position of advice columnist, with many male editors donning female personas. From these positions the editors, such as Gordon Stables in *Boys' Own Paper*, could still obsess about declining Victorian morality and the scourge of adolescent sexuality – masturbation. The Education Act of 1833 contributed to raising the levels of literacy, moving the advice column from an almost exclusively middle-class readership to a more diverse one. The emphasis on morality would remain; however, the columns became increasingly specialized in areas of health, beauty and personal problems at the turn of the twentieth century. In the aftermath of the Second World War, British problem pages were inundated with women seeking husbands, companionship and a desire for domesticity after the calamity of war. A similar crisis existed in Ireland for very different reasons. There was a widespread concern at the falling population brought about through a combination of emigration and an extreme caution and unwillingness to marry shown by many men and women. This unwillingness was largely economic, with parents refusing to hand over property to their sons until their old age. By that time, bachelors had often become unable to compete for brides with younger men, while women themselves often emigrated due to a lack of economic or marital prospects at home. An increasing number of men and women turned to newspaper lonely-heart advertisements in publications such as *Ireland's Own* and to the Knock Marriage Bureau to find suitable mates. The Knock Marriage Bureau was established in 1968. It was renamed the Knock Introductory Bureau and claimed in 2006 that it had facilitated 841 marriages.[11]

LONG-TERM PROCESSES OF SOCIAL CHANGE

Viewing the body and its sexual behaviour as shameful is a recent historical phenomenon. Norbert Elias identified a civilizing process between the fifteenth and nineteenth centuries in which manners and the relationship between the sexes became increasingly more formalized.[12] Elias focused on how bodily functions – such as eating, urination, defecation and spitting – and more intimate relationships within the bedroom all underwent a process of change. The result was a greater requirement of individuals to monitor and control their behaviour in the company of others. Starting with the upper classes, new standards at the dinner table and in the bedroom required greater levels of emotion management and consequently greater levels of shame and embarrass- ment. Elias dismissed reasons such as the demands of greater hygiene or health, since these civilizing tendencies occurred prior to a rise in such concerns. Elias connects these tendencies at the level of the individual to larger-scale transformations in the social structure, where the emer- gence of new classes and a decline in violence brought greater levels of interdependence and encouraged an associated consideration for others.

Norbert Elias argued that feelings of shame and embarrassment around sexual relations increased as part of the civilizing process.[13] This had be- come clearly evident later in history, in the difficulty with which adults spoke to children about sexuality. This difficulty was present within the Angela Macnamara column too, although the relaxation in talking about sexuality placed greater pressure on parents to engage in more open discussion with their children about the facts of life (Chapter 5). Elias explained that prior to the civilizing process, children, although subservient, had remained within the adult world.[14] Children dressed like adults. Adults would have made little effort to conceal their sexual behaviour or discussion from children, reducing the gap between the emotional and behavioural standards of adults and children. Little secrecy existed within the small living quarters of both adults and children.

Sexual relations were removed from public view. Elias wrote that 'in the civilizing process, sexuality too is increasingly removed behind the scenes and enclosed in particular enclave, the nuclear family'.[15] Sexual relations become surrounded by a wall of embarrassment. The sexual drive itself is also subject to greater control where adults are pressurized to privatize their impulses. Silence and secrecy descends as adolescents are imbued with the same restraint and control as adults who are unable to formulate the words to speak openly to their children about sexuality.[16]

Change occurs with the nuclear family too. Elias describes how it was not until the sixteenth century that an embarrassment became attached to a husband's extramarital affairs; until then, children born outside marriage were happily raised alongside those born within it.[17] As a result of a changing balancing of power between men and women in court societies, the extramarital relationships of women were also given a limited toleration in the seventeenth and eighteenth centuries.[18] Thus, while the civilizing process brought more restraint and control, it also offered opportunities for liberation.[19] Such liberation was grounded upon an expectation of self-control and restraint on the behalf of others which became an almost automatic response. Elias used the example of bathing costumes to illustrate how styles of dress could only have evolved when men and women were 'absolutely sure that each individual is curbed by self-control and a strict code of etiquette'.[20] The impact of the civilizing process on the lives of others was a greater split between intimate and public spheres. Sociology has remained less interested in intimate lives, with Anthony Giddens speculating that it is because they are 'less visible' than transformations in the public sphere.[21] This book redresses this balance, with the problem page offering a rare glimpse inside the intimate lives of the Irish.

BODILY SHAME AND INTIMATE LIFE

Studies of the Irish family confirm that such a legacy of shame and guilt had a devastating effect on the intimate lives of Irish Catholics. This work has contributed to an understanding of the Irish as somehow unique in regard to their sexual and emotional ineptness, a contention that I later challenge in this book. Studies have revealed that the inability of both men and women to disclose an emotional self within an intimate relationship led to high levels of dysfunction in romantic, parenting and sexual encounters. Nancy Scheper-Hughes, in her study of mental illness in rural Ireland, claimed that the body was more a site of fasting, penance and denial than a means of expressing and experiencing sexual pleasure.[22] Adults routinely referred to 'decent' and 'indecent' parts of the body.[23] She sees the devotion to Matt Talbot, a Catholic man who became an icon of the temperance movement in Ireland, as epitomizing the disdain in which the body was often held. After his death in 1925, Talbot's body revealed heavy chains wrapped around it to inflict self-harm as he moved.[24] Sexual and intimate relationships were fraught with difficulty as a result of such a negative understanding of the body. Scheper-Hughes paints a depressing picture, revealing a community where love was not a prerequisite to marriage and where men were 'awkward with women, troubled by sexuality'.[25] Married couples showed no outward affection for each other, often not even using each other's first name, and Scheper-Hughes concludes that it was socialization that led to the 'early orientation towards emotional distance and "sexual flatness" '.[26] Catholic sex educationalists John and Mary Ryan, writing in 1968, also described this cultural and religious legacy which has made us 'distrust and dislike our bodies', seeing the sexual organs as either 'bad' or 'holy' parts of the body.[27]

It was Conrad Arensberg and Solon Kimball's study of Irish family life, some thirty years before Scheper-Hughes, that has cast the longest and most influential shadow over a generation of work in this field.[28] It revealed that the needs of the rural economy dictated how men and women experienced sexuality, with a requirement for heirs and the needs of inheritance ranking far higher than the desires of the body or heart. Men were deemed to have lower sexual standards and were likely to lead girls astray. Arensberg and Kimball found that discussion about sexuality was confined to the 'laughter and hearty guffaws with which references of near any kind to sexual intercourse, sexual attraction and childbearing were greeted'.[29]

J.C. Messenger's study of an island community in the 1960s revealed that a common belief found amongst men was that a good woman did not enjoy sex, while the 'marriageable man ... is usually repressed to an unbelievable degree'.[30] The relationships between family members were also problematic, with Messenger speculating that the close mother/son relationship contributed to a Freudian scenario in which men avoided foreplay and the female breast, and frequently rejected women after sex.[31] For the women to whom Dorine Rohan spoke there was little appetite for or expectation of sexual satisfaction within marriage.[32] For men there was little hope that they could provide that satisfaction, with widespread ignorance of the female orgasm reported by men, although they most often complained about their wives' lack of interest in sex. Both sexes were limited in their exploration of sex within marriage, due to their inhibitions and a sense of an internalized shamefulness.

Authors such as Caitriona Clear are critical of this standard telling of the history of mid-twentieth-century Ireland, which lumps together a few anthropological studies and contributes to a narrative that positions women as 'completely powerless and silenced' during that period.[33] These studies remain the principle signposts by which scholars navigate themselves around our understanding of family life. Men are similarly positioned as patriarchal autocrats, and subsequent work, including my own, seeks to find other nuances in this one-dimensional story.

Whatever the underlying causes, the stage was set for often difficult courtships and married lives in which men and women were driven by desire but restrained by ignorance, guilt and a fear of such occasions of sin. What is significant is that thousands of people wrote to columns like Angela Macnamara's and availed themselves of a wide range of expert advice that gave them information and attempted to solve their relationship problems.

INFORMALIZATION

While the formalization of manners identified by Norbert Elias reached its height in the Victorian era, a slow process of informalization emerged in the twentieth century. Building on the work of Elias, Dutch sociologist Cas Wouters identifies a trend of growing permissiveness in the 1960s and 1970s when previous behaviours once frowned upon now became more socially accepted.[34] An informalization occurred in the rules of social conduct, leading to an emancipation of the emotional life of individuals, specifically in matters of sexuality. Greater freedom was expressed by people in their clothes, dancing, music and hairstyles, all of which find their way into Angela Macnamara's column where they become fault lines of intergenerational conflict.[35] While there was a decline in the regulation of how people conducted their lives there were also new rules of engagement with others, which stressed self-restraint and tolerated conflict, but only in a controlled manner. Greater inter-dependence within society brought social groups together in a way which was unfamiliar, reducing the social and psychic distance between people. Racial and class barriers between people started to be dismantled. Codes of manners acted as invisible barriers, granting and refusing access to the higher orders. The dangers of becoming *too* familiar with people were warned against in the manners books of the nineteenth and early twentieth centuries; such warnings disappear after the 1950s.[36] Wouters argues that the greater use of first names in social introductions and the spread of social kissing in the 1960s between people of only the briefest acquaintance were indicative of a greater intimacy and familiarity.[37]

Relations between the sexes were also part of this informalization. Cas Wouters argued that codes of manners and emotions changed between men and women in both dating and married relationships. Studying manners books since 1890 from four countries (the United States, Britain, Germany and the Netherlands), Wouters argues that all underwent long-term processes of informalization. These processes manifested themselves particularly in public disquiet in the 1920s at new forms of dancing that dispensed with the formality of the past and encouraged a more individualized, more limber use of the body.[38] Within courtship the decline of chaperonage at the turn of the twentieth century also signalled greater freedom for women from an intrusive external control over their behaviour.[39] Wouters's study illustrates how women successfully moved themselves out of the private domain and into the world of work and leisure, unhindered by this system of chaperones. Now the dating couple would have to chaperone and monitor their own behaviour, opening the door to a growing hysteria about increased 'necking' and 'petting' on dates or between couples now declared to be 'going steady'. Informalization brought a relaxation of manners, etiquette and deference towards elders and authority figures, a process which accelerated in the 1960s as the social and psychic gap between groups narrowed. Discussion and practice of premarital sex, unmarried cohabitation, homosexuality and pornography were all part of this wider informalization. This may have led to a more equal interdependence between the sexes, but this shift from the external supervision of behaviour within social life to a more internalized one also brought with it an expectation of restraint and self-control.

Cas Wouters also uses the concept of the love/lust balance to explore this shift in how men and women understood and acted upon this new regime governing their intimate lives. As traditionally defined, men were located at the lust end of this spectrum while women, predictably, were found on the love side. Wouters is interested in charting the move from a traditional lust balance to a situation where women more openly discussed their need for a more satisfying interplay between love, affection and sex in their relationships.[40] Using data from the Dutch women's magazine *Opzij*, Wouters shows how women sought a more satisfying love/lust balance, leading to a 'liberation' in sexuality, but this was followed by a formalization of attitudes in the 1980s. Crucially, as Wouters admits, men's reactions to these processes were not included because no comparable men's magazine existed.[41] Brinkgreve and Korzec carried out the first empirical study into the process of informalization.[42] Through the use of the advice column in the Dutch women's magazine *Magriet*, they studied the changing trends in advice and what these revealed about the power relationships between men and women, and between parents and children. As the women's movement progressed and women became more financially independent of men, the balance of power with men became more equal, thus having consequences for intimate relationships between the sexes.

I refer to Wouters's work throughout all the chapters of this book. The comparative nature of his work allows us to place changes in this love/lust balance in Ireland within a broader international context. It facilitates a greater understanding of how sexuality in Ireland slowly moved from a context of reproduction to one of pleasure and self-expression when this is viewed against an international backdrop. It also gives the experience of men's intimate lives equal attention to that of women. Cas Wouters's study goes some way to understanding how men and women answered questions surrounding this love/lust balance differently in Ireland compared to other countries. I argue that a distinct social and legislative context, which included the prohibition of contraception, allowed for a desire for greater physical intimacy between couples that had previously been denied to them (Chapter 5).

More recent studies have also explored intimate life in the 1960s and '70s. Betty Hilliard re-interviewed women from a previous study on urban family life in the mid-1970s, focusing on long-term processes of change in the women's lives and covering areas such as their married sexual lives and their relationship with Catholicism.[43] Hilliard revealed high levels of sexual ignorance among married couples and a belief held by women that it was sinful for them to refuse sex with their husbands. The views of men were not part of the remit of her study. My book builds upon work such as Hilliard's by including the voices of men. It also provides the analysis of data that contributes to a fuller under-standing of the intimate lives of women in this period. While studies of men's public lives have documented their successes in the political, eco-nomic and scientific worlds, scant regard has been paid to the intimate worlds they inhabited. I have previously explored the areas of sexual education, dating and relationships with gay men in this period.[44] My reasearch revealed that their communicative competence around sexuality was seriously impaired by their family upbringing and Catholic schooling, where they struggled to balance the potential freedoms which a more open, modernizing Ireland brought and the pull of tradition, family and community which held them back. I return to explore these stories and the lives of gay men who wrote to the column in Chapter 6.

IRELAND GOES GLOBAL

This book offers an opportunity with which to view Ireland's ongoing transition from a traditional, rural and conservative society to a more modern, industrial and secular one. The story of the economic trans-formation that occurred in Ireland during the 1960s has been well recorded, albeit sometimes simplistically. The publication in 1958, a year after Fianna Fáil returned to power, of the Programme for Economic Expansion by T.K Whitaker, Secretary of the Department of

Finance, sought to place Ireland in a position to benefit from growing world trade, encouraging foreign multinationals through a series of tax incentives.[45] There was a great urgency to do so. Unemployment had peaked in 1957; 78,000 people with families were out of work and living on unemployment benefit of 50 shillings (however large the family).[46] In the same year 54,000 people emigrated. The population dropped to 2,800,000 by 1961. During the years 1955 and 1958, two out of five construction workers lost their jobs, while the value of goods produced in Ireland actually decreased in these years; Ireland was the only country in the Western world where this was to occur.[47] The Irish economy would emerge from behind a wall of protectionist tariffs to compete equally within a more integrated European economy. The policy was designed to lessen Ireland's dependence on Britain as a trading partner.[48] J.J. Lee argues that it was this dependence on what was the worst-performing post-war economy, with growth rates half that of mainland European states, that hampered Ireland's ability to capitalize on rising world demand for its narrow range of exports.[49]

Tom Garvin argues that this change in policy and the subsequent growth of the Irish economy coincided with the decline of a political ascendancy led by de Valera who resigned in 1959 and others who clung to 'rural sentimentalities', economic insularity and moral and social conservatism.[50] The decision to embrace a free market economic policy required this generational shift in political elites to occur that could pose a challenge to the business, bureaucratic and religious monopolies that had profited from Ireland's social and economic protectionism.[51] Even Whitaker expressed surprise that a Fianna Fáil government 'so committed to self-sufficiency and protection, abandoned it all so readily', though he recognized the role of Sean Lemass, de Valera's successor in 1959, as being the 'great moving and dynamic spirit' in this change of policy.[52] This breakthrough for Lemass was, in Terence Brown's words, largely psychological, showing an ability to distinguish between the 'modernization and anglicization' of Ireland.[53]

It was this yielding of control to Sean Lemass and a new generation which ensured that the party remained in government throughout the 1960s.[54] Kieran Allen locates this '1958 turn' not so much driven by State bureaucracy as happening within a wider context of reforms that had begun in 1949 with the establishment of the Industrial Development Authority. Similarly, an agreement with the United States in 1955 on the expropriation of investments had laid the groundwork for the arrival of American multinationals. For Allen, this 'turn' was made more in consideration of reviving the native capitalist class, as grants and subsidies to foreign-owned firms were almost exclusively geared towards the export sector.[55] R.K. Foster also points to the existing internationalization of Irish economic affairs, given that by 1950 the county was already in receipt of £150,000,000 in grants and loans under Marshall Aid.[56]

Whatever the motivation or genesis, the gamble on the free market paid off. American and European firms established bases in Ireland. The value of Irish exports rose by 35 per cent between 1959 and 1960 alone. Emigration, which had epitomized the failure of the Irish State to provide for its people, was halted. Ferriter writes that 'while 44,427 people emigrated in 1961, only 12,226 did so in 1963'.[57] Previous obstacles to foreign-owned companies doing business were slowly removed, providing badly needed employment, although the percentage of those engaged in the industrial labour force remained low at just 15 per cent in 1961.[58] Such figures remind us that the social and economic transition within Ireland was gradual. Similarly, traditional practices of the past were slow to change. Tom Garvin's discussion of a survey carried out by American Jesuit Fr B.F. Biever in 1962 on religious beliefs revealed that almost 90 per cent of the respondents in the survey agreed that the Church was the greatest force for good in Ireland.[59] Crucially, it would be those respondents who had completed secondary education who would prove the most critical of clerical power – a small but growing constituency that would play a leading role in new social movements that would provide the future political and economic leadership of the country. I have previously argued that their emergence can be traced to the structural changes in European and American societies in the latter half of the twentieth century, which brought about the conditions suitable for a new form of protest to emerge.[60] There were new actors, new lines of confrontation, and new adversaries to be fought in a social and political climate that saw a decline in traditional class antagonism. As trade unions moved increasingly within the parameters of government towards social and political partnership, class conflict declined as a focus of mobilization, with workers challenging grievances through movements organized around ethnicity, sex and sexual orientation.[61]

In Ireland this era of social protest would mark the beginning of a cultural war between a new intellectual class, skilled in the art of the media, and a Church that stood steadfast behind the Vatican's pronouncements in premarital sex, contraception and homosexuality. It would be the letter writers to the Angela Macnamara column who would represent the collateral damage in this war, torn between the religious beliefs of their upbringing and new explanations proffered by those who rejected the Church's jurisdiction over how the body could be used as a source of pleasure. The battleground of this conflict would be played out in dark cinema seats, country laneways, and the marital bed where couples would set new limits on the range of sexual intimacies in which they would engage.

The tide was turning in this war. The power of Dr John Charles McQuaid, the Archbishop of Dublin, was waning. McQuaid had embarked upon an ambitious church-building project following his accession, with thirty-four churches built by 1965 to meet the demands of the growing city.[62] It was, however, McQuaid's preoccupation with the sexual lives of others for which he gained infamy during the later period of his career. He exercised his power – in conjunction with the political elite – with abandon, banning books and destroying the careers of public figures deemed to have violated the dictates of Catholic morality, most notably the writer John McGahern who was sacked from his post as a school teacher. Censorship was an activity in which the whole country could participate. Citizens were encouraged to forward books with highlighted text that they found objectionable to the board.[63] Angela Macnamara embarked upon her column just three years after Edna O'Brien's *Country Girls* was banned in 1960, a decision for which McQuaid personally took credit. Between 1946 and 1965 the total number of banned books was 8,000.[64] The list included the greats such as Hemingway and Sartre and also Irish writers, including Frank O'Connor and Sean O'Faolain. To understand the impact of Macnamara's public discussion of sexuality, even within the limits set by her editor, one has to understand the climate in which the Irish State denied its citizens access to even the least suggestive sexual material.

The same regime of censorship existed for films. Between 1962 and 1963 alone, thirty-nine films were banned. In 1957 director Alan Simpson was arrested and charged in relation to a 'profane' production of Tennessee Williams's play, *The Rose Tattoo*. But change was already afoot. Terence Brown suggests that the moral crusade of the censorship authorities actually increased, in terms of books banned, in the early 1960s, despite the introduction of an appeals board in 1946, suggesting a hardening of attitudes in the face of impending change.[65] Minister of Justice Brian Lenihan relented to pressure to reform the censorship laws by replacing the appeals board with a more liberal panel in 1964. The Censorship of Publication Board underwent similar change, first in 1956–57 but more radically in 1967 when an Act facilitated the unbanning of books after twelve years, a measure that brought 5,000 previously banned books into the public domain.[66] The trials and tribulations of the cultural elite remained, however, tangential to the everyday concerns of ordinary people. The ideas contained within much of this previously banned material would make their way into the pages of Macnamara's column as readers assessed new explanations and ideas with more traditionally held beliefs.

THE POLITICAL ECONOMY OF INTIMACY

Economic factors were also impacting on how Irish men and women conducted their intimate lives. Internal migration saw the population of Dublin rise from 472,935 in 1936 to 595,288 in 1961.[67] Terence Brown argues that it was women who disproportionately made this journey, and those who sought to make a permanent life for themselves in the city experienced a sharp adjustment to modern urban life.[68] The number of marriages rose from a low of 14,700 in 1957 to 16,800 in 1966, rising again to 22,000 in 1971. The age at which people decided to marry declined. Between 1961 and 1973 the mean age of marriage declined from 30.6 to 27.2 years for men and from 26.9 to 24.8 years for women.[69] The figures reveal how greater economic opportunity liberated adult children from their familial obligations and broke the financial hold that parents exerted over their choices of career and love (Chapter 5). Central to this liberation was a greater investment in education. The announcement of measures such as the free education scheme, school building and scholarship schemes and free transport saw the numbers in secondary education rise from 104,000 to 144,000 between 1966 and 1969.[70] The announcement of the establishment of Regional Technical Colleges in 1963 marked a commitment to producing a labour force that could adapt to the changing technological demands of a modern economy. The availability of third-year education remained firmly within the middle classes with lower socio-economic groups making up just 2 per cent of the population.[71]

The lives of women also changed at a slower pace. In 1961 women accounted for only 29 per cent of the workforce and were located in overwhelmingly female-dominated sectors of the economy.[72] Married women constituted only 5 per cent of that workforce.[73]

Measures such as the Income Tax Act of 1967 considered a married woman's income as part of her husband's for tax purposes, with married women paying more tax than their spouses or single people.[74] Wages, too, were lower for women. In 1960 women earned just 53 per cent of what their male counterparts earned, rising to only 59 per cent in 1971.[75]

The figures above were just one consequence of a number of State policies initiated since independence that recognized that the nation's common good would be best served by women being both encouraged and coerced to remain working within the home. Indeed, the granting of suffrage for women in 1918 would be the most progressive measure to take forward women's rights for decades. Laws such as the Juries Act of 1927 drew juries from ratepayers, effectively excluding women from serving. Books and periodicals that included information about contraception fell foul of the censorship legislation introduced in 1929. This restriction was further copper-fastened by the Criminal Law (Amendment Act) of 1935 that banned the importation, sale and advertising of contraceptives in Ireland. Two years later the new constitution outlawed divorce and enshrined women's 'special position' within Irish society.

The active political participation of women during the nationalist struggle, although largely conducted within traditional gender lines, diminished with the advent of the Free State.[76] Linda Connolly argues that to locate the emergence of second-wave feminism solely within the socio-economic changes of the 1960s neglects the continued impact that a number of women's groups, for example the Irish Women's Workers Union (IWWU), had in campaigning on issues such as barriers to jury service and women's employment in the civil service in the 1930s and 1940s.[77] For Connolly, any understanding of the history of Irish feminism has to pay particular attention to the continuities within the movement over a broader historical period than merely the emergence of new social movements in the 1960s.[78] When the UN Commission on the Status of Women asked non-governmental organizations in 1967 to examine the position of women in their respective societies and further pressurize governments into establishing their national committees on the status of women, a diverse range of women's groups came together. These included the Irish Housewives Association (IHA), the Irish Countrywomen's Association (ICA) and the Irish Council of Women (ICW). Following extensive lobbying, the first Commission on the Status of Women was established in March 1970 by Taoiseach Jack Lynch who had succeeded Sean Lemass as leader of Fianna Fáil in 1966. Its interim report a year later recommended the passage of legislation that would implement equal pay and remove the discriminatory marriage bar which forced women to retire from the civil service on marriage. This piece of controversial legislation has long been used as evidence to suggest a programme of legislative coercion that confined women to the domestic sphere. Revisionist accounts reject such a claim. Caitriona Clear argues that the policy was more 'a cynical attempt to make jobs available for young single men and women', pointing to the lack of comparative measures across the non-public employment.[79] In fact, she argues, women had been deserting the domestic sphere, with a substantial decline in women working in domestic service after 1940.[80] She suggests there is a need to address the question of 'which domesticity' historians are talking about in relation to de Valera's attempts to confine women within it. Similarly, a fall in maternal mortality had 'liberated' often the oldest daughter who would have been required to suspend her own ambitions to take care of younger siblings.[81]

The Commission on the Status of Women's (CSW) report remained moderate in tone, working within the conservative political system to achieve its objectives, a strategy that Linda Connolly argues would become seriously out of step with a new wave of the direct action protest of new social movements in the 1970s.[82] These strategies of protest would be employed to great effect by new groups within the women's movement, such as the Irish Women's Liberation Movement (IWLM). The IWLM drew its influences from activism around the world in the contentious political era in the late 1960s and the 1970s. It was a broad coalition of different groups but represented a break with feminist organizations of the past. It represented a new confrontational style of feminist politics that utilized its connections within the media to full effect, to garner maximum publicity for it activities.[83] While the key demands of the IWLM – equal pay, removal of the marriage bar and the availability of contraception – did not radically differ from the CSW, the methods deployed to achieve these aims did.[84] It would be the deployment of these direct-action tactics, like the 'Contraceptive Train' that saw members of the IWLM bring condoms through Connolly station in defiance of the 1935 Act prohibiting their importation, that caused rifts within the movement that would contribute to its very dissolution.[85] The formation of Irishwomen United in 1975 would bring together disparate elements of Irish feminism again in the struggle for the right to contraception and sex education to be made freely available to all under the banner of the Contraception Action Programme (CAP).[86]

Much legislative progress did continue, albeit slowly, throughout the 1970s. The Maintenance Orders (1974) Act, the Family Law

(Maintenance of Spouses and Children Act) of 1976 and the Social Welfare Act 1974 which transferred the legal right of children's allowance from the father to the mother all marked a significant redistribution of power between the sexes.[87] In Chapter 5 we see how the absences of these legislative measures in the 1960s contributed to a precarious financial position for married women in the home. Women were often forced by economic necessity back into the workforce where the barriers to their employment and equal status were being dismantled, particularly the repeal of the marriage bar in 1973 and the passing of the Anti-Discrimination (Pay) Act the following year.[88]

While *The Sunday Press* recorded the private, intimate lives at the back of the newspaper, surrounded by articles on the fashion and make-up of the season, the front page headlines proclaimed landmarks of Ireland's economic transformation. This was a new outward-looking Ireland. Aer Lingus launched its first transatlantic flight to the United States in 1960. *The Sunday Press* article of 13 September 1964 announced the building of five new regional airports throughout the country.[89] Things were truly, it seemed, looking up. The development of Shannon Airport and a more professional approach to marketing by Bord Fáilte (Irish Tourist Board) led to an influx of coach-tour visitors, with receipts from this new industry worth £80,000,000 by 1967.[90]

A front-page headline of 2 May 1965 marvelled at the opening of Ireland's 'first skyscraper' – Liberty Hall in Dublin. At 59.4 metres it still soars over the surrounding city, providing a headquarters for the Services, Industrial, Professional and Technical Union (SIPTU). *The Sunday Press* praised the political leadership behind such a transformation. In an article of 4 April 1965 the paper highlighted the 'young and vigorous men' Sean Lemass had selected to lead the country through this period of social and economic transformation. It was a transformation that would see the newspaper crammed full of advertisements for a whole new range of consumer durables from gas ovens to washing machines. These new durables created a greater demand for power and, despite the slow progress of the rural electrification scheme commenced in 1946, by 1962 96 per cent of areas designated for modernization had an electricity supply. The number of privately licensed cars on Irish roads had also increased from a mere 7,845 in 1945 to 156,000 in 1951.[91] A new Vauxhall Viva car cost £605 in 1963. The growth of car ownership would transform the dating lives of men and women, transporting them to dances and social events outside the surveillance of their immediate communities and facilitating a rare private location where couples could be intimate. While the growth of car ownership increased, funding for the underdeveloped road network did not and the result was a growing rise in fatalities on Irish roads throughout the 1960s, with a headline in *The Sunday Press* on 15 October 1967 pleading that 'the carnage must be stopped' after another four people died in a car crash in Dublin. The final tally of road deaths the following year would be 447.

Politically, Ireland would also play a greater role on the global stage. Ireland joined the Council of Europe and was admitted to the United Nations in 1955.[92] In 1960 Ireland's participation in peace-keeping duties with the United Nations saw an Irish battalion leave to the former Belgian Congo, and Ireland was a member of the Security Council in 1962.[93] The following year, Ireland would host the historic visit of President John F. Kennedy. Lemass had also clearly signalled his preference to join the European Economic Community (EEC), even making supportive speeches about the role of NATO, thought to be the greatest impediment to Ireland's entry. Ireland formally made its case for entry to the EEC in 1962, and although the application was thrown into turmoil by de Gaulle's veto of Britain's application the following year, the political ambitions of Ireland remained outwards.[94]

It was the global nature of the economics that would contribute to Ireland's growing workforce and fledgling economy feeling the full brunt of the peaks and troughs of free-market economics. The second programme for economic expansion (1964–70) was abandoned in 1967 while the third programme, according to Lee, was 'quietly shelved in 1971'.[95] The economic successes of the 1960s were short-lived. Increased living standards were jeopardized primarily by the oil crisis of 1973 which brought home the reality of laissez-faire economics. Financial mismanagement would also contribute to rising budget deficits and a spiralling national debt. By the end of the 1970s inflation and unemployment rates had risen and Ireland resumed the traditional role of being a net exporter of her people.[96]

'WE LOVE SEX ON RADIO KERRY'

While the stories of de Valera, Whitaker and Lemass have all been told, by themselves and by others, my focus remains on the private everyday lives of the men who navigated their way through a changing landscape of intimacy, love and sex. Capturing these stories was an important complement to the analysis of the problem page; one described through women's letters their difficulties in their intimate relationships with men and how they sought to 'fix' Irish masculinity, which the other revealed how men *themselves* understood the social world they inhabited. Despite letters printed in the national and local press soliciting men to come forward to tell their stories, the number of men responding remained low.[97] One spin-off from a letter published in the *Kerryman* was an invitation to appear on Radio Kerry's lunchtime show, hosted by Deirdre Walsh, to discuss the letters to the column and ask more men to come forward. After rejecting Walsh's invitation to 'have a bit of laugh' about the innocence of the letters people wrote, I asked whether the sexual content of some of the letters might be suitable for a lunchtime audience. 'We love sex on Radio Kerry', I was assured by Walsh. One man listening to the radio that day was 63-year-old Liam Ahearn. When I arranged to meet him outside Limerick city's train station he warned me to be on 'the look-out for an old man in green wellington boots'. And so it was; he had left work to come and talk to me. He explained, during the interview in his parked car, that his wife was now a mature student who also needed interviewees to complete an undergraduate thesis and he felt obliged to offer his assistance, as he well remembered the Macnamara column.[98] Ahearn was typical of the ordinary men who volunteered to speak to me, many admitting that the interview was the first time they had reflected on and spoken about their roles as boyfriends, lovers, husbands and fathers.

It was within the realm of the media that the hearts and minds of the Irish people would be won. The Catholic Church's ability to sustain a campaign of surveillance over how Irish people experienced sexuality in print and on the radio and television was limited. The decision to launch a national television service had been postponed by previous governments for fear of offending the Catholic Church, the Gaelic Athletic Association (GAA) and various Irish-language groups, each of which had expressed reservations about its cultural impact.[99] From the outset, leaders such as McQuaid had recognized the impact that television possessed in shaping public opinion, particularly in the area of morality. It was because of this knowledge, despite its reservations, that the Church supported the establishment of the television service in 1962, to offset the reliance of the Irish audience on the east coast on BBC programming. Louise Fuller notes that McQuaid had sent senior staff for television training in New York even before the first broadcast. He also established a Catholic press office in Dublin in 1965 and the Catholic Communications Institute of Ireland in 1969.[100] De Valera similarly struck a suspicious note in his address at the inauguration ceremony about the potential of television 'to influence the thoughts and actions of the multitude'.[101] Programmes like 'The Late Late Show' courted controversy several times during the 1960s, sparking the admonishment of the Church over guests and discussions seen to be anti-clerical in Irish society. From married women hinting at 'marital intimacy' on their honeymoons to Trinity College student Brian Trevaskis's criticism of Galway's new Cathedral and the bishop who commissioned it, 'The Late Late Show' and its host, Gay Byrne, continually made copy in the Sunday newspapers the following day, ensuring that ratings remained high.[102] This style of broadcasting revealed the end of the deference with which the clergy had previously been treated. It revealed a new society where values and moral codes would be publicly contested rather than prescribed.

Not all programming was as overtly challenging to Church authority. Television drama such as 'The Riordans' pushed social boundaries, tackling issues such as contraception, unmarried mothers and marital infidelity.[103] A storyline has the character Maggie asking the priest for advice on the moral implications of contraception. By suggesting that her decision was a matter of moral conscience, the storyline confirmed a recognized disparity between the discourse and practice of Church teaching.[104]

On radio, agony aunt Frankie Byrne broadcast her show 'Woman's Page' from 1963 to 1985.[105] A 'Dear Frankie' column was published in the *Evening Press*, where Byrne set about solving the problems of the nation with wry humour and a quick wit, becoming as well known as Angela Macnamara. While both shared the notoriety of being the nation's best-known agony aunts, Macnamara insisted that Byrne's show was principally for entertainment while her column was a more serious endeavour. Some of their letters and responses are compared later in the book. Byrne, a former public relations executive, certainly enjoyed entertainment, becoming a regular feature on Dublin's social scene. Her private life, exposed in a documentary after her death, showed her fondness for champagne and parties, but also a complicated relationship with a well-known married Irish broadcaster and former Irish Film Censor, Frank Hall, and the sadness she endured after the birth of their daughter, who was given up for adoption.[106] Angela Macnamara lived a very different life.

This book goes some way to analyzing the extent to which Ireland represented a special case in the arena of intimacy and sexuality. Were the Irish, especially men, unwilling or unable to self-disclose their needs for sex, intimacy or companionship in their relationships, and to what extent did that change throughout the 1960s and 1970s? The answer lies in a reassessment of the emotional and sexual repression narrative, but also in questioning an understanding of the 1960s as a period of exaggerated social transformation and sexual liberation. The result of this more balanced appraisal liberates men, allowing them to cast off the stereotypes of the past and to rewrite their own sexual and emotional histories.

NOTES

1. *Irish Times*, Health Supplement, 3 August 2010.
2. *Irish Times*, 9 September 2008.
3. P. Ryan, 'Researching Irish Gay Male Lives: Reflections on Disclosure and Intellectual Autobiography in the Production of Personal Narratives', *Qualitative Research*, 6, 2 (2006), pp.151–68.
4. In an RTÉ documentary, 'Dear Angela', broadcast on 24 April 1975, Macnamara explained that January of that year was a typical month, in which – in addition to the small selection of letters published in the column – she privately replied to over 200 letters; a further 1,000 anonymous letters went unanswered.
5. M. O'Brien, *De Valera, Fianna Fáil and the Irish Press* (Dublin: Irish Academic Press, 2001), p.86.
6. See P. Travers, *Eamon de Valera* (Dundalk: Dundalgan Press, 1994), pp.41–2.
7. Cas Wouters, *Sex and Manners: Female Emancipation in the West 1890–2000* (London: Sage, 2004), p.156. The concept of 'trend followers' is taken from W. Zeegers, *De Zonnige zijde van seks: De nawerking van positef beleedfde seksualiteit* (Leiden: DSWO Press, 1994), p.131.
8. C. Wright Mills, *The Sociological Imagination* (New York: Oxford University Press, 1959), p.8.
9. P. Atkinson and A. Coffey, 'Analysing Documentary Realities', in D. Silverman (ed.), *Qualitative Research: Theory, Method and Practice* (London: Sage, 2004), p.73.
10. R. Kent, *Aunt Agony Advises: Problem Pages through the Ages* (London: W.H. Allen, 1987), p.7.
11. D. Ferriter, *Occasions of Sin: Sex and Society in Modern Ireland* (London: Profile Books, 2009), p.351.
12. N. Elias, *The Civilizing Process: The History of Manners and State Formation and Civilization* (Oxford: Blackwell, 1994).
13. Ibid., pp.138–9.
14. Ibid., p.144.
15. Ibid., p.148.
16. Ibid., p.149.
17. Ibid., p.150.
18. Ibid., p.151.
19. Ibid., p.152.
20. Ibid., p.153.
21. A. Giddens, *The Transformation of Intimacy: Sexuality, Love and Eroticism in Modern Societies* (Stanford, CA: Stanford University Press, 1992), p.184.
22. N. Scheper-Hughes, *Saints, Scholars and Schizophrenics: Mental Illness in Rural Ireland* (Berkeley, CA: University of California Press, 1979), p.123.
23. Ibid., p.121.
24. Ibid., p.118. For a somewhat referential overview of the life of Matt Talbot, see E. Doherty, *Matt Talbot* (Combermere: Madonna House Publications, 2001).
25. Ibid., p.97.
26. Ibid., p.116.
27. J. Ryan and M. Ryan, *Love and Sexuality* (Dublin: M.H. Gill & Son, 1968), p.65.
28. C.M. Arensberg and S.T. Kimball, *Family and Community in Ireland* (Cambridge, MA: Harvard University Press, 1968).
29. Ibid., p.199.

30. J.C. Messenger, *Inis Beag: Isle of Ireland* (Prospect Heights, IL: Waveland Press, 1969), pp.68–9.
31. Ibid., p.78.
32. D. Rohan, *Marriage Irish Style* (Cork: Mercier Press, 1969), pp.69–74.
33. C. Clear, 'Women in de Valera's Ireland 1932–48: A Reappraisal', in G. Doherty and D. Keogh (eds), *De Valera's Irelands* (Cork: Mercier Press, 2003), p.104.
34. Wouters, *Sex and Manners*, pp.2–4.
35. Ibid., p.2.
36. Ibid., p.71.
37. Ibid., pp.80–4.
38. Ibid., p.21.
39. Ibid., p.49.
40. C. Wouters, 'Balancing Sex and Love since the 1960s Sexual Revolution', *Theory, Culture and Society*, 15, 3–4 (1998), p.187.
41. Ibid., p.190.
42. C. Brinkgreve, C. and M. Korzec, 'Feelings, Behaviours, Morals in the Netherlands: Analysis and Interpretation of an Advice Column', *The Netherlands Journal of Sociology*, 15 (1979), pp.123–40.
43. B. Hilliard, 'The Catholic Church and Married Women's Sexuality: Habitus Change in Late 20th Century Ireland', *Irish Journal of Sociology*, 12, 2 (2003), pp.36–7.
44. P. Ryan, 'Coming Out, Staying In: The Personal Narratives of Some Irish Gay Men', *Irish Journal of Sociology*, 12, 2 (2003), pp.68–85.
45. R. Breen, D.F. Hannan, D.B. Rottman and C.T. Whelan, *Understanding Contemporary Ireland: State, Class and Development in the Republic of Ireland* (Dublin: Gill & Macmillan, 1990), p.38.
46. D. Ferriter, *The Transformation of Ireland 1900–2000* (London: Profile Books, 2005), p.491.
47. J. Horgan, *Sean Lemass: The Enigmatic Patriot* (Dublin: Gill & Macmillan, 1997), p.176.
48. Breen et al., *Understanding Contemporary Ireland*, p.39.
49. J.J. Lee, *Ireland 1912–1985: Politics and Society* (Cambridge: Cambridge University Press, 1989), p.359.
50. T. Garvin, *Preventing the Future: Why Was Ireland So Poor For So Long?* (Dublin: Gill & Macmillan, 2004), p.33.
51. Ibid., p.67.
52. Horgan, *Sean Lemass*, p.176.
53. T. Brown, *Ireland: A Social and Cultural History* (London: Harper Perennial, 2004), p.234.
54. Ferriter, *Transformation of Ireland*, p.537.
55. K. Allen, *Fianna Fáil and Irish Labour* (London: Pluto Press, 1997), pp.107–8. For more detail on the establishment of the Industrial Development Authority, see Lee, *Ireland: 1912–1985*, pp.309–12. Lee argues (pp.344–5) that the IDA's chances of success were slim, given that the protectionist Control of Manufacturers' Acts remained in place. The Acts were finally removed in 1964.
56. R.K. Foster, *Modern Ireland 1600–1972* (London: Penguin, 1988), p.577. See also Lee, *Ireland 1912–1985*, pp.303–5.
57. Ferriter, *Transformation of Ireland*, p.542.
58. Garvin, *Preventing the Future*, p.252.
59. Ibid., p.253.
60. P. Ryan, 'Coming Out of the Dark: A Decade of Gay Mobilisation in Ireland, 1970–80', in Linda Connolly and Niamh Hourigan (eds), *Social Movements and Ireland* (Manchester: Manchester University Press, 2006).
61. A. Touraine, *The Voice and the Eye: An Analysis of Social Movements* (Cambridge: Cambridge University Press, 1981), p.13.
62. L. Fuller, *Irish Catholicism since 1950: The Undoing of a Culture* (Dublin: Gill & Macmillan, 2002), p.22.
63. Ibid., p.37.
64. Ferriter, *Occasions of Sin*, p.386.
65. Brown, *Ireland*, p.222.
66. Fuller, *Irish Catholicism*, pp.136–7.
67. Brown, *Ireland*, p.200.
68. Ibid., p.206.

69. Lee, *Ireland: 1912–1985*, p.360.
70. Ibid., p.326.
71. Ibid., p.363.
72. Ferriter, *Transformation of Ireland*, p.569.
73. Foster, *Modern Ireland*, p.581.
74. Ferriter, *Transformation of Ireland*, p.569.
75. Ibid., p.570.
76. L. Connolly, *The Irish Women's Movement: From Revolution to Devolution* (Dublin: Lilliput Press, 2003), p.65.
77. Ibid., p.67.
78. Ibid., p.92.
79. Clear, *Women in de Valera's Ireland*, p.107.
80. Ibid., p.108.
81. Ibid., pp.110–11.
82. Connolly, *Irish Women's Movement*, p.99.
83. Ibid., pp.124–8.
84. Ibid., p.118.
85. Ibid., pp.120–1.
86. Ibid., pp.130–54.
87. Ibid., p.108.
88. Ibid., p.106.
89. The midlands town of Athlone would discover that not all political promises are delivered on.
90. Foster, *Modern Ireland*, pp.581–2.
91. Ferriter, *Transformation of Ireland*, p.499.
92. Ibid., p.212.
93. Horgan, *Sean Lemass*, p.190.
94. Ibid., p.226.
95. Ferriter, *Transformation of Ireland*, p.353.
96. Ibid., pp.169–72.
97. Letters seeking respondents were published in *The Irish Independent*, *The Limerick Reader and* the *Kerryman*. Similar letters featured in the magazine *Senior Times*, aimed at the over-50s, and on the websites of the access programme websites of the NUI Maynooth and University College Dublin. I also targeted more specific avenues in recruitment. Following the idea of the 'trend follower' discussed earlier, I approached Accord, the Catholic marriage counselling services, asking whether any of their male counsellors who had read the column would be willing to particular, and some were. The motivation here was to tap into an understanding of the era from men who, theoretically at least, might be more proficient in talking about intimacy.
98. On a methodological aside, doing qualitative interviews in a parked car may not initially seem like the ideal location, given that eye contact is more intermittent because both interviewer and interviewee are sitting parallel to each other. In this scenario, however, rather than inhibiting rapport between us, I believe this situation facilitated much greater disclosure from Liam as he discussed topics that, at times, made him hesitant and uncomfortable.
99. R.J. Savage, Jr, *Irish Television: The Political and Social Origins* (Cork: Cork University Press, 1996), p.xiii.
100. Fuller, *Irish Catholicism since 1950*, p.129.
101. Ibid., p.128.
102. I refer to some of these scandals later in the book. The honeymoon feature on 'The Late Late Show' became known as 'the Bishop and the Nightie affair'. See Tom Inglis, *Lessons in Irish Sexuality* (Dublin: University College Dublin Press, 1998), p.39.
103. L. Gibbons, 'From Kitchen Sink to Soap', in M. Mcloone and J. MacMahon (eds), *Television and Irish Society: 21 Years of Irish Television* (Dublin: RTÉ/IFI, 1984), p.39.
104. Ibid., p.41.
105. P. O'Dea, *Dear Frankie* (Dublin: Mentor Press, 1998).
106. The 2004 documentary 'Dear Frankie' was directed by Gerry Nelson and broadcast on RTÉ television.

CHAPTER TWO

Introducing Angela Macnamara

Angela Macnamara was born in Dublin in 1931. Her father, George Little, was a doctor and historian and worked from his medical practice in their large family home in Rathgar. Her mother, Alice Mulhern-Little, worked full-time in their home. It was not a task she did single-handedly. During Angela's childhood her mother oversaw a household staff that included a nanny, a cook, a houseman and a woman employed once a week to do laundry. It set the scene for a largely idyllic childhood in a house bustling with activity. As well as being her father's place of work, their home was also where Angela was educated with her sister Mary, by a governess, Miss O'Riordan, during her early primary-school years. Its large garden contained a pavilion which acted as a playhouse for the children and a schoolroom during the warmer months. There was a tennis court and a teahouse where the family had lunch during summer, complete with a bell connected to the kitchen lest anything was needed. Such houses were reminiscent of an older 'upstairs downstairs' style of living, one which was quickly becoming obsolete. Macnamara recalls some embarrassment as a teenager bringing school friends to a house she saw as old-fashioned, filled with objets d'art, with reception rooms resembling a museum rather than a place for comfortable family living. It was a childhood where the countryside began at Terenure, a short distance from her home, where the family would picnic amongst the woods of Tallaght. A childhood of religious devotion where Angela remembered seeing photographs of their house, like much of Dublin, festooned with bunting and flags during the Eucharistic Congress in 1932.

This happy upbringing was disrupted by the death of her younger brother, David, in a traffic accident outside their home when she was 5 years old, the memories of which still linger. After David's death, Angela's mother gave birth to two further children, Frank and Leonard, who along with her older sister Mary completed the family.

Angela went to secondary school in the Convent of the Sacred Heart in Leeson Street, but while enjoying creative subjects she struggled in more academic ones, much to the disappointment of her father. Upon leaving school Angela considered three possible career options –

acting, Montessori teaching or journalism.[1] Her parents decided that acting was inappropriate, while Montessori would require training in England and was deemed unsuitable for a 17-year-old girl, leaving journalism as a possibility. Angela enrolled in a commercial course that specialized in typewriting, shorthand and bookkeeping. Her first job was in the National Maternity Hospital in Holles Street, working in the medical secretary's office and based in the Outpatients Department. She was paid £25 a month. The experience would allow Macnamara access to the most intimate details of people's married lives – 'people would confide in you once you were wearing a white coat', she recalls in interview. Angela embarked upon a busy social life of dating, dances and cinema, meeting her future husband at a party and becoming engaged at 21 years old. She left work a few months before she married, explaining that 'I just left, it was the thing to do. Few girls considered staying on at work. Today it's so different.' Angela Little married Peter Macnamara in 1953 and the couple had four daughters in the following seven years.

After the birth of her children Angela returned to writing. She had previously written reviews of children's books as a teenager and now wrote a series of articles on family life and being a mother of four children under the age of 7 for the *Irish Messenger of the Sacred Heart* magazines that were published in 1960 and 1961. The *Messenger* magazine had been founded in 1888 by Fr James Cullen, SJ, and enjoyed great popularity amongst the faithful. It contained readers' thanksgiving letters for favours they believed were received through their prayer and devotion, including the practice of the Nine First Fridays where penitents would attend confession and Communion on the first Friday of nine consecutive months. The magazine also ran a question-and-answer section, where readers wrote with questions about the propriety of their religious conduct, including whether an inability to see the altar meant they were not attending mass.[2]

The articles published by Macnamara in the *Messenger* focused on issues such as discipline and family prayer in the home. In her auto-biography, *Yours Sincerely*, Angela recalls rereading those articles years later and being struck by the old-fashioned style and ideas, deciding against showing them to her adult children.[3] In interview with me, Angela similarly expressed a difficulty in rereading pamphlets published during the 1960s, describing how she was 'horrified now at the sort of stuff I wrote and yet I can forgive myself because I was writing within a certain society'. These publications sparked invitations from schools to speak to final-year students about the challenges facing them and to hear their questions. Students were encouraged to place questions anonymously in a box – questions that ranged from the sinfulness of long kisses and wearing bikinis to the role of women outside the home.[4] Using the questions that emerged from school classrooms, Angela wrote a series of articles on these themes for the editor of *The Sunday Press*, Frank (Francis) Carty, which were published in six successive weeks. The topics and subsequent readers' questions were censored by Carty. When the paper received a large number of readers' letters during the six weeks of publication, Angela was invited to respond to the remaining letters in what would mark the beginning of her column. She received a lot of letters from boys asking about masturbation, which she describes as 'being completely out as far as the column was concerned'. Some people reacted with outrage to reading about sex in the column, even when the advice was couched in terms of Catholic moral teaching. The opportunity afforded Macnamara to begin a career in journalism, although in the documentary on her life she describes a stronger, faith-based motivation.[5] 'I feel this is the sort of work that Christians should be doing and as a Christian I am automatically called to help people where I can', she explained. Macnamara also wrote a similar series of articles on sex education for the *Farmers Journal*, of which only three were published, with the remaining three shelved due to the torrent of complaints from irate readers. As the popularity of the column grew and the volume of letters increased, Macnamara made the journey to the residence of the Archbishop of Dublin, Dr John Charles McQuaid, to seek greater support from Catholic agencies in dealing with the issues of sexuality. She recalls the encounter:

> In a short time a rotund and formidable nun swept into the room. She introduced herself. Almost straight away she advised me to give up both my schools' work and *The Sunday Press* column. She found them 'distasteful' … She told me that if I didn't give up the work she would advise the schools of her Order to cease inviting me. Then she stood up angrily and I thought she was going to bring me into the Archbishop. Instead she led me to the hall door and opened it.[6]

Macnamara believed that the Catholic Church's response to sex education was inadequate. Indeed, in the 1970s she was invited to speak to first-year seminarians in Saint Patrick's College, Maynooth, and

was genuinely shocked at the lack of knowledge the men
possessed about even the most basic aspects of women's physiology.
These very men would go forth from Maynooth in the coming years
and exercise a moral jurisdiction over women's bodies. She had to
tread a delicate line in her criticism. Such was McQuaid's power in
the 1960s that there is little doubt he could have exerted pressure
to have had her fired from *The Sunday Press*. Macnamara was also
writing a column for *Woman's Way* magazine, a popular weekly full
of articles on fashion, make-up, romance and sex. It came to the
attention of McQuaid through a meeting between the Bishop of
Galway, Dr Michael Browne, and the Archbishop's secretary, J.A.
MacMahon, in 1967.[7] Suspicion was aroused by the editorial staff,
which included a Mrs Caroline Mitchell, a Protestant and several
other members who were thought to be lapsed Catholics. Such was
the magazine's popularity that McQuaid received the advice that it
might be more prudent to advise women to exercise caution while
reading the magazine, rather than make an outright condemnation.[8]

Macnamara recalls: 'I was never critical of the Church in print, I just
felt the Church wasn't doing enough so I was going to push the boat out
a bit but I wasn't going to do it in an atmosphere of criticism ... the
editor wouldn't have accepted it anyway so I didn't do that.' Even when
her personal views were at variance with those of the Vatican, Macnamara felt it her responsibility to both publicly and privately observe
teachings of her faith. For her, as for most Catholics, it was the dashed
expectations of a liberalization of the Church's teaching on contraception
in *Humanae Vitae* in 1968 that created conflict between public and
private adherence. Macnamara explains how she was 'gob-smacked' by
the news. As a mother of four children she did not intend to have
another child and had believed that contraception would be approved
for use between married couples. In her column Macnamara did not
deviate from the position on contraception as laid out in *Humanae
Vitae*. Privately, she, like so many other couples, would struggle to maintain a sexual relationship within marriage while adopting cumbersome
natural family planning techniques approved by the Church. She
explained that 'for married people to relax in together in bed, seldom
making love to its natural conclusion, seemed to be pie-in-the-sky'.[9]
Macnamara recalled her own personal experience:

> It has to be remembered that I was at the very time myself work-
> ing all this through and we worked it out that we would have to
> investigate the infertile period and try and work this out in our

own lives and I found that very difficult and very unnatural and you ... we still stuck on in there with it and a certain amount of refusal of sex as well ...

It didn't work. Macnamara would go on to suffer three miscarriages in 1962, 1967 and 1968, the experience of which left her suffering from depression.[10]

The Catholic Marriage Advisory Council (now called Accord) launched its first training course for counsellors in 1967. Macnamara enrolled for the year's course, achieving her first counselling qualification. She admits that this rather basic qualification was late in her counselling career but that it contributed to a greater confidence in her chosen profession.[11] It did not, however, alleviate the disapproval with which this career had been regarded within Macnamara's broader family. Her parents and her siblings expressed their displeasure, but it was Macnamara's father who remained the most implacably opposed to his daughter's journalistic career. 'I was a source of embarrassment', Macnamara recalls.[12] There was also a class element to his objection. In interview, Macnamara said her father thought the column was 'to use a word from the time – common – as opposed to something more dignified ... I knew he disapproved but I didn't listen to that.'

The column would also influence the type of mother Angela Macnamara would be to her four children. Reading letters about young girls who had fallen pregnant, often rejected by their families, and about married women trapped within loveless or violent marriages, with little or no financial independence, made Macnamara an anxious, overprotective mother. She shared similar concerns for her daughters to some of those expressed through readers' letters, with Macnamara saying: 'I didn't want them to get into too much too soon but I didn't know what "too much" was.' As she didn't drink alcohol herself, being a member of the Pioneer Total Abstinence Association, Macnamara worried about the dangers of drinking for her daughters, who would socialize in different ways from her own generation, increasingly in pubs, which had been traditionally off-limits for women, and in mixed company. Nights were spent lying awake waiting for them to return home. She explains: 'I was getting a constant dose myself of the troubles of people and how it could all go wrong ... it created an anxiety in myself for my own daughters and I was looking at all the angles trying to protect to cover them and you know I'm sure they resented a lot of it ... really it was an exaggerated need to protect them for me ... I was far from being the perfect mother you know I forgive myself in retrospect – I suppose nobody is.' In a television documentary about her life, two of Macnamara's daughters explained how their peers often had preconceived notions of what they would be like, given their mother's notoriety.[13] One of her daughters recalled an occasion of 'boys producing the page of *The Sunday Press* at a dance and waving it around', although they believed such incidents were not significant in comparison to the good work their mother was doing.

CHRISTIAN COUNSEL

Angela Macnamara had an ambitious vision for her column. This came about quite literally by accident, when a car crash in 1973 confined her to hospital for a number of weeks and she struggled to keep up with the column from her hospital bed. The idea was to bring together a number of people interested in counselling by letter, train them with the help of some sympathetic professionals and establish an office space in Dublin from which the service could be run. It would be a large undertaking. The service would be called Christian Counsel and would become a registered charity. Macnamara rented a house from a religious order, the Brothers of Charity in Terenure. A group of volunteers were brought together who would act as ghost writers for Macnamara. A secretary was employed and fund-raising campaigns were initiated. Patrons were approached for their support, including the then Archbishop of Dublin, Dr Dermot Ryan. It was envisioned that similar counselling services would be established throughout the country. Macnamara found that, rather than having a decreasing workload, the counselling service increased it considerably. Key to this increase was Macnamara's insistence on signing every reply written by a volunteer. She already felt guilty because confidentiality had been broken by handing a letter addressed to her to a volunteer. Likewise, responses were being posted to readers that were written by volunteers, although signed by Macnamara. Macnamara felt owner-ship over all the replies, spending considerable time correcting and editing them before posting. In an article published in *The Sunday Press* on 27 April 1975 which describes the new counselling venture, Macnamara said that she would 'hate people to think I just sign these letters after all people had written them. It's not like that at all.'

As part of the guidelines for trainees, sample letters and replies were established, although such was the pace of social change in

Ireland that letters brought new problems every day an occurrence which Macnamara attributed to the spread of 'more secular and materialistic magazines and papers'.[14] A list of 'helpers' was devised. Counsellors could refer clients to professionals in a range of local areas. On occasion Macnamara would disagree with a volunteer's reply to a letter. Conflict ensued and resignations followed. By the late 1970s the counselling service was coming to a close after five years in operation. Macnamara, who had a hysterectomy during that time, was increasingly tired and unable to meet the growing responsibilities of managing the service, while unable to pass on those responsibilities to someone else – responsibilities no one else was willing to undertake. At the same time the column in *The Sunday Press* was also coming to an end for different reasons.

The volume of letters Macnamara was receiving had substantially decreased. Her editor, Vincent Jennings, responded by giving the column less space in the newspaper and demanding shorter replies.[15] 'He began by giving me less space and I smelt a rat that this was the beginning of the end', Macnamara recalled. Circulation was under increasing pressure from the *Sunday World* newspaper that offered a tabloid mix of entertainment, gossip and sexual scandal. Its journalistic style was summed up by its advertising slogan: 'We go all the way'; it proved to be successful, selling 200,000 copies in its first year, 1973. The paper came with a new generation of agony aunt – Linda – whose letters and replies were far more salacious than Macnamara's. Angela Macnamara thought that Jennings wanted her to become, in her words, 'more trendy', a request she refused. She continued: 'I was angry – I was angry and feeling, ok so he expects me to change ... and I'm not going to change for him so this is where my anger was.'

LIFE AFTER THE COLUMN

Macnamara continued to write articles for journals and magazines after the column finished in 1980. She continued to receive invitations from schools to speak to children and parents. She gave workshops to schoolchildren. Teachers also approached Macnamara, encouraging her to initiate the teaching of relationships and sexuality education in schools. This would be the next phase in her career. Macnamara found that school timetables did not allow for many day retreats and there was a growing demand for the 'nuts and bolts' of sex education. The issue of sex education in Irish schools would remain a contentious issue. While Macnamara had been encouraging of the use of the proper names to describe the sexual organs and the process of sexual intercourse, it was not until 1981 that a Catholic handbook, *Education in Sexuality*, was published that did so. The handbook describes sexual intercourse as the result of a loving, married relationship where the artificial methods of family planning are morally unacceptable.[16] Masturbation, pornography and homosexuality are discussed but also deemed morally wrong. There is no room for discussion of students' questions. In 1986 Macnamara published the first edition of *Ready, Steady, Grow!*, a book aimed at children aged 10 to 13.[17] The book continues a tradition of sex education within a Christian framework where the information is prefaced by three opening chapters containing biblical quotes and parables. There are discussions of puberty, the importance of manners and the danger of rejecting religion and of peer pressure. Masturbation, which repeats advice given in the original column, is seen as natural but needing to be controlled, or else it 'may be difficult for him to give his wife the time for gradual love-making'.[18] There is a discussion of sexual intercourse and pregnancy but children are told that 'God wants people to make him babies, but not until they are grown up and married', advice that might be potentially troubling to children of non-married cohabiting parents. Sexual intercourse is defined as for 'mature people who have made a commitment to one another to live together "for better or worse, in sickness and in health" until the end of life'.[19] There is a parallel recognition that couples do have sexual intercourse outside marriage but the 'Bible teaches that the ideal to aim at is to keep sexual intercourse for the committed relationship marriage'.[20] There is no discussion of homosexuality in the book except a brief reply in a question-and-answer section where children are told that 'despite their sexual disadvantage homosexual people can achieve success in anyaspect of life', and that teasing, rejection or showing prejudice to such a person is wrong.[21]

In 1995 Macnamara worked with St Brigid's National School in Greystones to produce a booklet on sex education which was widely distributed to schools throughout the country. It was written in conjunction with the Archbishop of Dublin's Education Secretariat and was recommended by bishops as the principle resource schools could use in their relationships and sexuality education. The description of sexuality presented to pupils is designed to foster Catholic values of love, marriage, parenthood and family life. Tom Inglis is critical of the programme for not working with children's existing understandings of sexuality which they may have learned from the media, or asking children what they would like to learn about sexuality – the implication being, he argues, 'that what they have already learnt or understood is either incorrect or inadequate'.[22] In 1999 Angela Macnamara published a guide for parents that encourages children's relationship-building skills.[23] It cover areas such as assertiveness, the role of the media in their lives, and establishes keeping sex for within marriage as the ideal to which their children should aspire. 'Far from being a modern liberation, sex before marriage can be a new tyranny', encouraging a lack of responsibility, Macnamara explains. In addition to these books, Angela Macnamara also made two sex education videos, one for boys and one for girls in the 1990s.

Angela Macnamara's last book, published in 2005, left the familiar field of sex education to offer her reflections on getting older.[24] There is some discussion about sex, specifically on the importance of intimacy among older couples when the pursuit of orgasm becomes less important.[25] Mostly, Macnamara's light-hearted message is about making the most out of older age, even through adversity, enjoying libraries and the courses they offer, the possibility of new friends, and keeping your house – and your mind – free from clutter. The topic of downsizing to a more manageable home was a topic with which Macnamara was well acquainted, having moved house in the year of her husband's death.

MACNAMARA AND ME

Angela Macnamara's principle concern in participating in a series of interviews with me for this book was that she wished that the letters would be understood within the social and historical context in which they were written. That is what good sociological enquiry is about. It is also how Macnamara understands what she has written. 'I feel justified in that I did my best with the situation that I had at the time, so I won't look on it with a more modern view' she explains. Not that it stops Macnamara's desire to continue to contribute to the current debate over how sexuality is spoken about. She continues: 'I'm totally aware how irrelevant my attitude now may be but I want to express it.' This book is one means of expressing those views. There is, of course, an inherent risk in participating in research: that of portrayal. Even when the most rigorous ethical guidelines about the treatment of respondents are applied, a process of analysis produces the researchers' account of a life, of a body of work. Of someone's life work. It is an onerous responsibility. Our lives are separated not just by generation but by religious faith, so influential in Macnamara's life and absent in my own. Angela Macnamara read all the chapters of this book prior to publication. She didn't always agree with my interpretation of what she wrote. Her comments are woven into the final work.

This is not a book solely about Angela Macnamara. It is about the lives of ordinary men and women as they make decisions that shape their intimate lives through dating, marriage and parenthood, seen through the prism of the column. This book is not nostalgic for the past, nor does it sneer over the innocence of the letters. Even at the time of writing the column Angela Macnamara was aware that her opinions were also considered irrelevant by a substantial section of the population.[26] Macnamara was well aware of the criticism. In a television documentary she describes how some people perceived her as 'something of a holy Mary, a do-gooder, I don't have any sense of humour'.[27] An article on Macnamara written by journalist Kevin Marron in *The Sunday Press* (24 January 1971) explains that 'it's no fun trying to help half the country, while the other half is laughing'. This fact reflected the reality of Ireland in transition: neither modern nor traditional, but a hybrid of competing attitudes. In the same article, Macnamara describes herself: 'I am not a square despite what many people think. I'm not conservative. I'm not the other extreme either. I'm liberal, sort of middle of the road.' Throughout this book there are elements of Macnamara's advice that range from conservative to liberal. She opposed censorship at a time when, between 1962 and 1963 alone, 408 books were banned in Ireland.[28] She opposed corporal punishment in schools, a practice that would not be outlawed for another twenty years. She spoke about the obligation on parents to impart sex education to their children so they would enter courtship and marriage with more information about sex than the previous generation, including herself, possessed. She wrote publicly about sex in a column that entered 400,000 homes every Sunday, occasionally displeasing the Catholic Church, particularly in the early years, before it was recognized that even McQuaid himself could not control the myriad of ways in which sex would be read about or watched on television. The advice was, of course, dispensed by Macnamara through the prism of the Catholic Church, motivated by her deep personal faith and a belief in the infallibility of its leaders. Macnamara remained steadfast in offering advice that was in compliance with that teaching, even, as the years progressed when the advice was often impractical, stretched credulity or went against her private beliefs on a topic.

NOTES

1. A. Macnamara, *Yours Sincerely* (Dublin: Veritas, 2003), p.33.
2. L. Fuller, *Irish Catholicism since 1950: The Undoing of a Culture* (Dublin: Gill & Macmillan, 2002), pp.30–2.
3. Macnamara, *Yours Sincerely*, p.50.
4. Ibid., pp.62–3.
5. 'Dear Angela', Radharc documentary first broadcast on 24 April 1975.
6. Macnamara, *Yours Sincerely*, p.84.
7. D. Ferriter, *Occasions of Sin: Sex & Society in Modern Ireland* (London: Profile Books, 2009), p.378.
8. Ibid., p.379. Angela Macnamara told me that she did not remember this incident.
9. Macnamara, *Yours Sincerely*, p.69.
10. Ibid., p.53–4.
11. Ibid., p.85.
12. Ibid., p.64.
13. 'Dear Angela'.
14. Macnamara, *Yours Sincerely*, p.108.
15. Vincent Jennings was appointed editor of *The Sunday Press* in 1968, succeeding Francis Carty. He was the youngest editor of a national newspaper in the country, aged 31. In 1986, Jennings was appointed general manager of the Irish Press Group of newspapers by the chairman, Dr Eamon de Valera. Jennings would later hold the positions of managing director and was chief executive when the company went into liquidation in 1989. He was also chairman of the Catholic Communications Institute and its publishing arm, Veritas, who would publish Macnamara's autobiography in 2003. Jennings died in 2010.
16. T. Inglis, *Lessons in Irish Sexuality* (Dublin: University College Dublin Press, 1998), p.41.
17. A. Macnamara, *Ready, Steady, Grow!* (Dublin: Veritas, 1996).
18. Ibid., p.61.
19. Ibid., p.79.
20. Ibid., p.80.
21. Ibid., p.112.
22. Ibid., p.46.
23. A. Macnamara, *Will Our Children Build Healthy Relationships?* (Dublin: Veritas, 1999), p.24.
24. A. Macnamara, *Reflections for the Golden Years* (Dublin, Veritas, 2005).

25. Ibid., p.103.
26. In a clarification, Angela Macnamara describes this section of the population as 'modern secular'.
27. 'Dear Angela', 24 April 1975.
28. Ferriter, *Occasions of Sin*, p.385.

CHAPTER THREE

Dancing, Dating and Courtship

INTRODUCTION

A great anxiety was evident on the pages of the Angela Macnamara column as young people and their parents sought how to best navigate the world of dating without falling prey to sin, pregnancy or a loss of character. It was a world that had already changed prior to Macnamara's arrival at *The Sunday Press* in 1963. The pace of this change would accelerate throughout the seventeen years of her tenure ushering in a transformation in how young couples related to their Church, their parents and their own bodies. Young people would increasingly see their bodies not as sources of sin, fasting or discipline, as many of their parents did, but as instruments of pleasure to be enjoyed in sexual intimacy, dancing and fashion. These changes were part of a wider transition from parental and community surveillance of dating couples to an internalized self-monitoring of behaviour; young people often juggled conflicting feelings of independence or obligation, lust or guilt.

The ritual and rules of the dancehall would give way to the individualism of the disco. Dating rules changed. Women approached men. Men approached other men. When Angela Macnamara started her career in relationship and sexuality advice she was often a lone voice in a world traditionally dominated by the Catholic Church, but it was a terrain that would become increasingly crowded as her tenure progressed. Young people were subjected to competing versions as to what constituted appropriate behaviour when dating and during their courtships. The rules governing dating would become more fluid, with couples drawing from alternative sources of advice published and broadcast in Ireland, advice they would increasingly use to interrogate the positions held by Angela Macnamara in her column.

While many embraced the new vista that had opened up, that would redefine dating, courtship and marriage, others clung to the certainties of the past. While change brought excitement and discovery to some, it brought great anxiety and unhappiness to others. Some young people, whom Angela Macnamara would describe as 'convention breakers', made new choices, often in defiance of the authority of their parents and the Church.[1] Not all of these choices brought the independence or fulfilment they expected. They did, however, forge new and more democratic relationships between themselves and their parents, between a religion they would observe and a Church whose authority they had started to question.

Angela Macnamara's reliance on advice that now felt reminiscent of the 1940s and 1950s would open her to scorn from those who believed that her column was hopelessly out of date for a generation of young people who were now influenced by new progressive social and cultural values. For others the column would be a valuable source of information, especially for those ignorant of sexuality and the facts of life, and it would become a resource for the Catholic faithful who often struggled to reconcile their religious beliefs with a changing dating landscape that demanded greater sexual intimacy and emotional disclosure.

IRISH DATING IN TRANSITION

Irish dating and courting practices were in transition in the early 1960s. Practices such as matchmaking are identified by Nancy Scheper-Hughes as having died out in the late 1950s.[2] A letter to Macnamara published on 15 November 1964 was from a recently engaged woman worried that she had no dowry to offer her wealthy fiancé. She was reassured that a dowry was no longer 'a 'must' nowadays' and that her boyfriend, if they loved her, would marry her whether she had money or not. This represented a shift where love moved more centre stage for young people choosing a mate over familial, religious or class obligations. Letter writers often disapproved of this tendency. A letter writer of 15 January 1967 thought that the happiest marriages had nothing to do with love but with 'down to earth economics'. Angela Macnamara also recognized this belief in what she describes in interview as the 'right match according to land ownership' in rural areas. This belief was part of a social system identified by Tom Inglis as having played a crucial role in maintaining the institutions of marriage and family during the nineteenth century and much of the twentieth century in Ireland.[3] The strict regulation of dating, courtship and marriage had allowed a sexual life only to a son who would inherit or a daughter who would have a dowry and marry. The influence of family and farming, however, would continue to exert an influence over dating and courtship throughout the 1960s. Because of both a reluctance to subdivide farms and fathers' unwillingness to sign properties over, inheriting sons were often discouraged from marriage and waited until middle age to inherit, finding themselves unable to compete with younger bachelors for eligible women.[4] Life history interviewee Patrick McGrath (75) recalls how his selection of a wife was also influenced by what was best for his family and the inheritance of his father's farm. It was also expected that his wife would look after his parents in their old age, help out on the farm and bring up their young children:

> I knew that I was to be at home on the farm; I knew I was to inherit the farm. I knew ... my parents who were still very active. I knew the type of girl that would suit them. I knew that. I also knew the girl I would marry would have to come into our house, their house and be with me and them while they were alive. I knew that was a pre-requisite ... Mary saw after those [his parents] during their illnesses and nursed them at home and both of them died at home about seven or eight years after we were married, they died within three months of each other and Mary nursed those, minded them and looked after them as well as the young children and that was accepted by her as normal and that's what she did.

Letters from agony aunt Frankie Byrne read on her radio show 'Woman's Page' from 1963 to 1985 also illustrated tension between married couples when presented with an opportunity to return to farming or to a mother-in-law. One woman from the country, now happily living in Dublin with her boyfriend, was distraught when she discovered he had inherited his uncle's farm and now wanted to return to a rural area twenty miles from the nearest town. Her boyfriend reassured her that she 'wouldn't have the kind of life my mother had to live – one of drudgery and hard work with no amenities and also almost primitive surroundings'.[5] The woman remained unconvinced. Another woman was unconvinced by an opportunity to move into a modern bungalow built beside her mother-in-law's house, although Byrne thought she was very fortunate to have such an opportunity.[6]

The concept of a newly married woman entering the family home of her husband was not restricted to the farming community. After my own parents' marriage in 1965, with low wages combined with little available credit for a mortgage, they lived with my mother's parents for five years, during which time my grandfather died in 1968. In 1970 my mother reluctantly moved into my father's family home in rural Co. Tipperary and nursed her ailing mother-in-law until she died the following year.

Angela Macnamara published a letter on 9 May 1965 from a newly married woman about how best to manage a much more difficult and controlling mother-in-law.

> Q. I am married a few months to a nice young farmer and we're living with his parents. His father is in bed all the time so doesn't give much trouble. His mother does not allow us any social life – not even the wireless. Though we have a car we're not allowed go to any place of entertainment. The reason is there would be money spent. I am fit to cry when I see the neighbours going to bingo.

> A. It's time someone spoke to that mother-in-law of yours – and spoke firmly – on the subject of justice and charity ... your husband should have a regular income which he and you can spend anyway you wish. There should be no question of looking for your mother-in-law's permission to go out ...

For D.S. Connery, the inability of sons to take the side of their new wives over their mothers had its roots in the dysfunctional relationship between mother and son, in which by 'pampering and then clinging desperately to her dear boy she makes him a victim of her possessiveness'.[7] Such possessiveness had also been identified by Alexander J. Humphreys, in his study of the Irish family in the 1950s and 1960s, and is thought to be responsible for preventing even larger-scale emigration from the land, obstructing the marriage of the inheriting son who often showed great reluctance to bring a new wife into the home while his mother was still alive.[8] Letters to Frankie Byrne's radio show also revealed a mother's desire to influence her son's choice of wife.[9] One letter was from a mother who was upset that her son's girlfriend was living in Edinburgh and had a very good job. She went on to describe her as 'very much the modern girl – beautifully dressed and I would imagine very sophisticated', whereas her son was 'a simple ordinary fellow', and she was convinced that their relationship wouldn't work. 'We lead a quiet life here and I'm sure it wouldn't suit her', the mother wrote. Frankie Byrne describes it as the 'classic situation of mother unwilling to untie the apron strings'.[10]

The greatest transition occurring within the field of dating in the 1960s surrounded the issues of surveillance and segregation of the sexes. Dancehalls had facilitated the practice of couples 'walking-out' together, afterwards deemed to be responsible for increased immoral behaviour. Letter writers to Macnamara encouraged a return to patrols policing country lanes to root out courting couples.[11] While Angela Macnamara disagreed with such measures and encouraged couples to police their own behaviour, her advice was for a mixture of segregation and surveillance, both by the couples themselves and by their peers. Parents did not trust their children. Neither did the Church. Therefore there was a combined duty to prevent young people from falling into a state of sin. Tom Inglis describes a religious and moral legacy in which boys were taught that contact with girls was problematic and potentially dangerous, and in which the best way to prevent falling into a state of sin was the 'strict segregation and supervision of the sexes'.[12] It was a lesson learned by the interviewees in this study. Patrick McGrath (75) said that as teenagers they were made to understand that 'from a boy's point of view girls were dangerous and from a girl's point of view boys were dangerous'. Segregation of the sexes – in schools and churches – was a means to control this dangerous and problematic relationship. Angela Macnamara laid greater emphasis on the supervision of the sexes by the wider peer group and also through the individual self-monitoring of behaviour. She believed that boys and girls were incapable of platonic relationships.[13] She believed that boys and girls should not be left alone together with nothing to do, nor be allowed to holiday together when dating.[14] Private parties were also ill-advised.[15] Parents, particularly mothers, had also internalized the supervision message, seeing it as their duty to protect their sons, and more particularly their daughters, from sin. One 18-year-old whose letter to Macnamara was published on 12 March 1966 complained of his mother's excessive supervision of his life:

Q. I am a boy of 18 doing Leaving Cert. I am not allowed go to dances, pictures or with girls. My mother says that teenage boys and girls never go together without sinning mortally ... Is it true teenagers always sin like this?

A. If parents have given their children a sense of responsibility, good positive sex instruction and love of God then they must allow them to become independent. Many teenagers are allowed out in the world without having received proper home-training. These are usually the ones that 'fall by the wayside'.

The segregation of the sexes continued long into adulthood, according to Nancy Scheper-Hughes, with seating in the local church distributed according to age, sex and marriage, and the physical space of the family home divided between husband and wife.[16]

THE PURSUIT OF ROMANCE

There was widespread dissatisfaction expressed by letter writers to the column about the limited range of social venues where young men and women could meet, socialize and date. This fact reflected the very different socio-economic climate which existed in Ireland in the 1960s. In the United States, by comparison, Cas Wouters reveals a dating culture that had evolved around the expansion of universities, boarding schools and other coeducational institutions in the 1920s which removed young people and their dating practices from family and community surveillance.[17] By contrast, full-time enrolments in Irish third-level education in 1963 were a mere 16,819 – hardly enough to launch a dating revolution, but change was slowly underway.[18] Connery also pointed to universities as one of the few places in Ireland where healthier, platonic relationships between men and women existed, where a boy and girl would 'seek each other's company for reasons of mind and personality'.[19]

It was, in fact, this changing dating scene that created anxiety and uncertainty among young people as they struggled to observe a range of informal rules that had to be navigated. This anxiety made its way into the pages of Angela Macnamara's column. Most letters concerned difficulties encountered within that cauldron of romance, the dancehall, although the life history interviewees revealed a wider range of religious, sporting and community groups where couples met.

The dancehalls that young men and women wrote to Macnamara about were different from what she would have experienced in the 1950s. There was a new optimism and affluence in Ireland in 1963. There was a desire for new entertainment; young people had rejected the dances of their parents in their local Parochial Hall in favour of a new generation of dancehall. Young people wanted more than the cards, draughts and the family rosary that had been so much a part of family life. They wanted more than the occasional access to the family wireless. The invention of the transistor radio contributed to a communications revolution in which young people had access to the latest music broadcast by stations such as Radio Luxembourg.[20] Changing tastes in music and fashion had filtered through from Carnaby Street and King's Road in London that challenged the more conventional and sombre styles of the 1950s. Harry McCourt claims that although the more outlandish fashions didn't catch on in Ireland, 'see-through blouses, crochet dresses, fishnet tights, hot pants and the mini-skirt sent male temperatures rising'.[21] The rule-bound dances of the 1950s would give way to a more informal, individual style of dancing synonymous with the Twist – launched by the international success of Chubby Checker's 'Let's Twist Again' in 1961. This new, more free style of dancing did raise a concern for modesty in the Angela Macnamara column, where she wrote on 27 September 1964 that 'the Twist and the Shake can be done in clothes that are too tight and with vigour that can be suggestive'. Other fashions, such as a trend for young women to wear tights with just a chunky sweater, were also deemed immodest in the column.[22]

Young people were undeterred and flocked to the newly built dancehalls, some resembling large sheds, that were mushrooming up all over the country. Vincent Power claims they changed Irish courting habits forever. Whereas 'youngsters cycled to local dances in the fifties', he wrote, they 'drove to ballrooms miles away in the sixties'.[23] This enabled young people to escape the surveillance of a local community and overzealous priests who were known to patrol county lanes, seeking out courting couples. Diarmaid Ferriter points out that the *Limerick Rural Survey* published in 1964 also reported 'the preference for young people for attending dances away from their own parishes' to avoid this surveillance by their families.[24] People now wanted to spend their recreational time not around 'things of the spirit', as Power suggests, like sodalities and Legion of Mary activities, but in the pursuit of romance in the dancehall.[25] This marked a broader cultural shift, identified by Steven Seidman, to young people finding fulfilment away from 'work and homemaking', and towards a more individual and personal quest for fulfilment encouraged by an expanding leisure industry.[26] The dancehall culture with its live bands would hold sway for much of the 1960s until yet again cultural habits changed. The failure to grant alcohol licences to dancehalls contributed to a drift of young people to newly built hotels that offered cabaret shows, discos and alcohol. Music tastes changed too, with the popularity of the electric guitar sounds of people such as Jimi Hendrix and Eric Clapton, while home-ground bands like Horslips and Bob Geldof contributed to a decline in the dancehall's popularity throughout the 1970s.[27]

Before these more individualized styles of dancing associated with the changing musical tastes of the 1970s became commonplace, letter writers were often dejected by their inability to dance and asked Angela Macnamara to suggest classes where they might improve.[28] For men, most anxiety revolved around asking a woman to dance. What if she was to say no?[29] What if she was to say yes – what sort of conversation should follow? Men often struggled with the conversation in which many women engaged at dances, believing it to be superficial and dull.[30] The following letter published on 18 August 1968 reveals how men struggled to learn the informal rules that governed the dancehall:

Q. I am a young man (25) and only started attending dances about four years ago. But I haven't got the right approach. In what manner should a boy ask a girl for a date, and how many dances should he give her before he asks her for a date?

A. When a man is starting his dancing years I think he will become self confident more quickly if he chooses partners who are quiet and less glamorous types of girls. Such girls are often the nicest ones, they are not so critical of men and they are pleased to be asked up to dance … To invite a girl to dance, simply approach and say 'Would you like to dance?' Don't complicate matters by thinking there is a formula. Pleasant good manners are the basic requirement.

Some women likened the experience of the dancehall to that of a cattle mart and objected to being appraised by men at dances; one letter of 3 November 1968 complained that they 'look us up and down as if we were cattle and then walk away'. Others, who deemed themselves to be attractive, were puzzled by men's lack of interest.[31] Angela Macnamara advised men who regularly attended dances that they must make 'a point of dancing occasionally with girls who are shy, lonely and not blessed with physical beauty'.[32] For young, politicized women like journalist and feminist Mary Kenny it was all part of a 'ghastly dance hall routine which I had no patience for whatsoever', while the very concept of 'waiting to be asked by a man to dance' was appalling to her.[33] It was her interest in politics that brought her into contact with a lot of interesting, exciting men 'without having to darn well dance with them!' Connery also describes the dancehall scene as 'operating like cattle fairs' where men survey the merchandise and choose. Both the men and women to whom Connery spoke often spent three nights a week dancing, leaving little money for anything else, but felt that this was their only opportunity to meet members of the opposite sex.[34]

For Patrick McGrath, while women were technically 'chosen', they would have made their interest in an approach known or could have availed of the 'ladies' choice' at a dance. He describes the scene:

> I remember it very clearly, the band started playing and all the girls lined up at one side and all the boys lined up on the other and they took time to vet each other across the hall and they chose a partner, sometimes the girls chose the man, in a nod is as good as a wink sort of way, so the choice was made … they went off dancing and there was the chat and then afterwards for those people as time went on or earlier then, they would say to the girl would you like to come out for a walk with me? … You'd go for a walk with the girl and you'd have a cuddle …

Power also recalls the often painful dating rituals of the dancehall. With the dance floor populated with existing dating couples, men and women surveyed each other across a largely empty space. Success was uncertain. Women often relied upon predictable lines of refusal – 'I'm too tired'; 'My feet are sore'; 'I'm waiting for my friend to come back from the ladies'; 'My fella's gone to get me a mineral'; and the old Dublin reliable – 'Ask my sister, I'm sweatin'.'[35]

Many women did say yes to a dance and yes to more intimate activity afterwards. It was this opportunity for morally dubious behaviour that had historically caused much public anxiety about the dancehall. The Public Dance Hall Act 1935 was introduced to regulate the holding of dances throughout the country. It required the applicant to apply to the Justice of the District Court for a public dancing licence which was evaluated on the facilities provided and also the age and character of the applicant. The Act was a recommendation of the Carrigan Report published in 1931 which called twenty-nine expert witnesses before a committee to give evidence in private on how the State might respond to perceived growing levels of moral degeneracy in Ireland. Central to this was the evidence of Rev.

R.S. Devane, SJ, who, according to Smith, had a 'seeming obsession with the dangers associated with popular amusements, especially the dancehall'.[36] For Devane, the spectre of young couples returning home on country laneways late at night provided both the temptation and opportunity for sin in a society where a lack of parental control, modern cinema and the privacy of the motor car were all deemed to be contributing to a moral decay.[37] The misuse of the motor car remained an important site in Penny Mansfield and Jean Collard's qualitative study of newly married London couples in 1988 who also struggled to find private and comfortable locations for sexual activity.[38] Conrad M. Arensberg and Solon T. Kimball also identified clerical displeasure at couples 'walking-out' after dances.[39] Ireland was not alone in acting against the perceived danger that dancehalls posed to the national good. According to Wouters, anti-morality dancing committees had been established in the 1920s in America which railed against the immodest shaking of the body present in many of the new dance crazes.[40] Similarly, in the Netherlands a government committee was established to investigate the dangers of dancing which was facilitating freer contacts between the sexes. The concern of government authorities centred upon a rejection of a more rule-bound dancing, with the adoption of styles which were seen to liberate the emotions, allowing for greater bodily movement and individual expression.

Displeasure with the conduct in dancehalls was not confined to the 1930s. Both men and women wrote to Angela Macnamara, disappointed at the moral behaviour of the other sex. A letter from a 22-year-old man published on 6 November 1966 described how he was 'appalled at the conduct, atmosphere and overcrowdedness of the dances' and that 'clergy, parents and teachers might be wakened up by an occasional visit to the dancehalls'. Macnamara agreed. In a reply published on 19 September 1965, to a woman who deemed dancehalls 'not places for decent, self-respecting girls to go', she agreed that 'the moral standard in dancehalls has certainly gone down' and advised parents to 'drop into a public dancehall after 10pm and see for themselves just what goes on'. It was, in fact, this low moral standard that was encouraging many patrons to attend, as this letter published on 31 July 1966 reveals:

> Q. Like all fellows who go with a girl after a dance, we try to go as far as we can with a girl. If a girl is 'soft' enough to give in, she needn't blame the boy for wanting all he can get. After all isn't that all most of us go with girls after dances for?

A. Unfortunately as proved by my mail, this attitude is not uncommon. Boys pour into public dancehalls when the pubs close for the sole purpose of picking up girls. If the girls were not as easily available as they are this scandal would not be continuing as it is.

Angela Macnamara saw alcohol as playing a dangerous role in undermining the control necessary for men to conduct themselves within appropriate moral boundaries; it was more likely 'to render him more ready to satisfy selfishly his insidious sensuality'.[41] For many life history interviewees, alcohol did not play a role in their social lives. Tony (63) described his love of music and dancing as his prime motivation for attending dances, first in two local tennis clubs and then in bigger Dublin ballrooms such as the Crystal and the National. As a member of the Pioneer Association he did not go to the pub beforehand, arriving much earlier than most of the men who did, a successful strategy allowing him to 'get a bit of dancing in with some of the girls'.[42] His anxiety about asking women to dance was probably a more common feeling than the bravado of the letter writer above:

> You'd be shy you know, you'd have to walk across that floor ... would she and yea you would be refused and have to walk [back] ... and then you'd have to ask someone else, all that awkwardness, there's a huge amount of awkwardness for me as a young man ... If she accepted the dance you'd see how you'd get on and very often it was just a dance and thanks very much but sometimes it would be do you want a dance or a mineral upstairs ... but if they said yes to that , that was the green light you know?

Of course, despite the potential awkwardness men and women were successful within the dancehall scenario, staring across a crowded room before plucking up the courage to approach, having a drink and maybe a cuddle on the way home. However, other life history interviewees described successful strategies that were less random. These revealed how these young men socialized in groups, often dependent on whether one of them had a girlfriend who, through her friends, would often provide dating opportunities for the others. In the case of James Kelly (70), he met his future wife after a friend suggested that he ask his sister to a dance. He explains that 'he [James's brother] was going with someone and my best friend was going with someone else and he said why don't you ask my sister. So I brought her to the New Year's Eve party in 1960, married in 1964.' Declan Staunton

(62), on the other hand, dated and eventually married his friend's ex-girlfriend – he describes himself as 'always having a kind of regard for' her – but not before contacting his friend beforehand. He says that 'I can remember writing to him and saying that we had met and that we were together and we may go out. And he said "Don't be stupid it is all over between us that is fine." ' Declan's early dating life revolved around walking up and down Dun Laoghaire pier or socializing in the local tennis club – a common meeting place for the men in this study. For others dating involved numerous trips to the cinema, to dancehalls and carnivals and, for James Kelly, attendance at novenas and visiting elderly relatives.

This idea of men and women socializing in mixed groups and casually dating was highly recommended by Angela Macnamara. She cautioned couples against becoming too serious too quickly, predicting that exclusive relationships or 'going steady' would involve couples spending more time on their own, with an increased risk of sexual exploration. She advised readers in one of her early articles published on 5 May 1963 that even after successive dates both parties should remain free to date other people:

> If a girl and boy have no intention or prospect of becoming engaged in the near future they are under no obligation whatsoever to each other. Both can date or be dated by anyone else they choose. They are quite free. Make no promises to each other.

Lest readers should interpret this advice as encouraging promiscuity over commitment, she continued that 'while advising teenagers to "play the field" and go out with plenty of the opposite sex, there must be no love making. If you want to deserve a bad name this business of making love with a different person every date will earn that bad name for you.' The encouragement to socialize and casually date in larger groups was similar to international dating advice. In the United States, Wouters suggests that columnists such as Amy Vanderbilt, writing in the 1960s, speculated whether groups of friends could monitor and chaperone their own behaviour, though realistically Vanderbilt recognized the tendency for couples to pair off when in company.[43] While both women dispensed similar advice, discouraging this trend for couples to pair off and go steady, what is noteworthy is how Vanderbilt's advice evolved over the next decade compared to Macnamara's. Nine years later Vanderbilt wrote that premarital sexual relations were a private matter between a couple, and that a girl considering such a step should receive information about contraception from her gynaecologist. Angela Macnamara, however, remained implacably opposed to premarital sex and to any sexual activity that she thought would encourage it. She also remained opposed to contraception, particularly for single women, which I shall discuss later in this chapter. Wouters believes that dating advice that encouraged people to date numerous partners without any commitment to engagement was unique to the United States, although similar advice is found in Macnamara's replies; both women tried to undermine the growing trend to go steady.[44] This overlap with American dating advice was due to Macnamara's regard for Catholic dating literature which became the basis of her own advice and which she also recommended to her readers.

Musical societies and sports clubs and religious organizations also provided venues for the men and women to meet. David Moloney's (63) job working in the civil service brought him into contact with a largely female-dominated workforce. Although he did date women with whom he worked, it was through his involvement with a musical society that he met his future wife. As a member of the male chorus in a production of *The Mikado* he became attracted to a woman in the female chorus, whom he asked out to a dance in the local cricket club after the final night of the show. He explains:

> The group were going and I had to bring somebody so I asked her and she was delighted and all very naive and simple enough, we went to the cricket club and danced the night away. And somebody had a car, she was dropped home and waved goodbye not kissed goodbye, and I went home. So that was the start of that particular relationship.

Religious organizations also provided opportunities for young men and women to socialize. Tony Fitzgerald (62) was a member of a boys' sodality in school which organized social events and outings with those in the girls' group; these were the first dances he attended and, coming from a single-sex school, they were an important means of meeting girls. For Patrick McGrath (75) the role of community organizations played a key role as he attended 'dances organised by Macra na Feirme and dances organised by the Pioneer Association ...the local GAA would have had socials, ICA had socials so you'd have the opportunities for attending those and meeting girls'. He described how he met his future wife when he was 22, at 'a Macra na

Feirme dance and I had known her family ... This girl appeared to me to be the type of girl that I would have been attracted to, so we danced, talked, we had a bit of a cuddle, it began from there really.' Patricia McElhone's book on the lives of six happily married Irish couples was written in 1977 to offset some of the negative exposure of Irish marriage in the media.[45] McElhone's interviewees revealed a range of venues – dances, sodalities and skiing – at which they met their spouses.

Macra na Feirme in particular was recommended by Macnamara as a venue for single young men and women and also features in the men's life histories as a social venue for those in rural Ireland.[46] It had been founded in 1943 with the establishment of three Young Farmers Clubs with the aim of providing education and more social activities that would make rural life more attractive.[47] Patrick McGrath (75) again describes the positive role that the organization had in his life:

> I was encouraged to join Macra na Fermie when I was sixteen, seventeen, and I also became involved in various studies in the Vocational School in Mitchelstown instigated by Macra na Feirme ... I took part in debating and public speaking at national level, I did a lot of drama as well ... Macra na Feirme stood for social activities, cultural and education and a whole range of things so the social opportunities were considered as hugely important and they saw to it that we had ample opportunities for socialising.

Hugh Ryan, former president of Macra during the period 1965–67, described how the organization served not only farmers but the wider community.[48] His local branch of Portlaoise opened its own hall in 1955, which served as a venue for social occasions and public dancing. He contends that there was a vital need, especially in rural Ireland, for more social outlets, apart from sport, that would allow men and women to socialize. In addition to dances Macra also organized 'field evenings' where members met on a particular farm and visited some local historical site in an attempt to bring together people with similar interests. Ryan describes how 'a number of members in my own branch were living in the town, working in the town and had no association with farm life at all'. Opening up Macra as an alternative venue for young people to meet was also facilitated by the opening of a tennis club attached to the hall, which proved popular among locals.

'STEALING THE PLEASURES OF MARRIED PEOPLE'

The Angela Macnamara column received a large number of letters from dating couples. These letters sought advice on what level of intimacy was permissible between them, and the writers ranged from teenage couples casually dating to those who were close to marriage. In all cases the advice from Macnamara remained consistent. She reminded readers that sex before marriage was always sinful, even when there was an intention to marry. Furthermore, readers should avoid situations and affectionate acts that might lead to sin. Even the act of holding hands with your boyfriend at the cinema held a potential danger of sin and she advised, in reply to a letter published on 30 May 1965, that the girl should 'be careful that this harmless little touch does not lead on and on to a petting session' and that people felt 'awkward and ashamed' to see courting couples behave like this. It was this 'slippery slope' argument, common in American Catholic dating advice, that was central to Macnamara's advice to couples. It was this near total prohibition on physical contact, however, that generated great anxiety amongst the faithful as they struggled to keep within their intimate parameters whilst generating ridicule amongst those that felt her column was now hopelessly out of date. Mary Kenny, for example, described her attitude to Angela Macnamara at the time as a mixture of 'laughter and derision', seeing the column as 'Peg's Paper' material – 'simple values for simple folk' – although recognizing that as modern women working in the media they thought they knew it all.[49]

Catholic dating advice is littered with analogies to eating, driving, faulty brakes and slippery slopes, all to illustrate to young couples that they might not possess the sufficient self-control to stop their lovemaking at just passionate kissing. Angela Macnamara's advice was no different and in one of her early articles published on 28 April 1963 she wrote:

> You feel hungry so you buy a steak, cook it appetisingly and as you sit down to eat it your appetite has reached a climax. But this time you know that, being on a serious diet, you are strictly forbidden meat. It was intensely stupid of you to have bought the steak to begin with. Now you must either be ill as a result of breaking your diet or suffer the disappointment of a frustrated climax. Can you see the connection between this and the sexual appetite?

It is unclear whether young readers could see a connection or cared either way as to the consequences. This advice is heavily influenced by the work of Catholic dating writers such as Monsignor George Kelly.[50] Passion, he suggested, could not be turned on and off like a tap and women risked being engulfed in desire unless they avoided passionate kissing in secluded locations. Angela Macnamara wrote on 28 April 1963 that such activities could cause a lack of control that may lead couples to 'steal the pleasures intended only for married people'. Kelly advised couples to plan their dates in advance and preferably to stay in the company of others, so that they could avoid the seclusion of a park bench or a parked car.[51] It was the woman who set the tone on a date and communicated her intentions through her dress, the amount of make-up she wore and her use of language.[52] How women dressed on dates was also an emotive subject in the Macnamara column, with an angry letter from a woman published on 25 May 1969 declaring that she hated the 'mini mini skirts and see through blouses' and that women had 'degraded themselves with such fashions'. In a reply to a letter on the same topic, published on 26 February 1967, miniskirts were also singled out by Macnamara, who said that 'girls that choose to wear immodest clothes are inviting boys to treat them cheaply'. There wasn't much that women *could* do that didn't hold the potential for the sexual arousal of men. Angela Macnamara explained in *Living and Loving* that 'through ignorance and thoughtlessness rather than badness girls arouse men by the way they dress, sit, move and the way they show affection inordinately'.[53] John and Mary Ryan also wrote of the role modesty played in having a loving attitude towards other people, as it 'guides us in choosing the clothes, cosmetics, postures and gestures which will best enable our bodies unobtrusively to express ourselves' to others.[54]

Overall, there was an informalization around how young people dressed at dances, often rejecting formality in favour of a more casual look, as described in a letter on 28 April 1974 from a woman who felt she always liked 'to dress neatly and tidily' but was 'passed by for someone who wears casual clothes'. For Cas Wouters, women's clothes – particularly the corset – had symbolized an increasing control over the body, whereas loose clothes became indicative of loose morals. The abandonment of such restrictive clothing and corset-like underwear from the 1960s onwards represented a liberation of the female body, but was undermined by a greater pressure to adopt a range of fitness regimes to mould the body into a desired shape. In Angela Macnamara's column, the informalization of clothes outside the dancehall caused disquiet too. Macnamara received letters complaining about the unsuitability of women's modern clothes in church. There was a growing trend among women not to wear hats at Mass, combined with a liking for shorter skirts that shocked letter writers.[55] A regular attender at Mass wrote to Macnamara on 13 July 1980, shocked that she was exposed to a woman's buttocks 'oozing through tight jeans'. Priests, too, were criticized for choosing to wear lay clothes while on holiday.[56]

Regardless of their dress or make-up, women wrote to Macnamara as if under siege from the amorous advances of their dates. Two women complained in their letter published on 10 May 1970 that men nearly 'always wanted to touch us immodestly under our clothes', and they wondered 'if we allow them, do they think we are cheap?' Macnamara was unambiguous in telling them that if the boys 'consider that you are cheapening yourselves, they are correct. You are.' Another 16-year-old girl's letter published on 12 September 1976 also complained that the boys she and her friends dated always tried 'to put their hands up under our skirts or inside our blouses'; although she refused such behaviour, her boyfriend dumped her as a result, telling her she was old-fashioned.

Given the lack of locations where dating couples could be alone, the cinema provided one such opportunity, though the following woman's letter published on 24 November 1963 revealed how she was both confused and excited about being intimate with her boyfriend in public.

> Q. My boyfriend makes love to me all during the pictures every time we go to a film. While I feel excited by this, I am embarrassed about going on like this in a public place. Yet I love him and don't want to lose him by being too prim and proper.

> A. Boys who take their girlfriends to the films, or anywhere else, and behave like this are displaying selfish lust, not love ... The shame so many girls feel about such behaviour is the instinctive reaction of a good girl to guard her purity.

Other women also found that agreeing to attend the cinema on a date was unwise if they were not willing to be sexually intimate. One woman, in her letter of 3 August 1975, humorously described the cinema as 'worse than a zoo' and said she was shocked at the 'carry-on of him as soon as we got into the seats'. Wouters had identified this realization that dates were both highly sexual and highly restrained in such a public place, and this had been hotly debated in manners books and advice columns in the United States from the 1930s.[57] Broader processes were at work too. Wouters's study reveals how until the beginning of the nineteenth century manners books warned against familiarity and encouraged the maintenance of social distance between both the classes and the sexes.[58] Such familiarity and a lack of external control could unleash dangerous impulses. A greater informalization of social relations brought change to what Wouters described as the '*balance of involvement and detachment* that is the, in the [*sic*] – social and psychic – proximity and distance between those concerned' (italics in the original).[59] It brought an associated growing level of intimate and emotional context between the sexes.

Similarly, other women were unsure whether there really was a sinfulness attached to passionate kissing where it did not lead to further sin, or where love or an intention to marry existed between the couple. A 21-year-old woman wrote in her letter published on 1 June 1969 that she still had no 'clear knowledge of the right and wrong of sex' and asked whether, because she and her boyfriend intended to marry, 'it is wrong for us to carry on like this outside marriage'. Another woman wrote on 14 February 1965 that she was being pressurized by her boyfriend to engage in greater intimacy because he believed that 'when a girl and a boy really love each other they should show their love physically as well as by company keeping', to which Macnamara again responded that 'passion cannot be turn on and off like an electric light. God designed passion between a man and a woman so that it would lead them, within marriage, to procreate children.' Even in a letter published on 11 November 1979 a woman still wondered whether it was sinful, when with her boyfriend, to 'touch one another intimately quite a lot'.

DANGEROUS IRISH WOMEN

It was not just men who were pushing for greater intimacy when dating. During 1968 Angela Macnamara published a series of letters from men complaining that women were now too sexually assertive and were responsible for lowering moral standards during courtship. I believe the letters were chosen by Macnamara to serve as a cautionary tale to women that seeking greater sexual intimacy on dates would lose them the respect of men and their peers. The letters were an attempt to stem a trend where women were no longer prepared to be the moral guardians of men's sexuality or take responsibility for the nation's perceived decline into moral degeneracy. For Lynn Jamieson, women's respectability and sexuality had traditionally lain in relationships where they 'lose themselves in love', refusing to be the initiators of sexual intimacy.[60] This tentative assertiveness in the sexual arena contributed to a contemporary era in which Angela McRobbie would later claim that young women were no longer slaves to love or victims of romance.[61]

A letter to Macnamara from a man, published on 9 January 1966, claimed that 'modern women by their immodest dress, their general behaviour in dancehalls and elsewhere have lowered their dignity to a state of shame'; the implication was that such sexual assertiveness would prove counterproductive when seeking to procure a husband. Another letter of 1 September 1968 assured Angela Macnamara that men would 'run a mile from a girl that is free with her favours', while one of 8 September 1968 declared that 'the girl who has no respect for herself and who will allow just anything to happen will not be treated with respect by the boy'. In the dancehall, women also stood accused. A letter of 7 November 1965 suggested that it was not only men who were responsible for the lowering of moral standards but also women, especially when heard to shout 'put down the lights' in dancehalls all over Dublin. Some men felt they had no other option but to succumb to the worldly ways of the modern Irish woman. A letter of 18 July 1971 suggested that in 'this permissive society if you don't make a pass at a girl they begin to think you may be queer' and this forced the writer to compromise his own moral principles in the search for a girlfriend; he claimed that 'to find a decent girl who is still a virgin is not too easy'. A letter of 4 November 1973 from a man agreed that there was 'hardly a girl that you would approach who wouldn't go to bed with you'. Another man, whose letter was published on 11 August 1974, thought that a lot of women 'welcome desire and encourage sexual experience before marriage', while a letter of 9 October 1966 revealed a man fearful that he may lose his girlfriend as he had been warned by his friends that she would 'get fed-up of me if I don't do something soon as she will be getting no sexual satisfaction out of our dates'. Letters to Frankie Byrne painted a similar picture. Men wrote 'disillusioned with the permissiveness of so many girls today', to which Byrne replied that it was 'a bit unfair to adopt such a puritanical attitude towards girls'.[62]

In *Living and Loving,* Angela Macnamara spoke of how 'nowadays girls tend to be intimate with men who are virtual strangers', and this facilitated married men 'picking up single girls in dancehalls'.[63] In the 1970s especially single women emerged as more dangerous figures who flirted and slept with men they knew to be married or had boyfriends.[64] Again, this letter of 4 July 1976 reveals that men were apparently powerless in the face of such sexual provocation:

Q. Would you please write something in your column about the married seducers that are filling our dancehalls ... The girls seem to have so little hesitation in flirting with the married man and it's not only mild flirtation ... I'm not blaming the men anymore than the women but men are, generally speaking, morally weaker than women. If provocative girls mad to get a man fill the dancehalls then weak men are going to make hay while the sun shines.

A. In all the current talk about women's lib I think we very often forget to consider women's strength and their consequent responsibilities. Once a woman sees herself as a 'man hunter' she tends, not only to lower her own dignity and lose the respect of men but also to encourage lowering the standards and sense of responsibility of men.

Angela Macnamara sought to advise men on what virtues to seek for in women. In her pamphlet *How to Choose a Wife,* women are humorously compared to cars; a man must be aware that once chosen, a woman, unlike a car, cannot be traded in. For Macnamara a man must choose both on more esoteric qualities than 'the thrill of a trial run along a modern highway' but, crucially, it was the 'right kind of woman' who must introduce a man to a wider understanding of love beyond the physical.[65] This belief that the 'right kind of woman' was always more interested in emotional intimacy contributed to a wider societal denial of women's sexual desire. Similarly, John and Mary Ryan described sexual attraction as where 'the female body excites the male body' but apparently not the other way around.[66]

Central to the letters quoted above and to the advice in Macnamara's pamphlet was the belief that women would potentially face a devastating loss of reputation if they engaged in sexual behaviour prior to marriage. Although Macnamara was sympathetic to the fact that women faced great pressure to marry and therefore often made themselves more sexually available to men to secure a husband, the publication of these letters aimed to convince women that men would never marry those with whom they had sex while dating. The importance of reputation was a key device used by Macnamara and the Catholic advice literature she relied upon to maintain what she believed to be appropriate moral standards in dating and courtship. Kelly devotes an entire chapter to the subject. At the centre of the chapter is the cautionary tale of Kathy. Kathy was 17 and after a date she found herself in a secluded location with a boy, where after some kissing and necking she had intercourse. Soon after this she was invited to another dance by a different boy and the same thing happened. Shortly afterwards, Kelly writes, 'Kathy's phone was ringing day and night.'[67] Her girlfriends refused to be seen with her. The only boys who dated her expected intercourse. Her reputation was ruined. These cautionary tales also made their way into American movie theatres. Lisa Lindquist Dorr's review of the film *Where the Boys Are*, released in 1960, follows the fortunes of four female college friends on vacation. The clear message shows how rejecting sexual experimentation with predatory men was the only sure way for the women to secure a boyfriend or husband. The one female character who rejected this message and had sex with the man she met ends up being identified as an 'easy score' and is passed around his friends as a sexual partner. By the end of the movie she has been raped and is suicidal.[68]

In the Angela Macnamara column, too, women who gave into men's demands for sexual intercourse were portrayed as being used and discarded. A letter from 'Hilary' published on 3 November 1968 described how she had been having sexual intercourse with her boyfriend but when she changed her mind and suggested they 'keep it till we marry' he laughed in her face and said 'Do you really think a fellow wants to marry the girl he experiments on?' Wouters's review of German advice columns revealed a similar message; in the 1950s, women were warned that premarital sex would be an impediment to marriage,[69] although the ultimate decision would remain a matter of conscience for the couple themselves.

The life history interviews lend some support to the view that couples were having greater levels of sexual intimacy, including intercourse, while dating. Patrick McGrath (75) describes meeting 'a number of girls who I went out with who wanted a little bit more than I was prepared to give' and wonders whether this was rare or unusual at the time, deciding unrepentantly that 'for better or worse I had very clear views on what I did and didn't do, always'. Describing his relationship with his first girlfriend, David Moloney (63) talks of his constant efforts to kiss and touch this girl, while she remained mostly resistant to his physical advances and only permitted him to 'slip my hand in under her bra at one stage and that would have been really good but that was it really'. This girlfriend subsequently joined a convent and became a nun, not an uncommon occurrence in Ireland, with 590 girls entering convents in 1966 alone.[70] Tony Fitzgerald (62) describes how he had intended to remain a virgin until marriage, before meeting a woman at a dance in 1972:

> I had been saving my virginity for when I got married ok? And ... not that I was getting that many opportunities, I probably wasn't recognising opportunities, if only I had those years back [laughs] on one occasion I met a girl at one of these dances just before I met my wife and she took me back to her place after a date or two and I had sex with her and that was the first time I had sexual intercourse with anybody and it was the only time I had intercourse before I got married.

Similarly, Eddie Staunton (56) had sexual intercourse for the first time aged 21 with his girlfriend, who he continued to see for four years. By contrast, for David Moloney (63) intercourse remained something more elusive that 'would have been nice ... but in my growing up it wasn't on the radar if that makes sense'. His sexual intentions with women were less ambitious, preferring to kiss, to 'have a relationship, to pair up, for her to be mine'. For Patrick McGrath (75) the concept of 'going too far' was never a temptation as he believed himself 'as being very safe within all that, there were very clear boundaries which I adhered to in any case and I was very happy to do that'; further-more, Patrick McGrath believed that there 'was a duty to protect oneself from being in this state of sin'.

GOING STEADY; GOING TOO FAR

Wouters revealed a general concern in the countries within his study with the trend of young couples 'going steady' – a phase of being 'engaged to be engaged'.[71] Ireland was no exception. Angela Macna-mara received letters asking two interlinked questions: did the fact that couples were 'going steady' change the range of sexual intimacies they could partake in and, in this regard, how far was *too* far? The very introduction of this language by Macnamara in her column was not without controversy, with a letter writer on 9 October 1966 angrily claiming that there was 'a lot of decent and innocent boys and girls still in the south of Ireland who have never heard of that filthy expression "going too far" until they read it in *The Sunday Press*'.

How 'far' a couple decided to go in exploring sex was often based on whether they described themselves as 'going steady'. Angela Macnamara repeatedly pointed out in the column that 'going steady' provided couples with no greater sexual rights than any other couple, lest this was seen as a potential loophole. Neither did the age of the couple. The concept of going steady – long courtships with no intention of marriage, or engagements with no fixed date to marry – was viewed with suspicion by Macnamara and other Catholic dating writers as potentially facilitating sex before marriage. Kelly warned that the longer the courtship, the greater the temptation that the couple will resort to 'sins of impurity'.[72] Angela Macnamara, replying to a reader on 5 May 1963, agreed that when there was no fixed date to marry 'they should end this "steady line" '. To another, on 10 November 1963, she advised that there 'should be a prospect of marriage within eighteen months', otherwise a long engagement would pose 'a great danger to purity'. To other couples who had become engaged and found it equally difficult to act in an appropriately restrained way, Macnamara advised on 5 March 1972 that they had the 'will to control the physical urge until the appropriate time for its expression' and that it would help if they were to 'avoid those places where the temptations are the greatest'.

A letter of 24 June 1973 challenged the idea that it could be wrong for a couple in love to engage in 'full sexual intimacy'. In response to a letter published on 17 August 1975 from a young man who was about to get engaged and was intimately involved with his girlfriend, Macnamara replied that the 'great mistake that many people make nowadays is to think that engagement gives licence for more and more intimate petting and they spend most of the time getting to know one another's bodies rather than controlling that very natural desire in order to give time to assessing their love in a much wider context'. The reference to control, so present in Angela Macnamara's advice, is reminiscent of American advice in the 1940s that suggests that love grows the more desire is restrained.[73] It was also a principle feature of Catholic dating advice in Ireland in the 1930s. **Rev. Martin Scott** warns that 'betrothal does not entitle a man to liberties' and that if his feelings are 'of such nature and strength that he cannot restrain it within proper bounds, it is to be feared that he is swayed by lust rather than love'.[74] For Kelly, the solution lay in learning to control your thoughts, most effectively achieved through the avoidance of certain situations and the use of physical exercise.[75] I come back to the role of physical exercise in Chapter 6, as it featured in advice commonly given by Macnamara to those confused about their sexual orientation. This inability to restrain oneself, to exercise control or defer gratification in a sexual context was also identified as a feature of the lower classes by Arensberg and Kimball in their study of rural Ireland.[76] Mary Kenny also commented on the central role that exercising control played in Macnamara's column, suggesting that, given her elite background, there must have been a class agenda, as 'the idea of control tends to be a more bourgeois idea'. For Weeks, with the economic expansion in the 1960s Britain was aided by a shift in moral attitudes 'away from the bourgeois virtues of self control and saving' towards a new consumerism particularly directed towards the 15- to 24-year-olds.[77]

The concept and logic of maintaining sexual control before marriage came under further scrutiny, particularly in the 1970s. Ireland would become influenced by international trends that suggested the importance of sexual compatibility between couples and the central role this played in a happy marriage. I return to how these trends influenced married couples in the next chapter, although a growing acceptance of the role sexual compatibility played in a relationship also influenced dating couples, particularly those who would have described themselves as 'going steady'. A letter of 22 January 1978 asks Macnamara: 'Why not have sex before marriage? Wouldn't it be too late if when you are married you find out that you are sexually incompatible?' Angela Macnamara responds that 'how two people react to sexual intercourse outside marriage would give no clear indication as to how they would react within the permanence of the marriage state'. Another letter of 16 September 1973 described how the writer and her boyfriend were reading an Irish newspaper 'which told of the huge percentage of failures of Irish marriages because of sexual incompatibility', a report which was influencing their decision to have premarital sex. This is a contention that Macnamara strongly rejected. She claimed in her reply 'that the majority of marriage failures come about not because the couple are incapable of sexual intimacy, rather because the couple are unable to face the burden of loving'. Macnamara had previously written that the 'importance of the physical was grossly over emphasised' through the media.[78] John and Mary Ryan, writing for an American audience, also raised the question of young people seeking physical intimacy before deciding to make a marriage commitment. They suggested that couples should not limit themselves to getting to know the body of the person while neglecting the social intercourse dimension of knowing someone through conversation, activities and 'physical demonstrations of intimacy'.[79]

Perhaps surprisingly, Mansfield and Collard's study of newly married couples lends some support to the idea that the experience of premarital sex was indeed very different and not representative of the sex that couples had after marriage.[80] There was an almost universal acceptance among the London couples that sexual compatibility had to be determined prior to marriage for these unions to be successful. Sex could not improve during marriage – couples were either compatible or not. Due to a lack of privacy, these couples most often had sex in cars or other somewhat uncomfortable locations where a fear of interruption or discovery was a possibility. The study revealed that women who had been enthusiastic about such sexual escapades were less so in the context of the privacy of the marital bed. Here, the regularity with which requests came from their husbands made some women long for the more restricted intimacy of their courtship, where the less than ideal context allowed both partners to say no to a sexual advance without it being interpreted as a rejection of the other.[81] Saying no within marriage held far greater significance. Indeed, as I discuss in the next chapter, many of Angela Macnamara's readers believed saying no to be sinful.

Another consequence of going steady was a growing trend for the couple to holiday together. In her replies to letters about this, Macnamara disapproved.[82] There was, she argued, greater sexual temptation for couples when left alone, temptation that would be multiplied by being alone in a hotel room on holiday. Macnamara published this letter on 30 June 1968 to convey the consequent anxiety resulting from such a trip:

> Q. I am 19 and I spent a weekend away with my boyfriend. We are both students. At the particular time of the month it was, I thought I couldn't conceive a baby, and there was no risk. We didn't even have complete sexual intercourse. But now I am worried sick.

A. Judging from the number of deeply unhappy girls who have written to me regarding a holiday spent alone with a boyfriend, I feel I must comment to save others from similar experiences. It seems to be considered smart nowadays to sneer at conventional morality. It is true that moral codes do change. But we all need some clear standards to look at when considering a certain line of behaviour ... When a girl agrees to sleep with a boy she is breaking a convention built up as a result of the experience of generations. Other girls did as you have done, and suffered the anxieties, fears and sense of guilt that led to the building of rules to safeguard others ... Most of the boys and girls going on holidays in twosomes are doing so because they are following the bad example of convention breakers. Your suffering is the result of your copying another couple(s) who thought they did not need the order of a disciplined society.

The life history interviews revealed that dating couples did not necessarily need to be physically separated from each other or constantly in the company of others to prevent a greater sexual intimacy. They had internalized a code of behaviour that successfully self-monitored how they conducted themselves. David Moloney (63) said:

There was one occasion when we went to Manchester for a week, my parents had a lot of resistance but we were just engaged at the time, her brother lived in Manchester and we went over ... we shared the same room, I think it was bunk beds, I think she was up and I was down but again nothing would have happened. Even being away didn't give permission for it to happen ... I vaguely remember Mary saying something like 'we are nearly there now, maybe we should just wait'.

Similarly, James Kelly (70) remembers going to a Fleadh Cheoil with his girlfriend, after becoming engaged in 1962, with a couple of friends who were recently married. He had previously described how their intimate life was restricted due to the difficulty in finding 'a sitting room available' or the fact that they didn't have a car. Upon arrival at their accommodation at the Fleadh they discovered there were only two beds, one for the married couple and one for them, but James described telling the guest house owner that they were not married and had decided to head home. Again, it would be wrong to think that such surveillance, self-imposed or external, was unique to Ireland. Mary Evans tells the story, in her book *Love: An Unromantic Discussion*, of an experience attempting to check into what she described as 'large international hotel chain' in Madrid in 1976 with her boyfriend, only to be quizzed by the receptionist as to their marital status.[83]

The decisions by the men in this study to avoid occasions when they might possibly be tempted to have sexual intercourse were influenced not only by a fear of pregnancy before marriage but also a belief, among some, that these sexual acts were inherently sinful. As a teenager, Tony Fitzgerald (62) describes how a fear of committing sin had become embedded in him through his Christian Brothers' education that saw him make regular trips to the confessional to seek forgiveness and tell the priest that he had 'kissed a girl, 40 times, 20 times ... I don't know if I'd say I had an erection because I don't know if I had that language but my honest belief was that it was a mortal sin to have an erection – a mortaler.' Declan Staunton (62) told a similar story, remembering how he had gone 'a couple of times to confessing that I had kissed a girl five times or something. And it would have taken a fair amount of effort to have gone to confession and say that.' For Eddie Cullen (56) the teachings of the Church had less resonance and influence over his life; he described how a belief that sex outside marriage was forbidden was 'a little bit outside of what I felt to be reasonable'.

DATING AND THE GREATER AVAILABILITY OF CONTRACEPTION

The greater availability of contraception, particularly in the 1970s, had a profound impact on the levels of intimacy between dating couples in Ireland. The importation, sale and distribution of contraceptives had been made illegal by the passing of The Criminal Law Amendment Act 1935. Chrystel Hug reminds us that Ireland was not unique in passing such a law. France too had banned contraceptive devices through a law passed in 1920 which remained in force until 1967.[84] It was also at this time that a growing discontent about the Catholic Church's position on contraception began to be heard. A new social context had emerged that prompted some theologians to urge a reconsideration of the Church's long-held views on contraception. This reconsideration was motivated by fears of overpopulation, the new role of women in society, financial strains facing large families and, crucially, the wide availability of oral contraceptives. Pope Paul VI's newly expanded commission of seventy-two members to investigate these concerns reported back that contraception was not intrinsically evil and that married couples should be free to decide on the issue themselves. Expectations of liberalization were dashed, however, when the publication of the document in July 1968 reaffirmed the Church's teaching on contraception. This reaffirmation would have a devastating effect on the moral authority of the Irish Church, particular among the young. Sales of the contraceptive pill had risen by 50% per cent in 1967 and a survey of final-year medical students at University College Dublin revealed that 88 per cent of students wished the Church to change its position on contraception.[85] Fergal Tobin explained how theologians, too, broke ranks with the Church, and Professor of Theology at University College Cork, Fr James Good, described *Humanae Vitae* as 'a major tragedy'.[86]

Angela Macnamara, although personally surprised by the encyclical, now had to reaffirm and support this teaching while developing counter-arguments to those Catholics who wrote to her who were no longer persuaded by or willing to obey the Church's position. The 'slippery slope' arguments of the 1960s also lost their potency when the likelihood of one of the greatest losses to one's reputation – an unwanted pregnancy – was removed, or greatly reduced. Macnamara seized upon this element of doubt about the reliability of contraceptives. A letter of 6 February 1972 published by Macnamara reflected the anxiety caused by a level of doubt after contraceptive use. The writer explained that '[my] boyfriend and I went "overboard". We did something we regret now ... He got contraceptives from a friend who was abroad. We are not sure if it worked.' A letter of 12 January 1969 revealed the certainty of an unplanned pregnancy:

> Q. I have been going with a boy who has been encouraging our use of contraceptive devices so that we could have sexual intercourse on nearly every date. To my horror I now find I've become pregnant. I told him and he now says he is engaged to another girl, and would not marry me anyway now that I am pregnant.
>
> A. It is well known that these contraceptive devices are not anything like one hundred per cent safe. Many girls have become pregnant in spite of such devices having been used. Also stories like yours indicate how little love there is in such

lustful relationships ... Now you must contact The Secretary,
Catholic Protection and Rescue Society, 30 Sth Anne Street,
Dublin 2. There you will be advised as to the best thing to do
and all arrangements for pregnancy, confinement, adoption
etc. will be made for you ... The services in this country are
excellent. Do not go to England.

Angela Macnamara also received letters from women who, after agreeing to have premarital sex with their boyfriends using contraception,
were now unable to get them to commit to engagement and marriage.
This argument against premarital sex was persuasive. Women could-
n't have it all: sex *and* the security of marriage which most still cov-
eted. A letter of 17 July 1977 described how a woman and her
boyfriend had 'been sleeping together for about eighteen months now
... but my boyfriend doesn't talk about engagement at all. Any time I
bring up the subject he says for one reason or another he is not ready
to get engaged yet' – to which Macnamara responds that 'relationships in which there is sex before marriage very often work out this
way. Quite simply if the man does not really love the woman and is,
perhaps, somewhat immature he can settle for a situation where his
physical needs are met and he doesn't have to take on any additional
responsibilities.' Some women wrote to Macnamara describing
themselves as not overly religious; they felt that if they could have sex
without the fear of pregnancy, they lacked an alternative argument for
refusing it.[87]

Angela Macnamara was fighting against a widespread belief among
letter writers that Ireland was now out of step with most modern
European countries where the use of contraceptives in premarital sex
was commonplace.[88] In letter of 4 April 1976, a 20-year-old woman
who had been asked by her boyfriend to have sex and mocked by him
as to whether she 'really believed such things in this day and age' –
about keeping sex for marriage – wrote that she 'hadn't any arguments
particularly since he said we could use contraceptives and I would not
get pregnant'. Macnamara replied that 'sexual intercourse before
marriage proves nothing about love ... Remember love does not grow
out of the experience of physical sex, rather does it grow from
controlling that urge.' The issue of sexual control had been brought
up angrily by a letter writer two months earlier on 8 February 1976;
she demanded that people had 'to stand up against this organised
degredation [*sic*] and abuse of women' and she sought a husband who
could 'control himself instead of a man who would bring me to a clinic

and have a metal coil inserted in me so as he could have more fun without the responsibility of another child'. Macnamara agreed in her reply that arguments put forward in the media had attempted to 'white-wash immorality and promiscuity' and thought, from her experiences of talking to women who had premarital sex with contraceptives, that they had 'found no lasting happiness, they experienced great insecurity, tremendous fear of losing him and strong feelings of guilt'.

Contraception had become a divisive issue in Irish society, even among the Catholic faithful. Couples also disagreed with each other. The following letter of 6 June 1971 reflected this tension and Angela Macnamara's attempt to counteract the persuasive influence of the media in society: 'We are due to get engaged in August ... Now I am very upset because my boyfriend does not agree with the Catholic Church on the subject of contraception. I agree ... Do you think we should not get engaged because of feeling so differently on this important matter?' Macnamara replies: 'As a Catholic you have no choice. The Pope has spoken and we must respond with faith and honesty ... You and your boyfriend will have to see a theologian about this matter and discuss it honestly and thoroughly with him. Don't be depending on the newspapers and television interviews for your education on this question.'

Parents were also concerned and somewhat misinformed about contraception and its possible use among their children. One mother who wrote a letter published on 30 April 1972 explained how she found a packet in her son's jacket and was shocked that he was using contraceptives, only to be told by Angela Macnamara in her reply that 'I cannot be sure whether or not the contents of the package was a form of contraceptive.' Macnamara also resorted to more alarmist strategies in *Living and Loving*, explaining that while 'people will tell you that with the advent of contraception there is no reason to keep your virginity before marriage', young people were at risk from vene-real disease and other serious health risks if they chose sex before marriage.[89] 'Medical people', Macnamara wrote, quoting both a senior lecturer in obstetrics at Birmingham University and a professor of obstetrics at Oxford University, 'suggest that there is a danger of cancer of the cervix (or neck of the womb) if young people engage in casual sexual intercourse.' Angela Macnamara issued such warnings because she recognized early on the potential that contraception held to usher in an era where sexual intercourse would become increas-ingly disengaged from procreation. She wrote that it was 'obscene to make a mystery into a play thing. To use the divine plan for procreation, in part or completely, as a form of selfish recreation is to vulgarise and profane the most personal, intimate and holy privilege man has been given by God.'[90]

Contraception was becoming a growing political issue in 1971. Senator Mary Robinson had repeatedly tabled bills to allow for the limited sale of contraceptives in pharmacies and hospitals. Her Criminal Law Amendment Bill 1971 was defeated by twenty-five votes to fourteen in the Seanad. The following year, the attempt by Labour's Noel Browne and John O'Connell to have the same bill read in the Dáil was also defeated. Events in the Houses of the Oireachtas were overtaken by a Supreme Court decision in 1973 which ruled that the ban on the sale of contraceptives was unconstitutional as it breached the right of marital privacy; a similar right for single people had been upheld in the American Supreme Court the previous year.[91] A change to the legislation was now inevitable and speculation as to the wording and the possible social consequences reached fever pitch.

This debate also found voice in Angela Macnamara's column. She was reluctant to enter directly the political debate on the shape of a forthcoming contraception bill, but a careful selection of letters was published in the column on 28 April 1974 from ordinary people who stood, in her words, in sharp contrast to the 'experts' who had sought to dominate the debate. One letter from an Irish woman living in London told of her experience of dating and sex there and predicted that Ireland would soon follow a similar pattern, where Irish couples 'set up "home" together without any marriage contract – made easy now with contraceptives doled out free, where it is impossible to meet a decent man at a dancehall whose first question ... is "Are you coming back to my flat?" "Are you on the Pill?" ' England is held as an example of a failed society, where promiscuity, infidelity and abortion were rampant, fuelled by a contraceptive culture that would wreak similar havoc on Ireland if not opposed. This recurring theme of Britain's toxic moral influence on Irish moral values was present throughout the column during the 1970s. A letter of 8 April 1979 told Angela Macnamara the story of a woman recently returned home from England who spoke of 'the immorality and confusion among children and parents alike' and said that contraception was 'totally out of hand and that one seldom meets happiness or fidelity in marriage ... She was suggesting that we are walking blindly into the same situation because we have not been adequately informed by the media or any other way. And that's true, we only get bits and pieces of information and the pro-contraception people get a lot of mileage in the media.' Angela Macnamara's published letters and her replies reflected her growing hostility to the media's reporting of moral issues, particularly contraception. It was a hostility shared by the Church. The comments of the Bishop of Kerry, Dr Kevin McNamara, at a dinner in London provided *The Sunday Press* with its lead story on 18 May 1980, in which the Bishop blamed the press, radio and television for promoting values that were alien to the country's heritage. He claimed that there 'are some very vocal people in Ireland today who would like people to believe that in matters of morality – especially family and sexual morality – everyone is a law unto himself or herself ... where people decided what was right or wrong without reference to the authority of God or the Church'.

The idea that Ireland's unique and superior moral values were under siege from a rising tide of moral depravity, primarily from Britain, had historic precedents, although it continued to lose traction as the 1970s progressed. Ferriter suggests that the extent of sexual revolution in Britain was, at least in the 1960s, greatly exaggerated and most likely to have been confined to London and the south-east.[92] Jeffery Weeks also confirms this exaggeration, claiming that British sexual behaviour had remained remarkably chaste, with births outside marriage only rising modestly from 5 per cent in 1955 to 8 per cent in 1967.[93] Weeks cites studies from the Latey Committee published in the 1960s and Michael Schofield's study that pointed to a high degree of conservatism, with a majority of young people still wanting to marry virgins and expecting their spouses to be faithful, and with boys saying that they would marry a girlfriend if she became pregnant. Weeks explains this gap between perception and reality through a hysteria that developed around the higher incidences of venereal disease that were being diagnosed and recorded that became equated with greater levels of sexual promiscuousness among the young. Crucially for Weeks there was also an automatic assumption that because there was a change in the behavioural styles of young people, expressed through clothes and music, there was also change in behaviour itself, which was not always the case. This argument could also be extended to Ireland during the 1960s and 1970s to explain the low levels of premarital sex identified in the column and in the interviews.

The perception of Britain as morally bankrupt remained powerful.

Irish-born priest Father Eoin Sweeney who worked in England in the 1960s suggested that Irish people under the age of 18 should be prevented from travelling to Britain, given the culture of sexual indulgence and the danger to their Catholic faith there.[94] Fergal Tobin also refers to a speech given by the Bishop of Cashel and Emily, Dr Morris, at an assembly for Catholic Boy Scouts in 1961, which returned to this 'moral siege' mentality, describing Ireland as a Christian country surrounded by paganism.[95] The bishop had requested, the previous year, that dance promoters would not hold dances on Saturdays, on the eves of Holy Days or during Lent.[96] It was a request that was repeatedly flouted during the decade. Letters from those who had emigrated to Britain certainly confirmed the existence of a moral chasm between the two countries. A letter of 25 January 1970 from a man who had emigrated to Britain described how 'the girls would make a fellow an animal in no time the way they go on'. Another letter of 8 August 1976 from a Mayo woman recently relocated to Manchester described how she felt odd because she did not drink or sleep around like the other girls in her office. In her reply, Macnamara agreed that 'the sort of behaviour you describe is quite common in big cities like England [*sic*]'. She responded similarly on 15 November 1970 to a man who had relocated to London from Kerry and literally saw sexual temptation on every street corner, explaining that 'people living in London have got used, gradually, to the blatancy of permissive trends'.

Catholic dating advice writers like Monsignor Kelly warned of the dangers of this 'birth control mentality' that saw married couples use contraceptives to delay having children until their careers had progressed sufficiently.[97] In a letter published on 24 October 1965 from a couple wanting to delay having children so that they could 'have our home properly fixed up', Macnamara is scathing, suggesting that 'the anti-baby neurosis of some young women today is, to me, positively unnatural and most unattractive'. She believed that it was the responsibility of young mothers to remain working full-time in the home to best guide children and avoid the prospect of Britain's latchkey kids, so starved of parental affection that they sought a different kind of affection in teenage sexual experimentation.[98] In her pamphlet *How to Choose a Wife*, Macnamara warns men to be alert to women who before marriage 'speak determinately of having only one or two children', as this may be indicative of a lack of generosity.[99] She returns to this subject in an article of 17 March 1974 in *The Sunday*

Press, where she writes of an 'anti-baby neurosis, the absence of a sense of joy and challenge in motherhood' prevalent among Irish women fuelled by a 'vague make-up-your-own-mind attitude about contraception [that] is causing more and more to violate the teaching of the Church, yelling for easily available contraceptive devices which facilitate empty relationships'. In another article published on 19 March 1978 Macnamara called on concerned citizens to rally against what she saw as 'the fruits of a permissive society by 'writing to government ministers, TD's and Bishops'. She advocated that people should write to the press and refuse to wait for the 'so called experts to form us'.

A further attempt by a Fine Gael government to legislate in line with the Supreme Court ruling came in 1974. The Control of Importation, Sale and Manufacture of Contraceptives Bill allowed for the sale of contraceptives in pharmacies to married people. The Bill was defeated by a combination of Fianna Fáil opposition and a division on the government benches. It would be a Fianna Fáil government that would finally introduce the very limited Health (Family Planning) Act 1979 that would allow for the provision of contraception to be sold to married people at pharmacies on prescription from their doctors.[100] It became law in 1980, the year Macnamara's column came to a close.

These legislative attempts to restrict the sale of contraceptives to married people were ineffective and unenforceable. In fact, as we shall see in the next chapter, the issue of contraception for married couples remained contentious. The evidence from the life history interviews reflects how the use of contraception was mediated by the age and location of the men but, more importantly, by the decisions that were made by the women they were dating. Eddie Cullen (56), the youngest man I interviewed, who had been having sexual intercourse with his girlfriend since he was 21, believed that contraception was 'the women's bit and she had better look after that so it never really entered my head'. During the sexual relationship with his future wife he remembers that they only used condoms 'three or four times' and that he was sure she was on the pill, although this was never openly discussed. For others, such as Declan Staunton (62), there was a recognition that 'condoms weren't available anyway or anything of that nature' so they waited until marriage to have intercourse and then used the natural family planning methods. Tony Fitzgerald (62) also spoke about the difficulty in getting condoms; he had relied upon the woman to procure one in his only sexual encounter before marriage. 'If I remember, she was a nurse', he recalled. Liam Ahearn (63) also recalled the special attraction that nurses held for rural dating men. Irish women who trained as nurses in Britain and returned home were known to him and his friends as considerably less sexually inhibited than local women:

> When I was dating there was a lot of women in Ireland going over to England nursing and other jobs and they would have been coming home quite frequently and when they came home if you ever had a date with one of the English girls, or girls that had been in England, one of the first things you observed was that she was very sexually experienced when she came back.

ROMANCE AND THE DECISION TO MARRY

Letters to Angela Macnamara revealed varied reasons why couples had decided to wed. For those whose premarital sex ended in pregnancy, marriage was often an option. The letters selected by Macnamara revealed the often dire consequences for women who chose this route; one woman wrote that her story should serve as a warning to 'young girls who think their men-friends mean love when they ask them to go too far in their sex behaviour before marriage'. Unexpected pregnancy was also a motivation for couples to marry in Mansfield and Collard's study.[101] Marriage under these circumstances was not something Macnamara advised. In a reply published on 1 March 1970 to a young man whose parents were pressurizing him to marry his ex-girlfriend of two months who was now pregnant, Macnamara advised: 'I don't think you should marry Susan if you don't love her, and will not be able to make her happy in marriage.' In the column there was also speculation, which Macnamara deplored, about couples whose babies were born only a few months after a wedding.[102]

Letters to the column revealed that Irish men were both affectionate and romantic in their courtship although, as I discuss in the next chapter, many women felt bitterly disappointed that this behaviour quickly faded after marriage. A letter of 11 February 1968 from a woman described how 'before marriage they had a romantic courtship ... spoke endearments, made promises of lasting affection, gentle embraces, thoughtful gestures', but she now realized that this 'pre-marriage charm is an act'. Another letter of 9 January 1966 described a boyfriend as 'affectionate', someone who 'demonstrated his love in various little chivalrous ways'. It was this period of courtship that Macnamara described as 'idyllic' and one which 'a woman in later life may look back to with bitter longing'.[103] It was also a period, identified by Francesca Cancian, where men remain firmly in control of the courtship aspects of the relationship, from initiating first contact and arranging dates to proposing marriage.[104] It is not until after marriage that women take over the responsibility for the relationship. One letter of 31 December 1967 described the letter writer's understanding of this transition:

> During the bachelor days they use 'love play' to cajole the girls. They are well able to think up compliments, endearments and fond affectionate touches at that stage. And little gifts come the way of most girls when the fellows are trying to win them. But once the knot has been tied at the wedding it's a sign for all the fond little gestures to be gradually dropped.

This emotional Irish man – both affectionate and romantic – is the one that Mary Kenny most identified with. It was Englishmen whom Kenny saw as being more unemotional, describing Irish men as 'great fun, great sense [of] humour', which was extremely beneficial in sexual relations as in everything else. The idea that displays of affection declined after marriage was, for Kenny, 'a universal experience' as opposed to an Irish one.

The view that all women entered courtship and marriage preprogrammed with a romance gene is not borne out by the men's life stories. Liam Ahearn (63), a Co. Kerry farmer, recalled how, on his third date, his girlfriend told him that she wasn't really into the flowers that he had brought her on their previous dates. Perhaps she thought he was 'too soft', he speculated. Other men in the study were also concerned that they would be perceived as soft. Eddie Cullen (56) described how he struggled with the whole idea of 'what a male romantic is ... because if you cross that line you might be seen to be of a different persuasion or something if you know what I mean, so is that about buying sexy underwear or is it about creating a nice atmosphere in the house or is it about perfumes and all that stuff?' He concluded that he would have equated romance with kindness, explaining that 'I would have shown romance in a different way, kindness would have replaced it ... I always wanted to be kind to my girlfriend so that would have been more romantic to me.' While he was confused about how to *be* romantic, meeting his future wife was a more traditional 'love at first sight' scenario. When out on a date with his current girlfriend one night, he saw a woman to whom he was immediately attracted: 'I said to myself in my own head that very night – "That is the girl I am going to marry" '. After six to eight months they were dating and they were married eighteen months later. Eddie Cullen was unusual in this regard. This concept of love at first sight was not something expressed by the other interviewees, for whom the more practical issues of compatibility, timing and economics would have played a central role. In Ann Swidler's study, her interviewees also revealed a similar reluctance to describe their courtship and the decision to marry in very romantic terms. Interviewees would more frequently talk of the decision as the outcome of a 'steady growth of support and friendship' or a feeling that the couple met at 'the right time' or, most dubiously of all, that both partners 'kind of grew on each other'.[105]

Angela Macnamara also warned couples that while romantic love was a 'very real part of love', it was only an intermittent part and 'romantic thrills must be limited and measured out' lest they dominate the relationship.[106] This issue of timing remained pivotal, with interviewees feeling, just before they met their future spouse, that the clock was running out on their chances of marrying. For others, like Liam Ahearn (63), timing would also be critical. Although he dated several women he never would have considered marriage until he deemed himself to be in a stronger financial position. He also felt, after years of a cautiousness and reluctance around relationships, that his age would soon be an impediment to marriage. He explained that 'I had a settling down period on my own, I began to realise that I'm pushing on a little bit now and if I get a chance again I better do something about it.'

It was a decision that Angela Macnamara would have approved of. In *How to Choose a Wife?* Macnamara advised that marriage should not be 'considered by a man who has no source of income, or whose income is inadequate'. She went further, writing that 'to get prematurely involved in an emotional "steady line" has been the downfall of the careers of many promising young men'.[107] Some twenty-one years later, Mansfield and Collard also revealed that among their respondents an improvement in 'occupational and economic status' often played a crucial role when deciding when to marry.[108]

Another interviewee, David Moloney (63), limited his concept of romance to 'things like Valentine Day cards', while Tony Fitzgerald (62) confessed that he 'wasn't one for buying flowers and chocolates and that sort of thing'. It was Patrick McGrath (75), the oldest of the interviewees, while recognizing the practical side of romantic attachment also described how he was 'idealistically romantic'. He continued – 'I had tremendous respect for girls ... I reckon the power of a girl at that time to influence a man, to bring sunshine into a man's world was absolutely there. And I would be imbued with the hope that I could do that for her as well.'

Although I argued in the introduction to this chapter that, for some, the 1960s and 1970s were a period of contention in which young people challenged religious and parental authority, creating new priorities for themselves, particularly in the fields of employment, love and marriage, none of the interviewees in this study dated or married women of whom their parents disapproved. Eddie Cullen (56) changed his feelings toward his first girlfriend of four years – a relationship which teetered on the brink of engagement – after his mother suggested that at seven years older the girl was perhaps too old for him. 'That planted a seed for me which stayed ever since', he pondered. Tony Fitzgerald (62) speculated that he was the victim of family interference when his girlfriend suddenly broke off their relationship: 'we had talked about getting married', he explained, and then 'she just suddenly pulled the plug, just pulled the plug ... She had a very interfering aunt, her mother was dead and this aunt was very interfering and whether that had anything to do with it.' This concept of heroic love overcoming family and community opposition to conquer all was largely absent from Ann Swidler's study too.[109] Her interviewees mostly married spouses of whom their parents approved. Such was this pressure, as I will discuss in Chapter 6, that gay men also maintained sexual relationships with women to avoid the censure of family and community.

CONCLUSION

In this chapter I have argued that a transformation occurred in the field of dating and courtship in Ireland. This process unfolded unevenly across the country. Some people quickly changed their dating behaviour to incorporate new levels of sexual intimacy facilitated by holidays alone with their partners, free from the surveillance of family and community, and by the greater availability of reproductive technologies such as the contraceptive pill. Angela Macnamara's column and the data from my interviews revealed that this shift to a more private relationship between the dating couple was enabled further by a greater use of the motor car that made it easier for young people to meet others outside their immediate communities. Direct family influence over young people's mate selection declined but the research showed that respondents rarely dated or married in direct defiance of their parents. Couples often remodelled their relationships around a more individualized code of moral ethics, frequently in conjunction with information they had gleaned from a range of alternative media now available in Ireland. In comparable experiences of advice columns in the United States and Germany, young dating couples were increasingly told that their sexual intimacy was a private matter of conscience. This represented a significant move from a more collective and rule-bound understanding of the morality of dating and courtship to one modelled and created through the use of alternative advice, the mimicking of peers, and the rejection and adaptation of Catholic teaching – one that would now more accurately reflect their lives.

The decisions that were being made by young people with regard to their intimate lives were occurring in tandem with broader processes of informalization in Ireland. Relationships, not only between the sexes but also between parents and their children, became more informal, a process that was mirrored in more relaxed and individual styles of dance, hair and clothes. The column and interviews chart these transitions in slow motion over a seventeen-year period and capture the anxiety people felt as they struggled to adjust to an alternative understanding of their own bodies and the desires within them that brought greater freedom and choice. They had to reconcile this changed understanding when sexually intimate with their dates and partners, a process which was disconcerting, particularly for men. This process was a sharper learning curve for those who had emigrated to Britain during this period and encountered a sexual permissiveness that they believed was far more advanced than in Ireland.

NOTES

1. 30 June 1968.
2. N. Scheper-Hughes, *Saints, Scholars and Schizophrenics: Mental Illness in Rural Ireland* (Berkeley, CA: University of California Press, 1979), p.102.
3. T. Inglis, *Lessons in Irish Sexuality* (Dublin: University College Dublin Press, 1998), p.29.
4. See D.S. Connery, *The Irish* (London: Eyre & Spottiswoode, 1968), p.166.

5. P. O'Dea, *Dear Frankie* (Dublin: Mentor Press, 1998), p.34.
6. Ibid., pp.38–9.
7. Ibid, p.167. Other letters in the column (e.g. 26 August 1973) also support this view that mothers-in-law often destabilized the married relationships of their sons.
8. A.J. Humphreys, *Urbanization and the Irish Family* (London: Routledge & Kegan Paul, 1966), pp.74–5.
9. O'Dea, *Dear Frankie*, p.18,
10. Ibid., p.18.
11. 12 April 1964; 3 May 1964.
12. Inglis, *Lessons in Irish Sexuality*, p.27.
13. 19 April 1964.
14. 16 May 1965; 13 March 1966.
15. 5 January 1964; 1 November 1964.
16. Scheper-Hughes, *Saints, Scholars and Schizophrenics*, pp.104–5.
17. C. Wouters, *Sex and Manners: Female Emancipation in the West 1890–2000* (London: Sage, 2004), pp.86–7.
18. P. Clancy, 'Education in the Republic of Ireland: The Project of Modernity', in P. Clancy, S. Drudy, K. Lynch and L. O'Dowd (eds), *Irish Society: Sociological Perspectives* (Dublin: Institute of Public Administration, 1995), p.468.
19. Connery, *The Irish*, p.179.
20. V. Power, *Send 'em home sweatin': The Showbands' Story* (Dublin: Kildanore Press, 1990), p.13.
21. Harry McCourt, *Oh How We Danced* (Derry: Guildhall Press, 1992), pp.20–1.
22. 24 November 1963.
23. Power, *Send 'em home sweatin'*, p.15.
24. D. Ferriter, *Occasions of Sin* (London: Profile Books, 2009), p.349.
25. Power, *Send 'em home sweatin'*, p.18.
26. S. Seidman, *Romantic Longings: Love in America 1830–1980* (London: Routledge, 1991), p.125.
27. Power, *Send 'em home sweatin'*, p.407.
28. 25 May 1969; 22 February 1970.
29. 13 September 1964.
30. 17 September 1967; 11 March 1973.
31. 6 February 1966.
32. Angela Macnamara, *How to Choose a Wife* (Dublin: Redemptorist Publications, 1967), p.15.
33. Mary Kenny, interviewed by the author, 1 April 2010.
34. Connery, *The Irish*, pp.177–8.
35. Power, *Send 'em home sweatin'*, pp.16–7.
36. J.M. Smith, 'The Politics of Sexual Knowledge: The Origins of Ireland's Containment Culture and the Carrigan Report (1931)', *Journal of the History of Sexuality* 13, 2 (2004), p.221.
37. Ibid., p.222.
38. P. Mansfield and J. Collard, *The Beginning of the Rest of your Life? A Portrait of Newly-Wed Marriage* (Basingstoke: Macmillan, 1988), p.80.
39. C.M. Arensberg and S.T. Kimball, *Family and Community in Ireland* (Cambridge, MA: Harvard University Press, 1968), p.207.
40. Wouters, *Sex and Manners*, p.21.
41. Macnamara, *How to Choose a Wife*, p.7.
42. The Pioneer Total Abstinence Association of the Sacred Heart was founded in Dublin in 1898 by Fr James Cullen, SJ. Members abstained from alcoholic drink, wore a membership pin and said the Pioneer Prayer twice a day. In the 1950s one in three Irish adults were members. In my own Christian Brothers' secondary school, the principal issued our entire class with membership pins and had a photograph taken for a Pioneer publication, though the percentage of my class that actually observed the pledge beyond that day was debatable. See D. Ferriter, *A Nation of Extremes: The Pioneers in Twentieth-Century Ireland* (Dublin: Irish Academic Press, 1999).
43. Ibid., p.82.
44. Ibid., p.88.

45. P. McElhone, *When the Honeymoon is Over* (Dublin: Veritas, 1977).
46. 27 May 1967.
47. See J. Miley, *A Voice for the Country: 50 years of Macra na Feirme* (Dublin: Macra na Feirme, 1994), p.15.
48. Hugh Ryan, interview with the author, 15 July 2010. Ryan was chairman of the Macra na Feirme executive from 1962 to 1965 and president from 1965 to 1967.
49. Mary Kenny, personal correspondence with the author.
50. Monsignor G.A. Kelly, *Dating for Young Catholics* (London: Robert Hale, 1963).
51. Ibid., p.73.
52. Ibid., p.75.
53. A. Macnamara, *Living and Loving* (Dublin: Veritas, 1969), p.25.
54. J. Ryan and M. Ryan, *Love and Sexuality* (Dublin: M.H. Gill & Son, 1968), p.70.
55. 12 November 1967; 26 January 1969.
56. 13 September 1970.
57. Wouters, *Sex and Manners*, p.89.
58. Ibid., p.71.
59. C, Wouters, *Informalization: Manners and Emotions since 1890* (London: Sage, 2007), p13.
60. L. Jamieson, *Intimacy: Personal Relationships in Modern Societies* (Cambridge: Polity Press, 1998), p.109.
61. A. McRobbie, *Postmodernism and Popular Culture* (London: Routledge, 1994), pp.164–5.
62. O'Dea, *Dear Frankie*, p.26.
63. Macnamara, *Living and Loving*, p.115.
64. 5 September 1976.
65. Macnamara, *How to Choose a Wife*, pp.33–4.
66. Ryan and Ryan, *Love and Sexuality*, p.7.
67. Kelly, *Dating for Young Catholics*, p.88.
68. L. Lindquist Dorr, 'The Perils of the Back Seat: Date Rape, Race and Gender in 1950s America', *Gender and History*, 20, 1 (2008), p.27.
69. Wouters, *Sex and Manners*, p.62.
70. 'Countering the Crisis in Religious Vocations', *Sunday Press*, 30 March 1975.
71. Wouters, *Sex and Manners*, pp.107–9.
72. Kelly, *Dating and Young Catholics*, p.110.
73. Wouters, *Sex and Manners*, p.106.
74. Rev. M. J. Scott, SJ, *Courtship and Marriage: Practical Talks to Young Men and Women* (Dublin: Office of the Irish Messenger, 1934), p.10.
76. Arensberg and Kimball, *Family and Community*, p.204.
77. J. Weeks, *Sex, Politics and Society: The Regulation of Sexuality since 1800* (London: Longman, 1989), p.250.
78. Macnamara, *How to Choose a Wife*, p.6.
79. Ryan and Ryan, *Love and Sexuality*, pp.74–5.
80. Mansfield and Collard, *Beginning of the Rest of your Life?*, pp.79–80.
81. Ibid, p.166.
82. 13 March 1966; 13 July 1980.
83. M. Evans, *Love: An Unromantic Discussion* (Cambridge: Polity Press, 2003), p.115.
84. C. Hug, *The Politics of Sexual Morality in Ireland* (Basingstoke: Macmillan, 1999), p.78.
85. Ibid., pp.86–7.
86. F. Tobin, *The Best of Decades: Ireland in the Nineteen Sixties* (Dublin: Gill & Macmillan, 1984), p.195.
87. 16 September 1973.
88. 16 January 1972.
89. Macnamara, *Living and Loving*, pp.7–8.
90. Ibid., p.12.
91. Hug, *Politics of Sexual Morality*, pp.96–7.
92. Ferriter, *Occasions of Sin*, pp.337, 362.
93. Weeks, *Sex, Politics and Society*, pp.253–4.
94. See Ferriter, *Occasions of Sin*, p.342.
95. Tobin, *Best of Decades*, p.41.
96. Ibid., p.18.

97. Kelly, *Dating for Young Catholics*, p.136.
98. 3 March 1963.
99. Macnamara, *How to Choose a Wife*, p.16.
100. Hug, *Politics of Sexual Morality*, p.114.
101. Mansfield and Collard, *Beginning of the Rest of your Life?*, p.66.
102. 25 March 1973.
103. Macnamara, *How to Choose a Wife*, p.10.
104. F.M. Cancian, *Love in America: Gender and Self-Development* (Cambridge: Cambridge University Press, 1987), p.94.
105. A. Swidler, *Talk of Love: How Culture Matters* (Chicago, IL: University of Chicago Press, 2001), pp.119–20.
106. Macnamara, *Living and Loving*, p.9.
107. Macnamara, *How to Choose a Wife*, p.8.
108. Mansfield and Collard, *Beginning of the Rest of your Life?*, p.64.
109. Swidler, *Talk of Love*, pp.121–2.

CHAPTER FOUR

Searching for Intimacy within Irish Marriage

INTRODUCTION

In this chapter I explore how women reconfigured and renegotiated a more satisfying balance between love, sex and intimacy in their relationships. The emotionally cold and distant husband was no longer acceptable to them. Nor were their unsatisfying sex lives. The letters to Angela Macnamara revealed a generation of women falling in love, dating and marrying in the 1960s and 1970s that expected more than their mothers did – wanting affectionate husbands and a more reciprocal sexual relationship, where sex was an expression of love, rather than a right or duty within marriage.[1] The letters bristle with anger against neglectful husbands who abandoned them for the pub night after night and whose control over the family finances allowed them only a meagre allowance, yet who expected their wives to be sexually available on request. This sexualization of marriage occurred in a context where couples, particularly women, increasingly sought advice from a body of expert literature on how to improve their relationships to secure a more satisfactory balance between love, intimacy and sex. These are what Cas Wouters refers to as 'lust balance' questions.[2] Traditionally these had involved a lust-dominated sexuality for men and a love-dominated relationship for women. That situation was now changing. In this chapter I will argue for a greater emphasis on the role of intimacy within this balance, where couples sought not just love or sex but a physical closeness where touch would not automatically be a precursor to sex. This particular desire for closeness had greater resonance within Irish relationships than those under consideration by Wouters, given the unique legal and cultural mores that provided the context in which couples practised sex. This 'intimatization of sex'[3] would be the hallmark of the renegotiation of the lust balance within Irish marriage.

Angela Macnamara's column recognized that through a lack of sexual education or a willingness to try harder, men had failed to satisfy their wives, deeming them as cold or frigid, rather than taking responsibility for their lack of arousal. The process of change would, however, be painfully slow. Both men and women lacked a communicative confidence to voice their sexual wants and needs, inhibited by a religious culture which taught couples to see their bodies more as a source of sin than as an instrument of pleasure. Through an unwillingness to use contraception, or a lack of opportunity to acquire it, sex continued to be associated with childbirth, or the fear of it, which hampered the couples' enjoyment of sex. Natural family planning methods created strain within relationships in which the spontaneity and enjoyment of sex was reduced by the introduction of charts and thermometers which were necessary to identify the safe period, preventing women from having sex at the time they most wanted it.

The life history interviewees revealed some similar problems in achieving a mutually satisfying sexual relationship and also a greater complexity in how couples negotiated improvements to their relationship. The analysis of the column and the interview data revealed a process of democratization. This democratization of personal life has been described by Anthony Giddens as 'less visible' because it does not occur in the public sphere.[4] The problem page data can give a greater visibility to and understanding of this dimension of personal life.

HONEYMOONS AND SEX

The opening lines of Ian McEwan's novel *On Chesil Beach*, in which his newly-wed protagonists Edward and Florence struggle to overcome their fears and have sex for the first time in 1962, reflected the similar fears of countless young couples of that age.[5] McEwan writes: 'They were both young, educated, and both virgins on this, their wedding night, and they lived in a time when conversation about sexual difficulties was plainly impossible.'[6] Although Florence had consulted 'a modern, forward-looking handbook' that was to act as a guide to new brides she remained nervous and somewhat nauseated by the details of sexual intercourse. Having sexual knowledge does not equate with being able to talk openly about sex, even to save your marriage. Their ignorance, defensiveness and inability to communicate during their bungled attempt to make love would jeopardize the future of Florence and Edward's day-old marriage.

The incident that occurred on RTÉ television's 'The Late Late Show' in 1966, that became known as 'the Bishop and the Nightie affair', brought the topic of honeymoon sex right into the nation's living rooms and has become a milestone in the discussion of Irish sexuality. It marked the transition of how Irish society started to talk about sex outside of a religious or romanticized understanding. The incident, where a recently married woman, when asked by chat show host Gay Byrne what colour nightie she wore on her honeymoon, divulged that she didn't recall whether she wore any on the night in question. The outrage expressed by the Bishop of Galway, Tom Ryan, at the explicit sexual nature of the incident was greeted with a mixture of both laughter and derision from a bemused public and sparked much media debate. Tom Inglis suggested that the incident's significance lay in the fact that sex was being spoken about, or at least implied, outside the traditional confines of the confessional.[7] For Mary Kenny too the incident was about stripping away the traditional romantic accoutrements surrounding the honeymoon to reveal its more primitive function – sex – for a generation that believed premarital sex was sinful.[8]

In a letter of 10 July 1977 a woman wrote that she had just completed a pre-marriage course in which 'very little was said about the honeymoon' and that, as a virgin, she remained anxious about her first experience of sex. Angela Macnamara's reply is the most explicit published in her column. It reveals how far the discussion of sex and the honeymoon had come in the public sphere since 1962, and the role that Macnamara's column played in both providing 'technical' information and contributing to the history of sexuality in Ireland:

> A young husband needs to be fully controlled in himself and have great patience in initiating his wife into the experience of sexual intercourse ... Some couples think that they need to have read all sorts of books on techniques but the main thing to remember when you are going on your honeymoon is that it is the starting point ... it may take a little time to achieve penetration ... it may hurt a little but don't be fearful because this is the normal experience of quite a number of girls and once the hymen is broken there should be no further soreness ... A lubricant such as K.Y. Gel is often very helpful when applied to the vaginal area.

Angela Macnamara's reference to sex manuals very much reflected a belief that sex was a crucial part of a successful marriage and there was great pressure on couples to become proficient in the technical aspects of sex. I return to this aspect of the sexualization of marriage, particularly among married women, later in this chapter. Life history interviewee

Tony Fitzgerald (62) described relying on a sex manual they had purchased before their marriage because there was 'an anxiety to 'get it right and do it right' on their honeymoon:

> I remember on our honeymoon, couldn't happen for the first couple of days because my wife ... I think she was having her period, it wasn't safe, we were using natural methods, there was no condoms ... I remember having a book lying on top of her telling us how to have sex ... on our honeymoon in Paris. That's the truth ... It was a learning exercise for us both.

For James Kelly (70) the everyday reality of married life intervened during the honeymoon to give a somewhat contradictory account of their first sexual experience as a married couple:

> We went to London, Paris, then Rome but we didn't do anything until we got to Italy and I was very unfamiliar with drinking and there was a glass of wine on the table and I thought I'd finish it and so we went to the bedroom and she was feeling a bit nervy so she went into the bathroom and then I went and when I came out she was fast asleep [laughs]. So [the] first time was difficult, it was painful, it worked OK, it worked well, there was no problem.

Patrick McGrath (75) remembered little anxiety but thought that 'anything you have to learn has awkward moments and you have to learn the mechanics of whatever it is, whether it is a bike or driving a car, you make mistakes I'm sure and you have to go on learning'. For David Moloney (63) the experience of sex during their honeymoon and early married life was difficult. He remembered:

> I just felt pressure for me on the honeymoon because ... out of the blue without any practice I am supposed to behave in some way ... I think I just made a mess of it really ... I mean I knew physically what to do but ... on top of all that you have the whole emotional package that goes with it and that is so important so it is not just one mammal doing it to another mammal, there's more to it than that ... I probably fumbled around during my honeymoon trying to do the physical activity bit thinking this is what you do and that would have caused some difficulty in the early stage of our marriage.

There was also a fear, according to David (63), that a negative sexual experience on their honeymoon would 'establish a pattern of bad behaviour' that would be difficult to rectify later.

This honeymoon experience was not unusual. Eugene J. Kanin and David H. Howard's 1958 study of honeymooning couples in the United States revealed that the deciding factor that influenced the success of post-marital sex was whether couples had engaged in premarital sex.[9] In the study, 47 per cent of women who were virgins on their wedding night reported that they were satisfied while this rose to 71 per cent of women who had engaged in premarital sex. A key influence on deciding whether the experience was pleasurable for women was whether they had achieved orgasm during intercourse.

The social construction of the honeymoon is identified by Bulcroft et al. in their review of sixty American magazine articles; while depicting the honeymoon as a pivotal experience, they warn of false expectations.[10] They reproduce an article by *Time Magazine* published in 1955, which warns that 'a good deal of alcohol, perhaps, or worse, the hangover from it six hours ago – these all make the male as ineffectual as he is ever likely to be ... at best there may be a hopeless fumbling effort, certain to complete the rout of a tense, ashamed and embarrassed girl'. As my interviews show, the embarrassment was not just confined to the brides. Other surveys drawn on by Bulcroft et al. referred to honeymoon tension caused by the husband's immaturity, insensitivity or sexual demands.[11] Their review of articles in the 1950s and 1960s often revealed mixed messages, with experts competing to give advice on how to achieve the perfect honeymoon. For women there was a mounting preoccupation with frigidity, while men were cautioned that the honeymoon may end in 'embarrassment, frustration and sexual impotence'.[12] It is perhaps thankful that many Irish couples embarked on their honeymoons in a blissful ignorance unaffected by expert commentary that may well have heightened their anxiety, with Patrick McGrath (75) declaring that 'it never occurred to me anyway that it wasn't going to work'.

Mansfield and Collard's respondents among newly married London couples, the majority of whom had sex before marriage, were faced with the dilemma of how to make the honeymoon special, given that the sexual significance of the night had been removed.[13] In tandem with that wish for 'specialness' the couples were relieved that their honeymoon night would not be their first sexual experience, since most reported that these had been awkward, embarrassing and uncomfortable. The couples attributed their disastrous first nights to a combination of inexperience, shyness and an inability to relax due to a lack of privacy.[14] For them the honeymoon acted more as 'mechanism of transition' between their single and newly married lives.[15]

'WOULD COURTING MAKE ME PREGNANT?'

The anxiety brought about by the sexual side of the honeymoon was intensified by the inadequate sex education with which couples embarked upon their married lives. Dorine Rohan described how a lack of information on the basic facts of life, except for dirty jokes and pornographic literature, had allowed couples to reach marriage in ignorance.[16] This allowed for a situation where pregnant young women were amazed to discover they could become pregnant outside marriage; where men had no understanding of the female body or *how* or *where* a baby was born. It was also the underlying religious culture, which imbued in children a belief in the immodesty of the body and the sinfulness of sex, that would damage their chances of having fulfilling sexual lives in adulthood. Betty Hilliard's respondents who gave birth in the 1950s and 1960s expressed a similar ignorance of sex and child-birth, with one woman who gave birth in 1966 believing that 'I thought that I would want to have one before I'd actually get pregnant.'[17] Other women had no concept of how their babies would be born. 'I hadn't a clue', one woman explained. 'I hadn't a clue and [my husband] hadn't a clue either where it was coming from.'[18] Connery's reproduction of a selection of letters from Angela Macnamara's other column, *Can you help me?* in the weekly magazine *Woman's Way*, confirms a picture of ignorance surrounding the basic facts of life. 'How is it some girls become pregnant before they are married?' one woman asked, while others wondered 'Would courting make me pregnant?' or 'Is it possible to have sexual intercourse without being aware of it at the time?'[19] Connery concludes that not only were young people given a distorted view of sex, they were also denied the most rudimentary information. This was also borne out in Patricia McElhone's interviews with six happily married Irish couples.[20] One of the couples, Paddy and Eileen, described how Eileen resisted all sexual advances in their three-year courtship, even refusing to be kissed if her arms were not folded in front of her. It transpired that she had received no sex education from her parents and believed that she could become pregnant from pas-sionate kissing alone.[21]

As a result, Rohan's interviewees too frequently described their sex lives in negative terms, telling how lucky they were because their husbands 'didn't want it very often'.[22] They felt resigned to marital sex lives which they found to be deeply unsatisfying. They recognized that this was not exclusively their husband's fault and as they were burdened by a feeling of guilt and shame about sex were often incapable of gaining any real satisfaction from it. One woman explained that 'I'd like to have a better physical side to my marriage but it's just hopeless. I was always taught that sex was dirty and sinful, and I have never been able to adjust.'[23] Men wrote to Macnamara, disappointed that their wives also had this view of sex as something dirty, degrading or unclean.[24] While in a response published on 21 September 1975 Angela Macnamara recognized that the wife in question 'may well be another victim of the defective education in our culture so that her upbringing has left her with a negative approach to marriage and sex', she did not acknowledge the central role of the Catholic Church in establishing and perpetuating such a culture. A letter of 6 February 1972 was from a man brought up in a family of boys where the subject of sex was never discussed; he wrote to Macnamara fearful that he would be unable to interact successfully with the opposite sex, preferring to remain with his male friends.

All but one of the life history interviews reported receiving little sex education when growing up, so that they entered their dating lives ill-equipped to make informed choices about sexual intimacy. They were paralyzed not only by this lack of education but also by a fear of committing sin. Eddie Cullen (56) remembers being in the bath, aged 8, and 'grabbing my mother's boob and I said "Mammy what are they for?" '. His parents responded to his earliest queries about sex with a book explaining the facts of life, which ensured that he didn't have to rely on the pieces of information circulated by boys at school through jokes or books. Other parents also made some tentative attempts at sex education. Declan Staunton (62) said that his father asked him on a drive back from the country 'if ever I needed to talk to him about anything and he would be available'. When I asked whether it was an offer he had taken up, he said: 'no and I remember consciously trying to make myself nod off in the car'. For others like Tony Fitzgerald (62) there was a widespread ignorance about all aspects of sexuality including childbirth and masturbation. Patrick McGrath (75) was brought up on a farm, and although not receiving any sex instruction from his parents he believed that he and others in a similar situation 'were aware of the happenings between the livestock [and] what happened in the procreation way'. Joanne Hayes, quoted in Tom Inglis's book on the Kerry Babies affair, also attributed her upbringing on a farm to her knowledge about sex: 'I didn't need to learn about the facts of life', she explained, '[because] at sometime or another you see it all enacted among the animals.'[25] Liam Ahearn (63) was also brought up on a small farm and described how in a family of five brothers and five sisters his parents' sexual relationship was audible in their house, and yet there was a 'cloak of secrecy' that surrounded speaking about sexuality in their home. He explained that there was a 'big crowd of us in a small house ... sometimes they'd start their intercourse down in the kitchen and they might just decide when we were supposed to be all asleep to move to the bed'.

DISCIPLINING MARITAL SEX

For couples who had embraced Angela Macnamara's message of sexual control in their dating and courtship practices, the arrival of their wedding day finally legitimated sexual intercourse within their relationship. Years of furtive fumbling in the cinema, in the car or in country lanes were replaced by the privacy and comfort of the marital bed. The exercise of self-control and the disciplining of married sexuality would, however, remain key messages communicated by the column. They would remain central to facilitating couples' use of natural family planning over artificial methods requiring periods of abstention. Angela Macnamara returned to analogy of food and warned readers of the consequences of sexual gluttony. 'The virtue of self control enriches married life', Macnamara wrote on 12 October 1975 in response to a man who accused the Catholic Church of repressing love within marriage, and added that to 'approach marriage in a gluttonous way and this gluttony for thrills can do two things – it can lead to selfishness and satiation'. Marital sex was, it seemed, a finite resource. She advised that a married man 'must learn to discipline his desire, to keep it in rein and gently initiate his young wife rather than overwhelm her'.[26] Similarly, in her book *Living and Loving* Macnamara writes of a woman's 'total surrendering of herself to her husband' during sex.[27] Women are portrayed as almost passive bystanders; sex is 'done to' them rather than with them, and they gain an emotional rather than a physical pleasure through sex. 'To make love excessively', Macnamara warns, 'is to misunderstand the needs of a wife.'[28] Letters such as one published on 14 December 1975 revealed a more complex picture of how married couples struggled to discipline their sex lives within a natural family planning framework:

> Q. I read about 'self-control in marriage' recently in your column ... we have four children inside these five years and we tried to space them using the safe period also the rhythm, all to no

use. The babies still came ... also my health was not as it should be. The stress and strain of four children got me down. Anyway to shorten my story my husband and I decided there was only one way out for us 'Catholic style', to abstain from sexual intercourse. That was twelve years ago. Of course I know I could have done the other thing, have plenty of sex and a baby every year, but I could not face that life either. Does the Catholic Church care about sex starved Irish marriages?

Angela Macnamara's reply was to again encourage the use of natural methods of family planning and to cast doubt on the long-term medical effects of the contraceptive pill, suggesting that future generations may be impotent or infertile from its use.

All but one of the interviewees relied upon natural family planning during their marriage. David Moloney (63) was the most adamant that the discipline required did not have a negative effect on their relationship; he described how 'it was not a strain at all, it was a mindset, I mean it is not an issue because people do not have sex every night of the week every month'. He continued: 'there are quiet times and there are active times'. But for Tony Fitzgerald (62) it was the very sexual culture that existed in Ireland, which was characterized by denial, self-control and a lack of education, that made the adoption of the Billings method and the restraint it required in their marriage unproblematic:

We never had an issue around that [the Billings methods]. In reality neither of us had much of a sexual history in terms of full intercourse. We probably were quite restrictive in how we expressed ourselves sexually, it was fairly traditional. We wouldn't have been of the experimental kind and it never crossed either of our minds and if it crossed her mind she never said it ... so I think I just muddled along in that sense of what we knew.

In Rohan's study she described how the withdrawal method or coitus interruptus was a common form of contraception, although the 'rhythm method', the only form of contraception sanctioned by the Catholic Church, was also popular despite its low rate of success.[29] For many couples to whom Rohan spoke, the rhythm method was abandoned early on as husbands 'got fed up waiting' three months to determine when regular ovulation occurred. Hilliard's respondents often had the same experience, with one woman describing how husbands 'wouldn't wait until your time of the month ... they would want their little bit of fun and you wouldn't want to in case you got pregnant'.[30] It was this waiting that caused some strain in married relationships. When asked whether Billings had created tension in their marriage, Declan Staunton (62) agreed that it had, adding that 'it normally would have been that I would have liked to have sex and particularly after our first daughter was born, Fiona would have been concerned that she would get pregnant too soon'.

The RTÉ documentary 'Too Many Children?', first broadcast in October 1966, revealed stories of ordinary women struggling to cope with the physical and emotional burden of large families they had little role in deciding to have, and the views of medical professionals on family planning. Again this was a landmark broadcast challenging a prevailing view of the Catholic Church that large families were the will of God. In the programme Father Enda McDonagh admitted that the rhythm method and the associated calendar and temperature checks did damage the spontaneity of love.[31] Other contributors such as Dr Ivor Browne and Dr Declan Meagher expressed little confidence in the success of the rhythm method which, although it only worked for a minority of women, was the most widely practised method of birth control in Ireland at that time.

John and Mary Ryan's book *Love and Sexuality* was widely available in Ireland but never recommended by Angela Macnamara.[32] While the Ryans agreed with Macnamara in dissuading couples from premarital sex, using much the same language, they disagreed that the rhythm method was a viable option for family planning. The Ryans stressed the need for responsible parenthood on the basis of age, health and finance and believed that to characterize those couples who rejected the rhythm method as lacking in self control or merely wanting to pleasure them-selves without the responsibility of a child as unfair. They described sexual intercourse as the 'intimate self giving and receiving through the body', a process which was undermined by the rhythm method which 'depersonalised and dehumanized' their sexual relationship.[33] As discussed in Chapter 2, this was, in fact, close to Macnamara's private opinion on the topic. The Ryans believed that educated Catholics saw little difference between preventing conception through the rhythm method and preventing pregnancy using other forms of contraceptives. The Ryans recognized the anguish caused by the Church's teaching to married couples, priests and doctors.[34]

McElhone's interviewees described similar difficulties in negotiat-ing their sex lives around the Billings method.[35] One wife told how her menstrual cycle was abnormal, with the result that she had thirteen pregnancies during her marriage. She described how she often abstained from sex completely for nine months yet felt guilt at refusing her husband sex and at being a source of temptation to him. Her husband explained that he was disappointed that she would never take the initiative in sex, which left him feeling unloved.[36]

Rohan found a much more liberal attitude towards contraception among urban couples, with many using whatever form of birth control they could locate.[37] This is in contrast to the men I interviewed and reflects how those who responded to advertisements asking them to talk about their relationships in the context of Angela Macnamara were more likely to be what I have described as 'trend followers'. As discussed in Chapter 3, there was a remarkable abdication of responsibility around family planning among some of the men, such as Eddie Cullen (56), when dating and in marriage; they believed this to be primarily within their wives' jurisdiction.

LOVE, MONEY AND THE 'MARRIED BACHELOR'

Married relationships came under increased strain when husbands failed to distribute equally the household income. Some husbands had continued to live as they had when they were single and enjoyed their bachelor lifestyles of drinking and sport, while women often found it increasingly difficult to stretch the remaining household budget to cover necessities. Women resented being left alone in the evening, often after spending the day at home.[38] Many women, particularly those unable to drive, were dependent on their husbands who may or may not have taken them to visit relatives or to the cinema. At a time when not every home had a television, married men frequently retreated to the pub to watch it, leaving their wives at home with their children.[39] This unhappiness made its way into the Angela Macnamara column. A woman describes the unfairness which characterized her domestic life in a letter published on 11 October 1970:

> Q. The 'Boss' visits the local each night in case he misses some valuable information which would boost his prowess as a breadwinner. He visits the cattle marts briefly (two or three times a week) spending the greater part of his time on the 'high stool' discussing politics or football ... On the rare evening he spends at home he is restless and edgy, the children must be quiet and respectful. Daddy must choose the TV programmes – regardless.

A. Sometimes it is difficult to keep firmly and fairly in mind that
    husbands who treat their wives as you so clearly outline, have
    reasons, perhaps painful reasons, which they themselves don't
    recognise or understand, for their inability to love and give
    themselves to their wives and families ... These men have not
    been educated to recognise the tremendous influence that can
    be exerted by the father of a happy family. They have, from the
    cradle, been 'brain-washed' into all sorts of false notions
    of what is 'soft' and 'unmanly' and 'sissyish'. The tough,
    emotionless, unyielding despot is, for them, the real man.

The Catholic marriage advice that Angela Macnamara recommended to
her readers prepared newly married women for the scenario outlined
in the letter above. Pierre Dufoyer tells women that men will never
share their greater interest in marriage and family and would
always put their careers and the pursuit of social prestige outside the
home first.[40] Men would thus want to spend more time outside the
family home than within it. Dufoyer described how 'man is by his temperament inclined to external activity and cannot content himself with
the occupations of the home. The woman limits her world, if not will-
ingly at least more easily to the home ... a man feels more confined if
he spends too much time in a house.'[41] Newly married women must
understand their husband's needs for his 'external activity' and yield
to it. By adopting such a strategy a wife will, according to Dufoyer,
benefit from a wider view of the world seen through the eyes of her
husband. Patrick Baggot agreed, but believed that such
behaviour must not be misconstrued by women as a lack of love for
them.[42] Just because a man requires distraction, companionship and
novelty outside the home it does not show a lack of love or respect
within their relationship. It is a characteristic of a newly-wed woman
to resent those things which she sees as a rival for her husband's time and
affection. Baggot advised wives to understand this element of a man's
character rather than challenge it and warned that it is a woman's
possessiveness which is most likely to irritate her husband.[43] The
bachelor lifestyle of married men had also been identified by previous
research on the Irish family. J.C. Messenger's study revealed that men
were slow to abandon the camaraderie of sports and drinking with their
male friends.[44] Women, lacking a similar social network, remained in
the home where their lives revolved around their duties as a mother
and housekeeper. Husbands were most often found in pubs or at céili
– both off-limits to married women. This problem was not exclusively

rural. Alexander Humphreys also identified the time married men spent drinking outside the family home as the greatest strain on marital relations.[45] Humphreys did agree that, among younger married couples, women were reluctant to be left at home as their husband socialized while other couples enjoyed socializing together as a couple.

Mansfield and Collard's study emphasized the resentment felt by wives who led a restricted social life and who were expected by their husbands to be attentive and available when they finished work.[46] It was 'coming home late' from work that was deemed a destabilizing influence on the married relationship at home. Letters to Frankie Byrne's radio show also revealed married full-time mothers unhappy at being excluded from their husband's work. 'There's a whole world out there and I'm not part of it', a woman wrote to Byrne; she felt jealous that her husband mixed with 'glamorous girls in his office and sophisticated business women'.[47]

Angela Macnamara's letter writers resented the personal sacrifices they would make to balance the books, and, most relevant here, they resented the continued sexual demands their husbands made upon them, reducing intercourse to a duty to be endured with men who no longer held their respect. A letter of 27 March 1966 was from a woman who wrote that while she was anxious about stretching her housekeeping budget, 'he smokes twenty cigarettes a day, has a morning snack in town every day with his friends from the office and goes out one night a week with the "boys" to the local.[48] Then he "can't afford" to give me pocket money. I have to nearly beg for the price of a lipstick or a pair of nylons'. Another letter of 16 June 1968 described how a woman had to ask for extra money for basics such as her bus fare or to get her 'hair set or buy any little things for myself', and this was often refused. One woman's letter of 21 October 1979 described how she was forced into the job market because she had 'no money for myself at any stage. I couldn't even buy a pair of tights Angela.' It is significant that a letter about entering the workforce came towards the close of the column. Angela Macnamara had previously been hostile to married working women, suggesting that a couple should never become dependent on a woman's earnings.[49] Women with independent income would represent a decline in the economic dependence on their husbands, increasing the role that love and intimacy would play. Macnamara's advice to women in this financial predicament was not to sacrifice expenditure on themselves but rather to reduce the quality of the cuts of meat or other foodstuff they bought for the home, telling their husbands that this was all they could afford on the allocated money. Rev. David A. Lord had previously warned dating couples in his book *M is for Marriage* to watch for signs of both tightfistedness and extravagance:[50]

> A young couple considering marriage will be extremely wise to watch each other's attitudes towards money. If the man is tight-fisted he will grow more tight-fisted after marriage. If the girl is wasteful and extravagant, she will not improve with the years.

The distribution of household income has been identified as a source of marital conflict in previous studies. The study of working-class families in the coal-mining region of Yorkshire in the 1950s by Dennis et al. revealed a widespread agreement between couples that the husband would pay his wife a fixed amount for housekeeping while keeping the remainder for himself.[51] The conflict ensued when the household wage was not adequate to maintain a decent standard of living for the family and also provide money for the husband's recreation.[52] The task of administrating the family finances nearly always fell exclusively on the women, who were more likely to sacrifice their own personal items of expenditure to balance the books. The result was that this further restricted women's social life to calling on neighbours or family while their husbands seemed to prefer to stay outside the home when not eating or sleeping – although the television had reduced this habitual tendency to go out.[53]

Joanna Bourke's study of working-class communities in Britain during the twentieth century revealed a more complex side of this financial precariousness.[54] Women, she argued, knew that their authority was grounded in their husband's physical dependence on them and resisted male interference in the domestic sphere.[55] The parlour in the house symbolized the housewife's power in the home, where its use was carefully monitored and inappropriate behaviour was not tolerated. The room came to represent the housewife's success at budgeting, showing that there was excess money for more luxurious furnishings.[56]

In Ireland the reality was that Irish State policy actively discouraged women's labour-market participation. Measures such as the marriage bar, introduced after a committee of inquiry into health insurance, removed married women from jobs in the public sector and forced them to forgo entitlements to insurance benefits. The State was strongly influenced by a British 'male dependency model', where Irish women were not treated as individuals in their own right but as dependents within the marital family unit.[57] Women even required their husband's signature to cash their children's allowance cheques. Nuala Fennell's exposé of the silence that surrounded the many failing Irish marriages also included the precarious position of women who were financially dependent on their husbands, a situation supported by the State.[58] This financial control over women deprived many of their dignity in begging for more money for often the most basic personal items. Nancy Scheper-Hughes writes of rural women concealing money from their husbands which they had earned from the sale of eggs or butter.[59] As they were not entitled to benefits in their own right – such as unemployment assistance – and other rates of payment were always lower than men's, financial protection for women was assumed to take place within the family unit. The letters received by Macnamara suggest that this was not always the case.

My own grandmother – always a prudent saver, even on a low income – concealed the existence of a Post Office saving account from her husband. My grandfather, who was often found in the betting shop and greatly averse to saving of any kind, learned of the existence of the saving account after his sister-in-law saw my grandmother depositing money in the Post Office. When confronted, my grandmother denied its existence, claiming that she never had extra money to save. Unconvinced, my grandfather searched the house in pursuit of the alleged savings book which remained undiscovered, hidden under the lining beneath his fireside chair.

THE GROWING IMPORTANCE OF LOVE AND INTIMACY WITHIN IRISH MARRIAGE

In the previous chapter I highlighted those women who wrote to Angela Macnamara in praise of their romantic boyfriends in courtship but who had quickly became disillusioned within marriage.[60] Letters to Macnamara now revealed how male affection was deployed, often only as a precursor to sexual intercourse which, in turn, made the women emotionally withdrawn from their husbands. The letters also cast doubt on whether love – particularly for men – was really a prerequisite to marriage at the time.[61] Dorine Rohan's interviewees expressed a similar disillusionment.[62] Sex was more often brief, unaccompanied by any tenderness, and this accelerated women's distaste for sex as a purely animal act, while their husbands construed this as the women being cold or frigid.[63]

A yearning from women to renegotiate this relationship between love and lust in their marriages – wanting female-centred sex accompanied by a physical and emotional intimacy – can be identified in the column. Importantly, it was women themselves who often withdrew the intimacy of physical touch in their relationships, for fear that this would be misinterpreted by their husbands as an invitation to sexual intercourse. At a time when couples were struggling to plan their families through natural methods, of which abstinence was a part, the stakes were too high for women who did not want to become pregnant again. The desire of women that emerges in the column is for this 'intimatization of sex' rather than the sexualization of marriage identified by Steven Seidman in the United States, where sex is seen less as a 'symbol of love or a marital obligation than as a sensual basis of love and marriage'.[64]

Crucially, women were advised both by Angela Macnamara and a broad range of dating literature not to *ask for* or *expect* expressions of love and intimacy within their marriages. There were two trends within intimate life that Macnamara was attempting to influence. Firstly, there was a romanticization of love, where people longed for a more expressive display of love within marriage rather than the mere fulfilment of spousal duties. Secondly, there was a sexualization of love. Tom Inglis identifies this trend too, where marriage started to lose its spiritual dimension and became inseparable from 'erotic longings and pleasures of sex'.[65]

Other women wrote to the column with more urgent concerns. Angela Macnamara believed that marriage was for life. Never once in seventeen years did she advise a letter writer to separate from their spouse, even in cases of domestic abuse, such as in the following letter of 27 June 1965:[66]

> Q. My husband strikes me and slaps me across the face when he is angry about something. I don't mind being struck so much but I wish he wouldn't do it in front of the children ... How can I tell them what good Catholic home life is like? I don't fight back or hope any more. I've been so hurt and disappointed in marriage that I don't care what happens and I'm depressed. I am only 32 and if I'd my life to live again I wouldn't marry. Problems only begin when you marry.
>
> A. I can quite understand your feeling as you do when things have been so hard for you. I am so sorry about the difficulty you are having but admire your wisdom in wishing to make

things better for the sake of your grand family. I am also sorry for your husband. He must be suffering some personal frustration or disappointment which is making him take it out on you. I don't think 'fighting back' is the answer. You must try to get to the root of the trouble. When did all this begin and why? Confide in a priest who would advise you and help your husband too. I know you feel bitter and disappointed because love has gone out of your marriage. Can you be unselfish enough – and it takes great spirit – to love your husband and show him that you need him? Do little things he likes you to do and praise any effort on his part. Your doctor, too, may be able to help you get over your depression. Be frank with him. Then do pray, and keep praying no matter how you feel. God will surely give you peace.

While Macnamara's glass may be permanently half full, her advice here is an extraordinary ask of this woman. The belief that anti-depressants, prayer and praising the husband who was beating her would improve this woman's situation was dangerously naive and reflected Angela Macnamara's rather sheltered, secure, upper-middle-class existence. It was, of course, the absence of women's refuges in Ireland in the 1960s that severely limited the options available to women in these circumstances. Replying to other women who were dismayed at the lack of emotional reciprocity with their husbands, Macnamara sought to reassure them that this lack of emotional reciprocity was, in fact, a common feature of married life. The advice again reflected Macnamara's reliance on a number of Catholic dating and marriage guides from the US, France and Ireland, which she also recommended to her readers.[67] She accepted the underlying premise of these texts: that the different natures and psychologies of men and women had led to misunderstandings and false expectations within marriage. A solution to this suggested in Wouters's study shows how manners books in the Netherlands between 1939 and the 1960s attributed the introduction of co-education in facilitating the freer contacts between the sexes.[68] In Ireland, the answer to the absence of male affection lay in the re-education of men about the emotional needs of women and the ability to communicate those needs to their spouses – a clear indication that the 'complementary' roles within marriage were lacking. This letter of 1 December 1968 is typical of the frustration felt by many women at their husbands' lack of affection:

Q. I've a good husband but he never shows me affection beyond a small kiss in the morning and when he comes home. He never gives me a warm hug of affection or rarely makes an affectionate comment, or tells me of his love. He only does these things when he wants the marriage act, so I don't feel they are affection then. I seek all my affection from the children and I notice many wives do likewise. Can I change my husband as I feel I am making myself be cold towards him to try and lessen my need for his affection?

This sentiment is also identified by the married women who contributed to Rohan's book on Irish marriage; these women talk of lavishing their attention and affection on their sons to fill an emotional void caused by their husbands.[69] Children's rights author John Holt rails against this emotional abuse of children in his landmark text.[70] Holt claims that children are used as emotional crutches by adults who have been starved of human contact and affection. Children have little say in being picked up, hugged and patted by adults they do not even like.

In her reply to these letters Angela Macnamara does not blame men for their transformation from affectionate suitors to neglectful husbands, or women for failing to be more assertive in communicating their needs. This is in sharp contrast to American articles reviewed by Wouters which suggest that from the mid-1960s women were encouraged to actively express their anger which, rather than being negative, was an essential part of conflict management in intimate love.[71] For Macnamara, women should praise their husband's minimal efforts rather than demand more emotional reciprocity. Such advice was reminiscent of a feature of advice columns identified by Wouters prior to the 1960s where women remained largely submissive but negotiated their relationships through sweet-talking their husbands as opposed to direct confrontation.[72] Angela Macnamara does let men off the hook here. It is 'not part of a man's natural inclination or temperament to be so warmly affectionate', she replies. The displays of tenderness through courtship were a means to an end, a conquest. In marriage, Macnamara writes that men are often burdened by a greater responsibility in the world of work and will 'allow desire to take the place of affection in his love making'.[73] More controversially, perhaps, Macnamara suggested that within marriage there is always a mutual exchange of sex for affection:[74]

He will be ready to give her affection (in token and gesture), companionship, praise, encouragement and constant unasked for reassurance that she is very much needed and loved. In return his wife will give herself to him with fullness of joy in their physical relationship, satisfying his needs (greater in this sphere than hers)

Pierre Dufoyer similarly identifies this 'desire for conquest' which drives men above and beyond their masculine psychology to perform acts of gallantry to secure the woman's agreement to marriage.[75] It would appear that men and women were reading from very different romantic scripts. Dufoyer confirms to young men, to whom the book is directed, that the romantic phase of their lives will generally end in their mid-thirties as they turn to their ambitions outside the family home.[76] In his view, it is women who are at fault. Driven by a hyper-sensitivity that encouraged them to view their husbands more critically after marriage, women focussed on each failing and slight against them. Rohan's interviews with married men reveal how they too apportion some of the blame for an absence of romance to their wives.[77] One man described how his wife criticized him for being unromantic while still having curlers in her hair, wearing a five-year-old nightdress with scorch holes from the fire and an old cardigan with only one remaining button. The life histories also reveal that it wasn't only men who changed between courtship and marriage. Liam Ahearn (63) described how he found the transition to marriage difficult:

I found it hugely difficult to settle when I got married. I'd say the biggest change I found was that my wife went along with some of the things that we would like to do and were doing together before we got married and when we got married she said 'we've enough of that' like we used to go to the local for a drink. You know I thought she was happy enough but I did realise immediately after we got married that she wasn't a pub woman at all, and isn't a pub woman today and she just went along with me.

Anthony Giddens sees men as 'laggards', historically excluding themselves from the transitions occurring in intimate relationships.[78] The concept of romantic love has always had an ambiguous relationship with men's desire for, and access to, sexual conquest. For Giddens they have misunderstood a basic prerogative of modernity – where the self, including an emotional self, becomes part of a reflexive project which is constructed and reconstructed over the life course. For women, romantic love becomes both a tool of oppression and also a key means with which to actively interrogate masculinity.[79] The letters on the subject of unemotional husbands may well reveal the naive, gendered expectations of some romantic newly-weds; indeed, other women are scornful of them as needy 'immature women who require praising', but they represent a refusal to compromise on the romantic vision which they have been sold.[80] Angela Macnamara's column and other print and broadcast media contributed to this romanticization of love, a development not welcomed by all. A letter of 15 January 1967 castigated Macnamara for filling young girls' heads with thoughts of love and romance 'to the detriment of practical living'.

For the women in the Dennis et al. study on Yorkshire miners in the 1950s, romance offered a refuge from the humdrum routine of daily life, the struggles with money and the dissatisfaction they felt with their husbands.[81] Some could barely recognize their husbands as the attentive romantic men of their courtships. One woman explained that 'I'll go over and sit next to him when he comes in from work and he'll say to me "Can't you find somewhere else to sit and let a man read the paper in peace".'[82] The women often expressed a preference for the weekly women's magazines and paperback novelettes that carried stories of dashing romantic heroes and passionate embraces.[83] Janice Radway's study on reading romance novels also found a preference for stories about love and sex within the confines of monogamous married relationships.[84] What is significant is that these magazine love stories, which had always avoided any sexual description, now started to have a growing emphasis on sex as opposed to love.[85] This fiction would gradually mirror the reality of many women's intimate lives. Macnamara had remained suspicious of the influence of romance novels on women, particularly concerned that they might cause them to be less cautious when in intimate situations with men. She warned that 'if you let your imagination wander or be stimulated by reading cheap romantic stories you may begin to imagine things that could happen on your next date'.[86] Angela Macnamara was concerned that the wider availability of books and films would have a damaging effect on young people, a concern shared by the Catholic Church. She continued: 'this is why books, films, television and magazines which encourage such imaginings are a very bad diet for young people ... the church has our best interests at heart when she advises us to avoid bad books, films and entertainments'. The Catholic Church, of course, was not just advising its flock to *avoid* such publications; it had been actively supporting some of the strictest censorship laws in the Western world. There was a widespread belief among the Macnamara readership that the Censorship of Publications Act of 1967, which loosened the restrictive climate governing the media, had flooded Ireland with pornography, particularly from Britain, that was corrupting young people.[87] There is little doubt that the Act did contribute to a growing openness and discussion of new and controversial ideas, even those that ran counter to Catholic social teaching. Angela Macnamara, in a reply to a letter writer on 28 January 1973 who was concerned about the spread of pornography, wrote that 'censorship is not the answer, we must educate people to become their own censors' – although in her reply on 1 May 1977 to a woman who had forwarded 'filthy magazines sent to her son', Macnamara stated that she had 'sent the magazines to the Office of Censorship of Publications'.

Connery had an equally bleak outlook on whether young Irish women could actually distinguish between fact and fiction: 'The girls are particularly susceptible to the dream world cajoleries of films, advertisements, popular magazines and pop idols. Their heads have little inside them but thoughts of boys, dates, dances and the ways and means of achieving popularity.'[88] Connery does recognize that these very films and popular magazines have changed the expectations of a cohort of girls reaching maturity who will have little tolerance for a neglectful 'bachelor husband' in their marriages.[89]

Joanna Bourke's study of working-class culture corroborated Angela Macnamara's belief that young people would mimic the actions of their Hollywood screen heroes.[90] A 21-year-old shorthand typist confessed that films made her more receptive to lovemaking and made her feel like kissing a stranger, although she never did. An 18-year-old bank clerk grew impatient with the local boys who courted her, preferring the dashing lovers of the big screen. Another girl also felt more receptive to lovemaking after watching films, though few girls believed the depiction of 'love at first sight' on their cinema screens.[91]

Other women had more radical solutions to their loveless marriages than romance novels. A letter to Frankie Byrne described how a 50-year-old woman in a relationship with a cold and selfish man had embarked on a short affair with another married man. Though they ended the affair, the woman had remained unhappy ever since. Frankie Byrne advised her to 'look for ways to change your life even more radically now – while you still have your energy and your remarkable ability to function without self pity'.[92] Byrne does not reproach the woman for her affair. Byrne was at the time conducting a long-term relationship with a married man herself. To another married woman engaged in a relationship with a married man Frankie Byrne advises: 'He sounds to me like the eternal youth who balances out domestic responsibility with extra-marital romps, but in the end always opts for home because that's where he keeps his pipe and slippers.' She continued: 'I think you want this man as an escape route out of your own wretched marriage and in my opinion, you haven't a hope with him.'[93]

Crucially, the letters from these romantics and Angela Macnamara's replies represented a considerable challenge to the existing balance between love and lust. The letters contribute to a growing trend within Ireland that saw women enter into both a public and a private dialogue with men about the importance of emotions like love and intimacy within a successful marriage. This set in motion a process where relationships would be built upon the reciprocal exchange of love, intimacy and sex. As couples attempted to renegotiate the traditional love/lust balance there were new opportunities but also responsibilities to monitor and supervise the conduct of their own relationships against a greater democratization of personal life throughout the column and beyond.

FROM A 'RIGHTS AND DUTIES' DISCOURSE TO A SEXUALIZATION OF LOVE

The analysis of the letters reveal that often the sex lives of married couples were motivated not by a desire for individual or reciprocal sexual fulfilment, but rather as a procreative and potentially sinful 'duty'. Over the course of the column's publication this would change. Neglectful husbands who had abandoned their wives for the pub several nights a week and expected sex on their return were unacceptable but left women feeling resigned to their fate. In a letter of 22 May 1977 a woman describes how her husband had abdicated all responsibility for their children and the running of their house. She explained that her husband 'has never shown me that he loves me. He has no love for either me or his children ... he thinks that using me as a sex instrument is loving me. That's all love means to him.' Angela Macnamara apportions blame to the mothers of husbands like this who 'had been spoiled at home by mothers who doted on them and did everything for them. So they turned out to be irresponsible husbands and fathers, quite unready to really give themselves in marriage in any way other than the physical.'

Other wives complained that their husbands couldn't even wash themselves.[94] Hygiene was also a feature in Rohan's book on Irish marriage, with her respondents suggesting that the unwashed smell of their husbands contributed to their lack of interest in sex.[95] For most women their enjoyment of sex was mediated often by their fear of pregnancy, guilt or the economic burden of an expanded family. A woman in a letter of 16 November 1980 describes how she has not had 'sexual intercourse properly for a long time for fear of conception ... we have used the withdrawal method to avoid pregnancy but I have always felt guilty. I cannot bring myself to go to confession as I cannot put into words to a priest just what I do.' Indeed, Macnamara reveals during interview that it was women's avoidance of sex as a crude method of contraception or, as she describes in the column, as a punishment for their lack of affection that angered men and further damaged the relationship.

By contrast, Wouters's study showed that both the introduction of the pill and an expected self-restraint had contributed to a decrease in the fears and anxieties surrounding sex.[96] The use of contraception by newly married couples in Kanin and Howard's study had a clear class dimension, with two thirds of middle-class respondents employing a method of contraception, as opposed to one third of working-class respondents.[97] There were also higher rates of contraceptive use among those couples (74 per cent) who had no premarital sex in their relationships compared to those who had (46 per cent), which the authors attribute to these latter couples 'feeling "ready" for children'.

For the Yorkshire women in the study by Dennis et al., birth control was not widely available.[98] One woman, Jean, described by the authors as having aged beyond her years after multiple miscarriages, told how she had bought condoms in the chemist but her husband threw them in the fire, stating that they took 'all the enjoyment out of sex'.[99] Jean, however, got little enjoyment out of sex herself, being told by her husband that she was 'cold'. When she learned about the availability of the contraceptive pill in a local clinic she thought that there was something unnatural about it but, more importantly, felt that her husband wouldn't approve. Few women in the study claimed that they got any real satisfaction from sex with their husbands, while in the absence of contraception the use of the withdrawal method made the possibility of female orgasm even more remote.[100] Dennis et al. argue that most married couples had 'no intimate understanding of each other' except when they climbed into bed together at night for sex that both parties often described as disappointing.[101] They argue that it would be impossible for women to enjoy sex under a dominant ideology which saw them only as objects of lust, mothers and domestic servants.[102]

Joanna Bourke's study similarly reveals that Irish married women were not alone in having difficulty in obtaining information about or access to contraception.[103] She writes that as late as the 1950s the Medical Women's Federation reported that out of twenty-seven British medical schools only four provided medical undergraduates with lectures on contraception.[104] Letters to Marie Stopes, reviewed by Bourke, reveal that for many women, especially up to the 1960s, abstinence was regularly practised as a means of family planning. The opening of birth control clinics in Britain was also unevenly dispersed around the country, where there were difficulties in finding suitable premises in communities with high unemployment who struggled to pay for the services. Bourke argues that the reliability of contraceptives was an issue for women and that after abstinence the most common form of contraception among working-class communities was abortion. This process was made safer after the passage of the Abortion Bill through Parliament in 1967.[105]

Dating guides had traditionally encouraged women to yield to men's greater sexual demands within marriage. Pierre Dufoyer warns women to expect men's greater need for sexual intimacy with 'rhythmical frequency'.[106] Angela Macnamara acknowledges this in interview. On the occasion of her own marriage, her mother advised her on the subject of marital intimacy that 'men want more and you just have to give it to them'. This was just one part of a greater patriarchal dominance within the home. Macnamara believed that even strongly opinionated women expected their husbands to assume the role of the head of household, for 'he is more suited by nature to exercise authority and she to accept it'.[107] This advice reflected an understanding of that time of the rights and duties of a married woman in relation to her husband. Hilliard's study of married women's sexuality in the 1970s similarly reveals this 'strong sense of a husband being entitled to the sexual availability of his wife'.[108] Women were, at that time, conditioned to expect little control over their fertility or their sexual lives. The sinfulness of refusing one's husband and a fundamental belief in the shamefulness of the sexual act influenced women's enjoyment of sex. This letter of 30 October 1977 reflected the experience of some of Hilliard's respondents and the wider societal view:

Q. I confessed to my doctor that I was not always ready for sex
with my husband. He told me to ACT as if I liked it and never
refuse my husband. Well! I should have got an Oscar as I acted
myself into a large family and a breakdown. Now I have
retired from the acting profession. I clean the house, cook the
meals, look after husband and children and accept all sexual
advances passively. My husband seems to believe there can be
no love without sex and so I'm considered frigid. My husband
has never said 'I love you', never given a kiss without
expecting sex.

Sexual relationships were further complicated by a genuine suspicion, by
some men, of women who displayed an interest in or enjoyment of sex.
Baggot argues that men considered it 'part of the wife's bargain to fall
in with their needs and desires'.[109] Wouters had also identified this trend
in advice columns in the 1930s in the Netherlands, where women were
portrayed as indifferent to sexual intercourse.[110] He suggested that in
the United States women were curtailed by a double standard that
blamed women for sexual transgressions.[111] Ireland was no different in
this regard, although the consequences – like incarceration in religious-
run Magdalene homes – proved far more severe.

As the letter writer of 30 October 1977 revealed, women often
participated in sex even when they found it distasteful, seeing it as an
unpleasant necessity in order to achieve the much-coveted home and
family. More worryingly, the following letters, published on 1 June
1969, 16 August 1970 and 4 April 1976 respectively, show that women
often didn't feel that they had a choice of whether to refuse sex or not:

Q. Have married men the right to force themselves on their wives
in any kind of way? His demands are excessive and certainly
unusual and he gets mad if I don't give in to him any time he
wants, and fires things around. I am sure that what he does is
sinful. Can there be any sexual sin in marriage?

Q. Hasn't a wife a duty to fulfil her husband's physical needs in
marriage, even in later years?

Q. Mine is a rather silly question but at least it's short. I just want
to ask is it ever right for a wife to say no to her husband's
advances?

Another woman in a letter of 2 November 1980 described how her
husband had to 'get sex regularly ... there's no love making or petting,

just sex. I can't refuse him.' During interview with me, Angela Macnamara spoke of letters from women who had refused sex with their husbands and 'had to put up with the fact that he would masturbate in bed beside them which was really disgusting to women ... and I couldn't print something like that. But when I had the opportunity, when they enclosed stamp addressed envelopes, of writing privately.' Life history interviewee Patrick McGrath (75) also commented on this tension between a lack of sexual education, fear surrounding sex as sinful and the sense of sexual entitlement men felt for their wives that existed within marriage at the time:

> It was exacerbated by the religious things, by the fear that was in people about sex, a feeling that sex was dirty and people had to do it in the dark whatever ... I remember the Angela Macnamara column, there were women who were very very disappointed with the man who had now ownership over her and had been married to her now. He was entitled to it you see. He knew nothing about it but he had to have it. Big problem. Big problem for both of them.

This sense of sexual entitlement was also reported by some of Hilliard's respondents reflecting on their married lives in the 1950s and 1960s, with women describing how they were 'reared in a time when we had to obey our husbands, we couldn't refuse them' while others 'felt it was a sin to refuse him his rights'.[112] The documentary 'Too Many Children?' also featured women who expressed little choice in having large families. One woman described how she got married in 1956 and had had a child every year since then. 'The babies just come around every year', she said, as if powerless to exercise control over her own body. Another woman was similarly dismayed with her large family: 'I just couldn't stop, I just kept on having them.'[113]

Economic growth, urbanization and the expansion of third-level education all contributed to a changed context in which people would conduct their intimate lives.[114] Armed with a new knowledge derived from books, especially self-help manuals, magazines and television, analysis of the column reveals how this was translated into a growing dissatisfaction with marital sexuality for many. Primarily this would be among married couples, especially women, but later the population as a whole. This was in contrast to Wouters who had charted a more open discussion about sexuality among both single and married women.[115] Indeed, it must be remembered that Wouters's data was drawn from

Opzij, a radical feminist magazine and in sharp contrast to Angela Macnamara's conservative outlook. In both cases this process of sexualization of love would be neither linear nor continuous, with the advent of HIV/Aids – and, in Ireland, the Kerry Babies Case – redefining sexuality and the body in the 1980s.[116]

THE BRITTLE STATE OF IRISH MARRIAGE

The state of Irish marriage came under increased scrutiny, particularly in the 1970s, with a greater public awareness of the unhappiness which many couples experienced. In an article published in *The Sunday Press* on 9 December 1973, Dr Noel Browne dramatically claimed that married couples were 'forced to live in a continual cock-pit of mutual self-hatred'.[117] Other published articles highlighted the plight of deserted wives.[118] Rohan wrote about relationships that had broken down but not broken up.[119] This was in sharp contrast to the situation in the four countries under review in Wouters's study.[120] All had simplified the procedures for obtaining a divorce which, combined with a declining stigma and more financial assistance for women leaving relationships, contributed to a lessening of the dependence women felt upon their husbands. Within the life histories that I collected, only one man had separated from his wife. Tony Fitzgerald (62) separated in 1987 and explained that, even then, he 'didn't know one other separated person in Dublin or Ireland, not one, not one ... I was very isolated and that was a very difficult time for me.'

As the 1970s progressed there was a greater discussion in the Irish media about the role that a happy sex life played within marriage. Even within *The Sunday Press* there was a parallel discussion of sexuality which was very different to Macnamara's. Journalist Gillie Kennealy's article published on 11 May 1975, 'Put the Love Back into Sex', claimed that married couples were no longer going to put up with a sexually unsatisfying relationship. People's expectations of marriage had increased, she wrote, with young people wanting a career and personal fulfilment and a satisfying sex life. She argued that it seemed that 'a mutually enjoyable sex life is more important than some people traditionally believed'. She refers to the 'bang-bang' attitude that men still have to sex and the belief that sex is always obligatory – that every touch, every kiss, must lead to sexual intercourse. Women were now feeling that they were sexual failures because popular glossy magazines put so much emphasis on the ability to achieve orgasm. *The Sunday*

Press's main rival, the *Sunday World*, had been publishing a more salacious problem page of its own, contributing to this trend.[121] Angela Macnamara, in a response of 12 October 1975, agreed that Irish society had moved on from a situation where 'the woman was never to admit to getting sexual pleasure from sexual intercourse' to a culture where the woman was under pressure to respond to sex in a way designated by the sex advice literature. This belief in the centrality of women's orgasms to a successful relationship would continue in the following decades, with research on the content of men's magazines referring to 'women's constant demands for better orgasms'.[122] Mansfield and Collard's male respondents also stressed the importance to them that their wives achieved orgasm during sex, a need often greater than among women themselves.[123] While this may indicate either the arrival of this more female-centred sexuality or that the female orgasm had become synonymous with an accomplished male sexual perform-ance, in practice the traditional roles of men and women during sex seemed more resistant to change. There was disagreement among cou-ples in Mansfield and Collard's study over who should initiate sex, with men, who had often taken the lead role in courtship, wanting their wives to show more initiative. Women described how, when their husbands initiated sex, it was often devoid of endearments.[124] Men reported that sex was the only arena in which they could verbalize their emotional selves, including the endearments their wives longed to hear. Women placed as much emphasis on foreplay as on intercourse itself.[125] The sexualization of love and marriage in an era of sex manuals and multiple orgasms, of equal rights for women in the boardroom and the bedroom, of self-disclosure and self-autonomy, created a tightrope which couples struggled to walk. In the absence of self-disclosure, couples were often left guessing the needs, wants and desires of the other. In Mansfield and Collard's study this tightrope was summed up, with women wanting men to be 'dominating in a gentle way' and women wanting men to 'take initiative but not take over'.[126]

Kennealy's articles reinforced an emerging view within Irish society that placed a satisfying sex life at the centre of a successful marriage. They also highlighted how much Angela Macnamara's column now seemed out of date, a development that did not go unnoticed by her editor.[127] Macnamara remained somewhat suspicious of the role sex manuals could play in improving marital sex. On 28 October 1973 she advised a young man intending to marry, who was worried that his use of such material maybe sinful, that to 'reread these passages for the purpose of making oneself aroused' was not proper for a man on the cusp of marriage. John and Mary Ryan saw a role for these manuals in teaching the husband and wife how to get the most pleasure out of sexual intercourse, but thought the explicitness of the diagrams and the level of detail could potentially be off-putting to young women, contributing to their reluctance to fully engage in sex.[128] Furthermore, the Ryans felt the manuals did not emphasize that sexual intercourse was not just a physical act but one in which body and spirit were united.

This process of a greater sexualization of love had emerged earlier in the United States. Seidman's review of the role sex manuals played in the sexual ideology of the 1960s argued that they conveyed multiple meanings of sex as reproduction, love and pleasure.[129] Those manuals from the 1950s still located sex within reproduction, but stressed its central importance to a happy marriage and it was this sexualization of love and marriage that contributed to a greater culture of eroticism. It was only in the 1960s that sex began to be explored as an act of pleasure and self expression.[130] Sex was seen not as an expression of love or reproduction but something for the exclusive exploration of pleasure and self-expression. By contrast, the seemingly liberal discussion of the Kennealy column still located the pleasures of sex within the context of married relationships. For single women, even in the United States, Seidman notes the persistence of the 'good girl' in the 1970s who is neither sexually assertive nor lustful, concealing and controlling her sexuality to avoid the disapproval of both men and women.[131]

James Kelly (70) was sanguine about the course of his sexual married life, believing that 'the reality about sex is that people become used of it and the magic disappears to a certain extent and it's often a question of intimacy, being together and sharing, which is the wonderful part'. Most of the interviewees did accept that while there was a greater availability of information on improving marital sex, it was difficult to break free from established patterns of sexual behaviour in the early stage of marriage. It was this concept of intimacy that James spoke about, quoted above, that often eluded both men and women who believed that such expressions only occurred within the bedroom, before and after penetrative sex. Angela Macnamara spoke of this in interview with me, believing that men, particularly, misunderstood that 'making love doesn't only take place in bed ... it's going on all the time prior to going to bed, also in the sense of the woman feeling loved before she even goes to bed'. The difficulty for couples was this disjuncture between sex and intimacy. As Macnamara explains: 'if the man couldn't have the lot – penetrative sex – then he wasn't interested in anything else ... He wasn't interested in half measures.' The life histories reveal that while this may have been a feature of early married life, a broader conception of sexual intimacy did emerge later in marriage.

As the column progressed into the 1970s the letters reveal men and women's greater desire to discuss sexual difficulties within their marriages and seek solutions to them. Women who wrote to Angela Macnamara were dismayed by their inability to achieve orgasm and the speed with which their husbands did. They were saddened by the gulf that often existed between their sexual relationships and the lack of emotional or intimate connection with their husbands. In a letter of 31 July 1977 a woman wrote: 'I feel a terrible change in our lovemaking ... It takes about fifteen minutes now and immediately afterwards my husband goes to sleep ... I've tried to tell him to be more slow but he says he reaches climax.' Another letter of 13 April 1980 expresses a similar dissatisfaction:

> Q. How I would love if my husband made love to me. Now I don't mean if he'd have sex – he's always ready to have sex ... I mean if we have sex it only takes a short time and I feel little or no response. I don't think Irish men in this country know how to make love.

> A. I understand the hurt that is caused a lot of women by their husband's lack of understanding of the primary needs of a wife ... A woman can best respond to a man if she has been tenderly loved, spoken to with loving words, gently caressed; her physical arousal takes place under such loving circumstances.

This idea that women's sexual desire could only be aroused within such an emotional and romantic context as described above by Angela Macnamara was already being sharply criticized in the United States. Alma Birk, writing in *Cosmopolitan* magazine in 1968, argued that such an understanding of women's sexuality is disempowering and stigmatizes women who find sex outside a context of love.[132]

Often Angela Macnamara's letter writers even struggled to escape a view of sexuality as something dirty and sinful. Others lacked any communicative competence to express their sexual wants to their husbands who, often through ignorance or selfishness, were disinterested in more reciprocal, female-centred relationships. In a letter of 28 December 1975 a woman asked Macnamara whether it was wrong if she masturbated, being so dissatisfied with her marital sex life. The trend towards more female-centred sexual relationships also remained slow internationally. Wouters's review of sex research in the Netherlands revealed that up to 50 per cent of Dutch men continued to have an aversion to clitoral stimulation in the early 1970s, although this had declined to 20 per cent ten years later.[133] In Ireland men wrote to Macnamara, often saddened by their wives' lack of interest in sex.[134] James Kelly (70) revealed the willingness of some couples to negotiate their sex lives so that they were more female-centred. He relates that 'orgasm wasn't reached by penetration for my wife so that [intercourse] wasn't the central feature of our sex life' and that 'she was happy to modify my means to accommodate that but [it] wasn't a major issue'. The modification James spoke of was that he gave his wife oral sex to achieve orgasm, although when I asked him whether this was reciprocal he said that 'he thought it rude to ask' for oral sex. For others like Tony Fitzgerald (63) the very concept of oral sex didn't register within their marriage – 'didn't know it existed ... never crossed our minds', he explained, a situation that only changed when he separated from his wife. It was when he 'started to see other women that I experienced [oral sex] and I started to catch up on the sexual revolution'.

The majority of letter writers to Angela Macnamara sought not to end their relationships but to take advantage of new opportunities to improve them. Unlike proponents of an individualization thesis that saw a declining kinship influence over family members and the elevation of choice in intimate relationships bringing greater fragility and risk to them, the analysis of the column reveals continuity in strong bonds of love and connectedness between family members.[135] Contemporary studies still support this view. Neil Gross's critique of theorists supporting this detraditionalization of intimacy within society cites many studies in which Americans overwhelmingly believe in the concept of a 'soul mate' and reveal a higher regard for love within married relationships now as compared with the 1960s.[136] A changing economy allowed a woman who had always felt financially dependent on her husband to return to the workforce.[137] A married women in her mid-fifties asked if it was too late to discuss with her husband why she gets so little pleasure from sex.[138] These letters represent some evidence of an actual renegotiation of relationships, although it is a limitation of the documentary methodology I have used in the book that in some cases it is difficult to ascertain whether the column represents just a more open *discussion* of sexuality rather than a *transformation* in individual practice. This letter from a woman on 4 March 1979 reflects this dilemma when she asks for Macnamara's advice as to why she and so many other married women simply don't enjoy sex:

> Q. I am married six years now and for quite a long time I have found that I do not really enjoy sex, but it's only lately that I've realised that the majority of married women I speak to don't enjoy it that much either. It doesn't seem to matter whether they are on contraceptives or not. They just don't enjoy it very much. It's hard to know what's wrong ... It can't be natural that so many women do not enjoy sexual relations. It's not even that our marriages are unhappy ... A number of us are very happily married and we still can't enjoy sex. Can you suggest any reasons for this and anything we could do about it?

> A. Long ago, though not that long ago, women were given to understand that it was not proper for them to enjoy sexual relationship and that the enjoyment was only meant for men! Even one generation ago women were given to understand that men should be given 'their rights' whenever they wanted them, irrespective of how the woman felt or what might be her needs ... Arousal for a woman is a much more complex thing than it is for a man ... The man may be hasty, his desire greatly increased. He may approach his wife without real sensitivity and without having a concrete realisation that she still needs all the sort of loving that she needed prior to marriage before she is ready physically and emotionally for sex ... Well what can you do? ... the first is that the husband and wife must talk together ... then take steps to set up a situation in which leisurely, comfortable lovemaking is possible.

Angela Macnamara does not, in this reply, suggest that the couple refer to a growing amount of literature aimed at learning and improving the knowledge and skill of both partners to enable them to give maximum pleasure during sex. Instead Macnamara relies upon the belief that women always need the right *emotional* context for good sex to occur, a belief that was widely challenged outside Ireland. There is no doubt that women were leading this quiet revolution, facilitated by a changing social and political context – one in which the feminist movement played a key role. Angela Macnamara interpreted some of this self-development as evidence of a rising individualism. In an article of 30 November 1975 she claimed:

> In our society today, self expression, self development and self fulfilment are emphasised ... We are living in a time of individualism. This encourages selfishness, which is the very antithesis to love. It can never be right to develop oneself at the expense of others.

Love requires us, Macnamara writes in a reply on 11 September 1977, to be 'other centred' as opposed to self-centred. A few months before, in a reply on 31 July 1977, she wrote that 'self has to become background and this is very hard ... The world is always telling us "do your thing", to seek pleasure for ourselves, to get and possess and have.' It was, however, usually women who were blamed for pursuing individual fulfilment, rather than the men who had neglected those needs in the first instance. Francesa M. Cancian and Stephen L. Gordon's review of American magazine articles on marriage also confirm the persistence of a message of 'self-sacrifice more than self-development'.[139] Cancian and Gordon's study traces a shift in how love and anger were expressed in women's magazines over an eighty-year period. They identify how a belief that the avoidance of conflict through self-control was a natural expression of one's femininity gave way to an understanding of conflict and disagreement as a normal part of married life. It marked a transition from advice, also present in Macnamara, where women were encouraged to use their feminine wiles to persuade and cajole their husbands, often sacrificing their own interests in order to preserve their marriage. Now the expression of anger became the sign of a healthy marriage. They argue that the normalizing of disagreements in marriage 'contributed to more equal power between the sexes'.' Such voicing of anger did, however, have to occur in a controlled manner most often described as 'constructive'.[140] This idea is reminiscent of Wouters's 'controlled decontrolling' of emotions where there must be willingness to 'tolerate and control conflicts, to compromise'.[141] It was also a process that was interpreted differently by men and women. Mansfield and Collard's male respondents told how they interpreted their wives' desire to 'talk and clear the air' as an indication that they were looking for a fight.[142] The wives in the study expressed disappointment that their need for self-disclosure was not always shared by their husbands, many of whom said they had no need to confide in anyone. Other men in the study found such 'monologues of self disclosure' boring.[143]

Swidler also tackles this challenge, in which the free choice that enabled individuals to freely select their marriage partners could also be the freedom that would end the relationship.[144] She identified different cultural understandings that attempt to reconcile this tension between individual fulfilment and commitment. Two of these understandings – the disciplined self and attuned selves – reflect similar tensions in the column, where Macnamara resisted the tendency, of women particularly, to develop greater autonomy within their marriages. Swidler's concept of the 'disciplined self' is revealed through her interviewees' willingness to make their marriages work despite any emotional incompatibility or desire to fulfil an individual want detrimental to their relationships.[145] Through a disciplined act of willpower her interviewees – who were often deeply religious – believed that their marriages were based not on their individual desires but on a greater selfless commitment to Christianity. Many letters to Macnamara revealed couples who also willed and prayed that their relationships would work, often against huge odds, believing that their individual wants were secondary to the sacramental commitment they had made in marriage. Others believed it was God's will that they suffered in unhappy marriages, a sacrifice that would be rewarded in heaven.

Rohan's interviewees often similarly believed that marriage was to be endured rather than enjoyed or resisted. One Irish mother of nine commented on the sexual side of marriage: 'whoever said you were supposed to enjoy sex? Sure aren't we all here to suffer, and the more we suffer in this life [the] better it will be for us in the next.'[146] Swidler refers to the transition towards a more 'therapeutic ethic' where individuals try to understand what they *really* want in marriage when freed from religious, family and community obligations.[147] It was this development that Macnamara tried to prevent from gaining a foothold in Irish marriage. This individualism, referred to by Swidler as the 'Me Decade' of the 1970s, increasingly became a currency in which the media and ordinary couples in Ireland spoke of their relationships.[148] What is crucial in understanding the Macnamara column is that while people did start to develop these autonomous selves in their marriages, they did so often to better the existing relationship, not to end it. Swidler's interviewees similarly pointed to how, through developing oneself and making oneself happier, this was not incompatible with making their marriages happier too.[149] It is evidence like this that is consistently ignored by the pessimism of prominent detraditionalization of intimacy theorists.

I argue that a consequence of renegotiating marriage to achieve a more satisfactory balance between love and sex led in turn to a greater equality within peoples' intimate relationships. For Giddens, it is the principle of autonomy that is central to the emergence of the pure relationship within personal life.[150] Autonomy is the result of the 'successful realisation of the reflexive project of self' which enables individuals to act in an egalitarian way and see that self-development of others presents no threat, nor is it done at the expense of others. Rather than being the antithesis of love, as Angela Macnamara claimed, such development may hold the key to the pure relationship. People remained in such pure relationships 'solely for whatever rewards that relationship can deliver'.[151] My reference to Giddens here is made cautiously. The economic parity necessary for the advent of the pure relationship in Ireland had not yet been fully realized. Women's participation in the labour market remained low (around 30 per cent) by international standards.[152] Also, in the absence of divorce, couples did lack a socio-legal context to pursue relationships of this kind. That said, it is my contention that the realignment of intimate relationships in Ireland during this period through the focus on mutual self-disclosure, free and open communication, a greater prohibition of physical violence and the exploration of sexual pleasure did lay the foundations of the pure relationship in late modern Irish society. There is, of course, debate about whether such a relationship even exists, whether aspects like mutual self-disclosure are always positive and whether these transformations that Giddens locates in late modernity were actually present some fifty years previously.[153]

Angela Macnamara may have regretted the advent of greater individualism but she recognized that Irish marriage had changed forever. In advising happily married women who were still not enjoying sex with their husbands she suggested on 4 March 1979 that 'at least some women and possibly quite a number of men ... haven't yet got used to the new understanding of marriage partnership'. This 'new' understanding is in opposition to a more traditional rights and duties discourse governing sex and implies a more equal partnership within intimate life.

CONCLUSION

In this chapter I have argued that a transformation occurred within the realm of personal and intimate life for many married couples during the period 1963–80. The use of the letters to Angela Macnamara has allowed access into this private domain to chart what I argue has been a renegotiation of the traditional balance between love and sex. It is, however, a renegotiation that came later to Ireland compared to other Western countries. Several reasons contributed to this. The early segregation of the sexes increased the level of awkwardness between them. As adults, government policies controlling laws on contraception and divorce mediated their experience of sex often more as a reproductive duty or a fear of an increased economic burden than an exploration of pleasure. This often created a greater need for intimacy – for touch and closeness – within relationships than was identified by Wouters's comparative study, for example. The result created an unnecessary strain within relationships that delayed a move to more mutual pleasure and a wider process of a sexualization of love. With high levels of religious observance, a higher proportion of married couples than in Wouters's study could have been identified as 'trend followers' for whom greater levels of anxieties surrounded sexual exploration.

Women have spearheaded this exploration. It has brought with it many unintended consequences. By raising intimate problems in a public forum women were reshaping the social, political and economic context in which they lived their lives. The solutions lay in a new body of expert advice, Angela Macnamara included, that encouraged women to reveal their emotional and sexual needs within marriage. This context changed men also. Their intimate relationships changed as they responded to or contested women's 'new' needs within marriage. This chapter brings a much-needed visibility to the emotional lives of men, through both their own problem page letters and those of the women who sought to navigate relationships with them. The gaze inside some Irish marriages revealed how these new options, both economic and emotional, opened up a greater world of possibility for fulfilment.

NOTES

1. My understanding of this range of emotions as socio-construct is influenced by Deborah Lupton. Like her, my interest is in how emotions are played out within the 'lived experience' of relationships where they are mediated by existing constructs of gender and power. How we experience and express emotions in these everyday practices becomes part of a gendered self which is constantly (re)constructed. See D. Lupton, *The Emotional Self* (London: Sage, 1998), p.38.
2. C. Wouters, *Sex and Manners: Female Emancipations in the West 1890–2000* (London: Sage, 2004), p.124.
3. I am grateful to Betty Hilliard for this term.
4. A. Giddens, *The Transformation of Intimacy: Sexuality, Love and Eroticism in Modern Societies* (Stanford, CA: Stanford University Press, 1992), p.184.

5. I. McEwan, *On Chesil Beach* (London: Jonathan Cape, 2007).

6. Ibid., p.3.

7. T. Inglis, *Lessons in Irish Sexuality* (Dublin: University College Dublin Press, 1998), p.39.

8. M. Kenny, *Goodbye to Catholic Ireland* (Dublin: New Island Press, 1998).

9. E. J. Kanin and D.H. Howard, 'Postmarital Consequences of Premarital Sex Adjustments', *American Sociological Review*, 23, 5 (1958), p.560.

10. K. Bulcroft, R. Bulcroft, L. Smeins and H. Cranage, 'The Social Construction of the North American Honeymoon, 1880–1995', *Journal of Family History*, 22, 4 (1997), p.447.

11. Ibid., p.479.

12. Ibid., p.478.

13. P. Mansfield and J. Collard, *The Beginning of the Rest of your Life? A Portrait of Newly-Wed Marriage* (Basingstoke: Macmillan, 1988), p.80.

14. Ibid., p.166.

15. Ibid., p.108.

16. D. Rohan, *Marriage Irish Style* (Cork: Mercier Press, 1969), p.78.

17. B. Hilliard, 'Motherhood, Sexuality and the Catholic Church', in Patricia Kennedy (ed.), *Motherhood in Ireland* (Cork: Mercier Press, 2004), pp.141–3.

18. Ibid., p.141.

19. D.S. Connery, *The Irish* (London: Eyre & Spottiswoode, 1968), p.174.

20. P. McElhone, *When the Honeymoon is Over* (Dublin: Veritas, 1977).

21. Ibid., p.55.

22. Rohan, *Marriage Irish Style*, p.69.

23. Ibid., p.74.

24. 21 September 1975; 16 October 1977.

25. T. Inglis, *Truth, Power and Lies* (Dublin: University College Dublin Press, 2003), p.147.

26. A. Macnamara, *How to Choose a Wife* (Dublin: Redemptorist Publications, 1967), p.12.

27. A. Macnamara, *Living and Loving* (Dublin: Veritas, 1969), p.6.

28. Macnamara, *How to Choose a Wife*, p.12.

29. Rohan, *Marriage Irish Style*, pp.78–9.

30. Hilliard, *Motherhood, Sexuality and the Catholic Church*, p.144.

31. See Connery, *The Irish*, p.172, for a discussion of the programme.

32. J. Ryan and M. Ryan, *Love and Sexuality* (Dublin: M.H. Gill & Son, 1968).

33. Ibid., pp.162, 165.

34. Ibid., pp.66–7.

35. McElhone, *When the Honeymoon is Over*, p.65.

36. Ibid., pp.66–7.

37. Rohan, *Marriage Irish Style*, p.97.

38. Examples of such letters include 26 March 1967; 18 February 1968; 5 December 1971; 17 April 1977; 11 December 1977.

39. 26 March 1967.

40. P. Dufoyer, *Building a Happy Marriage* (London: Burns & Oats, 1962), p.53.

41. Ibid., p.75.

42. P.A. Baggot, *Unspoken Problems of Married Life* (Dublin: Irish Messenger Office, 1965), pp.41–2.

43. Ibid., p.44.

44. J.C. Messenger, *Inis Beag: Isle of Ireland* (Prospect Heights, IL: Waveland Press, 1969), pp.68–9.

45. A.J. Humphreys, *Urbanization and the Irish Family* (London: Routledge & Kegan Paul, 1966), pp.143–4.

46. Mansfield and Collard, *Beginning of the Rest of your Life?*, pp.190–1.

47. P. O'Dea, *Dear Frankie* (Dublin: Mentor Press, 1998), p.30. O'Dea does not give a date of broadcast for Frankie Byrne's advice.

48. Examples of other letters on 'tight-fisted' husbands were published on 10 September 1967; 12 November 1967; 25 January 1970; 26 April 1970; 21 April 1974; 9 December 1979.

49. Macnamara, *How to Choose a Wife*, p.21.

50. Rev. D.A. Lord, SJ, *M is for Marriage and More* (Dublin: Catholic Truth Society, 1962), p.10.

51. N. Dennis, F. Henriques and C. Slaughter, *Coal is our Life: An Analysis of a Yorkshire Mining Community* (London: Eyre & Spottiswoode, 1956), p.187.

52. Ibid., p.191.

53. Ibid., p.204.
54. J. Bourke, *Working-Class Cultures in Britain, 1890–1960: Gender, Class and Ethnicity* (London: Routledge, 1994).
55. Ibid., p.70.
56. Ibid., p.66. Bourke's discussion of the parlour is drawn from Walter Southgate, *That's the Way It Was: A Working Class Autobiography 1890–1950* (London: New Clarion, 1982), p.67.
57. N. Yeates, 'Gender and the Development of the Irish Social Welfare System', in A. Byrne and M. Leonard (eds), *Women and Irish Society* (Belfast: Beyond the Pale Publications, 1997), p.147.
58. N. Fennell, *Irish Marriage: How Are You?* (Cork: Mercier Press, 1974), pp.25–80.
59. N. Scheper-Hughes, *Saints, Scholars and Schizophrenics: Mental Illness in Rural Ireland* (Berkeley, CA: University of California Press, 1979), p.102.
60. 26 March 1967; 18 February 1968; 5 December 1971; 17 April 1977; 11 December 1977.
61. This was also identified in Scheper-Hughes, *Saints, Scholars and Schizophrenics*, p.97.
62. Rohan, *Marriage Irish Style*, pp.70–1.
63. Not all research conveyed such a negative portrayal of women's enjoyment of sex. Joanna Bourke uses interviews conducted with wives of soldiers in the 1940s by Slater and Woodside to illustrate that many reported high levels of sexual satisfaction, with one third of women stating that they 'always' experienced orgasm. Other women reported a desire for sex, with only a few expressing disappointment. See Bourke, *Working-Class Cultures*, pp.50–1.
64. S. Seidman, *Embattled Eros: Sexual Politics and Ethics in Contemporary America* (New York: Routledge, 1992), p.28.
65. T. Inglis, *Truth, Power and Lies: Irish Society and the Case of the Kerry Babies* (Dublin: University College Dublin, 2004), p.147.
66. Violence was also a feature in the lives of Hilliard's respondents, of whom one in eight had experienced severe violence in their marriages. See B. Hilliard, *Micro-Processes of Social Change: Aspects of Family Life in Late Twentieth Century Ireland* (unpublished doctoral thesis, University College Dublin, 2010), p.120.
67. For example, G.A. Kelly, *Dating for Young Catholics* (London: Robert Hale, 1963).
68. Wouters, *Sex and Manners*, p.73.
69. Rohan, *Marriage Irish Style*, p.68.
70. J. Holt, *Escape from Childhood: The Needs and Rights of Children* (Harmondsworth: Penguin, 1974), pp.80–1.
71. Wouters, *Sex and Manners*, p.159.
72. Ibid., p.148.
73. Macnamara, *How to Choose a Wife*, p.10.
74. Ibid., p.9.
75. Dufoyer, *Building a Happy Marriage*, p.70.
76. P. Dufoyer, *Marriage: A Word to Young Men* (New York: P.J. Kennedy & Sons, 1963), pp.14–5.
77. Rohan, *Marriage Irish Style*, pp.44–5.
78. Giddens, *Transformation of Intimacy*, p.60.
79. Ibid., p.2.
80. 21 May 1967.
81. Dennis et al., *Coal is our Life*.
82. Ibid., pp.229–30.
83. Ibid., pp.207, 231.
84. J. Radway, *Reading the Romance: Women, Patriarchy and Popular Literature* (Chapel Hill, NC: University of North Carolina Press, 1984), pp.73–5.
85. See Dennis et al., *Coal is our Life*, p.232.
86. Macnamara, *Living and Loving*, pp.28–9.
87. See 4 January 1970.
88. Connery, *The Irish*, p.177.
89. Ibid., p.169.
90. Bourke, *Working-Class Cultures*, pp.34–5.
91. Ibid., p.35.
92. O'Dea, *Dear Frankie*, pp.48–9.
93. Ibid., 56–7.
94. 18 August 1968; 27 January 1980.
95. Rohan, *Marriage Irish Style*, p.114.

96. Wouters, *Sex and Manners*, p.126.
97. Kanin and Howard, *Postmarital Consequences*, p.559.
98. Dennis et al., *Coal is our Life*, p.208.
99. Ibid., p.208. Hilliard's respondents also reported an unwillingness among their husbands to use contraceptives, with one man refusing to sign a consent form to enable his wife to have the coil fitted. See Hilliard, *Micro-Processes of Social Change*, p.79.
100. Dennis et al., *Coal is our Life*, p.231.
101. Ibid., p.228.
102. Ibid., p.231.
103. Bourke, *Working-Class Cultures*, p.56.
104. Ibid., p.56.
105. Ibid., p.57.
106. Dufoyer, *Building a Happy Marriage*, pp.59–60.
107. Macnamara, *How to Choose a Wife*, p.23.
108. B. Hilliard, 'The Catholic Church and Married Women's Sexuality: Habitus Change in Late 20th Century Ireland', *Irish Journal of Sociology*, 12, 2 (2003), pp.36–7.
109. Baggot, *Unspoken Problems of Married Life*, p.21.
110. Wouters, *Sex and Manners*, p.125.
111. Ibid., pp.140–1.
112. Hilliard, *Motherhood, Sexuality and the Catholic Church*, p.146.
113. Connery, *The Irish*, p.171.
114. See Inglis, *Truth, Power and Lies*, pp.132–5.
115. C. Wouters, 'Balancing Sex and Love since the 1960s Sexual Revolution', *Theory, Culture & Society*, 15, 3–4 (1998), pp.187–214.
116. The Kerry Babies Tribunal was established after the discovery of two dead babies in 1984. Suspicion fell upon a single woman, Joanne Hayes, who was having a relationship with a married man. Her confession and that of her family to the crime, which it was later proven they did not commit, led to an enquiry about allegations of police misconduct. The tribunal of enquiry brought about a forensic investigation into the sexual conduct of Hayes which became a modern witch-hunt of a sexually transgressive woman. See T. Inglis, *Truth, Power and Lies: Irish Society and the Case of the Kerry Babies* (Dublin: University of Dublin Press, 2003). The 1983 abortion referendum was a divisive campaign to place a ban on abortion in the constitution. Although passed, the ambiguous wording has led to four further constitutional amendments. See T. Hesketh, *The Second Partitioning of Ireland: The Abortion Referendum of 1983* (Dublin: Brandsma Books, 1990).
117. Noel Browne was previously a reforming Minister of Health, 1948–51. He continued to champion issues such as women's and gay rights. See N. Browne, *Against the Tide* (Dublin: Gill & Macmillan, 1986).
118. 13 January 1974; 27 January 1974; 23 June 1974.
119. Rohan, *Marriage Irish Style*, pp.43–63.
120. Wouters, *Sex and Manners*, p.149.
121. The *Sunday World* was launched in 1973 and would mark the end of *The Sunday Press*'s dominance of the Sunday newspaper market with a unique combination of sport, gossip and entertainment. Its agony aunt column, *Dear Linda*, blurred the lines between problem-solving and titillation. See M. O'Brien, *De Valera, Fianna Fáil and the Irish Press* (Dublin: Irish Academic Press, 2001), p.132.
122. A. Rogers, 'Chaos to Control: Men's Magazines and the Mastering of Intimacy', *Men and Masculinities*, 8, 2 (2005), p.185.
123. Mansfield and Collard, *Beginning of the Rest of your Life?*, p.168.
124. Ibid., p.166.
125. Ibid., p.168.
126. Ibid., p.167.
127. Macnamara's editor, Vincent Jennings, declined to be interviewed for this book.
128. Ryan, *Love and Sexuality*, p.82.
129. Seidman, *Embattled Eros*, p.32.
130. S. Seidman, 'Constructing Sex as a Domain of Pleasure and Self-Expression: Sexual Ideology in the Sixties', *Theory, Culture & Society*, 6 (1989), p.303.
131. S. Seidman, *Romantic Longings: Love in America, 1830–1980* (New York: Routledge, 1991), pp.153–4.

132. Ibid., pp.145–6.
133. Wouters, *Sex and Manners*, p.126.
134. 16 October 1977.
135. Proponents include U. Beck, *Risk Society: Towards a New Modernity* (London: Routledge, 1992); U. Beck and E. Beck-Gernsheim, *The Normal Chaos of Love* (Cambridge: Polity Press, 1995); Z. Bauman, *The Individualized Society* (Cambridge: Polity Press, 2001); E. Beck-Gernsheim, *Reinventing the Family: In Search of New Lifestyles* (Cambridge: Polity Press, 2002).
136. N. Gross, 'The Detraditionalization of Intimacy Reconsidered', *Sociological Theory*, 23, 3 (2005), p.302.
137. See 21 October 1979 and 17 August 1980.
138. See 15 February 1976.
139. F.M. Cancian and S.L. Gordon, 'Changing Emotion Norms in Marriage: Love and Anger in US Women's Magazines since 1900', *Gender and Society*, 2, 3 (1998), p.310.
140. Ibid., p.320.
141. Wouters, *Sex and Manners*, p.2.
142. Mansfield and Collard, *Beginning of the Rest of your Life?*, p.187.
143. Ibid., pp.171–3.
144. A. Swidler, *Talk of Love: How Culture Matters* (Chicago, IL: University of Chicago Press, 2001), p.137.
145. Ibid., p.139.
146. Rohan, *Marriage Irish Style*, p.67.
147. Swidler, *Talk of Love*, p.143.
148. Ibid., p.148.
149. Ibid., p.144.
150. Giddens, *Transformation of Intimacy*, p.189.
151. A. Giddens, *Modernity and Self-Identity: Self and Society in the Late Modern Age* (Cambridge: Polity Press, 1991), p.6.
152. E. Smyth, 'Labour Market Structures and Women's Employment in the Republic of Ireland', in A. Byrne and M. Leonard (eds) ,*Women and Irish Society: A Sociological Reader* (Belfast: Beyond the Pale Publications, 1997), p.64.
153. L. Jamieson argues that there is considerable evidence to suggest that the greater concern with the concepts of intimacy, equality and privacy in marriage and family life existed since the 1940s; for example, see E.W. Burgess and H.J Locke, *The Family: From Institution to Companionship* (New York: American Book Company, 1945). Jamieson is also critical of Giddens's dismissal of Foucault and Bauman, who focus on the regulatory and dependent roles that experts can play including an almost obsessive incentive to self-disclose. See L. Jamieson, 'Intimacy Transformed? A Critical Look at the "Pure Relationship"', *Sociology*, 33, 3 (1999), pp.479–81.

CHAPTER FIVE

Children: Seen and Heard

INTRODUCTION

It was not just the relationships between dating and married couples that experienced change in the manner in which intimacy was explored and understood during the 1960s and 1970s. Other family relationships were changing too. A wider process of informalization was taking place which challenged the power imbalances between older and younger people and between lay and expert professionals in Irish social life. Informalization ushered in a new relaxation of etiquette and social customs that governed the lives of individuals, particularly the relationship between the sexes, ending a formalization of manners embarked upon since the sixteenth century.[1] This informalization process intensified in the 1960s. A transformation was also occurring in how parents and their children related to each other.

In this chapter I look specifically at the experience of children and young adults who asserted themselves during the 1960s and 1970s, seeking greater freedom from their parents in their choice of career, sexual partners and fashion. Children challenging their parents' authority was, of course, a feature of social life before the 1960s. However, I argue that this challenge to parental authority in Ireland in the 1960s coincided with a fundamental shift in how children were perceived less as heirs, farmhands or a form of social security for their parents in their old age and more as individuals determined to chart their own course in the world, freed from the social and familial constraints that held back previous generations. Old orthodoxies were being challenged and new questions were being asked of parents that dared not be spoken a generation before. Parents faced questions in answer to which they increasingly had to defend their religious beliefs and the associated moral code which governed their relationships. Children had more questions, gleaned from greater access to information about sex and religion from a wider variety of television, newspaper and magazine sources, including Angela Macnamara's column. The economic austerity of the 1950s gave way to a greater affluence that facilitated a greater focus on individual fulfilment in relationships and careers. Increased access to education enabled those ambitions to become reality. Some parents who wrote to Angela Macnamara were distressed and anxious at the new challenges their children would face and their own incompetence in navigating them through a new world. Letters to the column revealed a perception that increased wealth had spoiled and indulged children who were previously economic assets to their households, leading to a decline in respect for their parents and other authority figures. Mothers wrote anxiously about how they would guide their children through a childhood so radically different from their own without the full participation of their husbands in their upbringing and the dire consequences that might ensue. Parenting itself emerged as a skill to be learned rather than an intuitive practice.

Some parents reacted to the new challenges with old methods. Attempts to restrict the freedom of children or to use physical force to uphold the parents' will were strongly resisted by children and by Angela Macnamara. Letters to the column revealed that some young people had rejected domineering parents who sought to curtail their personal freedoms and restrict their recreational activities outside the home. There was also a rejection of corporal punishment in the home and in schools as old styles of parental discipline and authoritarian teaching methods were increasingly challenged. The State would soon follow, banning corporal punishment in schools in 1982.

A new world of parenting slowly emerged, but how different was it from what had gone before? Anthony Giddens argues that greater democracy is not just a feature of his concept of the 'pure relationship', which is marked by an emotional and sexual equality where both individuals stay so long as the relationship is satisfying both their needs, but also extends to a transformed relationship between parent and child, based on equality, respect and mutual self disclosure.[2] I question whether this new world of parenting represented just a change in the language used and if parents had substituted a traditional form of authority and surveillance for more covert means under the guise of democratic parenting. I explore these transformations, focusing on why relationships between parents and children changed during the period of Angela Macnamara's column and the impact this had on wider gender relations within the family.

TOWARDS DEMOCRATIC PARENTING

Anthony Giddens argues that the extension of democracy in family life is not just a process within exclusively sexual relations but a process that extends to 'friendship relations and, crucially, to the relations of parents, children and other kin'.[3] For Giddens, democratization within the family requires equality, autonomy, mutual decision making and freedom from violence. In his view, parents will 'still claim authority over children ... but this will be more negotiated and open that before'.[4] Giddens believes that the concept of 'permissiveness' is inaccurate to explain the transformation within parent–child relationships that goes beyond a more lax style of parenting.[5] He believes something more profound has happened to these relationships, where intimacy has replaced parental authoritativeness. They represent a break with the past when child-rearing manuals encouraged parents to remain largely aloof from their children to prevent a dilution of their authority. Now, Giddens argues, the parent–child relationship holds the potential to be a democratic one.[6] In the transition to adulthood this relationship will now have to be negotiated on the basis of voluntarism.

Julia Brannen et al., writing in 1994, agree that if parents want to maintain good relationships with their children they have to 're-create ties on the basis of equality and reciprocal liking, trust and understanding'.[7] However, they argue that parents do not relinquish their authority or power in the parent–child relationship; rather, the 'control mechanisms' undergo change.[8] A new mechanism of surveillance emerges, so that parents expect to be informed of their children's activities through mutual consent, under a guise of supporting their child's transition to independence. Children respond by withdrawing certain pieces of information from their parents. The Brannen et al. study also reveals other shortcomings in extending Giddens's model to the parent–child relationship, where the flow of communication is also mediated by the sex and class of the children involved. Fewer daughters, for example, reported higher levels of satisfaction with their relationships with their fathers.[9] Young women also showed a higher propensity to disclose personal information to their parents than young men did. The willingness to disclose also varied according to ethnic origins, with children of non-indigenous parents less likely to disclose to their parents.[10]

These findings are replicated in other studies. Solomon et al. also explored these changing relationships between parents and children in a study of seventy families, of whom over 50 per cent described 'being there' and 'talk' as the most important aspects of being in a family.[11] It was also this mutual disclosure of information between parents and their teenage children and a growing tendency for parents to treat their children as adults that transformed the relationship from a hierarchical one to a more equal, friendship-based one.[12] Children sharing information about puberty, boyfriends and girlfriends was seen to epitomize this renegotiated relationship as parents recognized their children as emerging adults, equal in status to them.[13] Solomon et al. are also critical that Giddens does not acknowledge the inherent power differentials between parents and their children before they embark upon this democratic process in their relationship.[14] The evidence from the Solomon et al. study suggests that tensions exist between the authority that parents hold and their desire for this open communication. A number of their respondents were well aware that their parents had mixed motives in encouraging them to disclose, facilitating a subtle form of surveillance. Indeed, many children knew that the more they disclosed the 'the more they risk losing control over the private lives'.[15]

For Ulrich Beck, children are an impediment to individualization, in their cost, commitment and their monopoly of attention of their parents, yet they are at the same time irreplaceable. For it is at times of instability in relationships where partners can come and go that children, according to Beck, can offer the 'last *remaining, irrevocable, unexchangeable primary relationship*' (italics in the original).[16] Children become the last bastion in the fight against loneliness as opportunities for love gradually fade. Within relationships some children become the focus of an unprecedented energy and commitment directed at them by their parents. As I discussed in the previous chapter, traditionally children were seen as an almost inevitable by-product of marriage – sometimes desired, sometimes not. Giddens claims that we are now 'in the era of the "prized child", where children are no longer an economic benefit but instead a major cost', leading to profound change in child-rearing practices.[17] Viviana Zelizer also traces the historical emergence of this economically 'worthless' child.[18] Her study traces the transformation in the economic and sentimental value of children in the United States between the 1870s and 1930s. While a child born in nineteenth-century rural America was greeted as an additional farm labourer, the middle classes lessened their need for their children's income and protection in old age by taking out insurance and constructing trusts to protect this economically worthless child in the future.[19] Families relied on earnings derived from child labour, which remained an important source of additional income for working-class families until the 1960s when, Zelizer argues, children joined the ranks of the economically worthless.[20]

This concept of the changing economic and sentimental value of children is central to understanding what made the transformation of the parent–child relationship in 1960's Ireland different from what had gone before. In Chapter 3 we saw that Macnamara recognized that families no longer demanded a dowry upon their daughters' marriage, reflecting a wider transformation in the character and fabric of rural Ireland. Alexander J. Humphreys understands the rural family as both an economic and social unit, with shops and farms run predominantly as family enterprises 'employing' adolescent and adult children.[21] This resulted in the continued subordination of children to their parents, and a situation in which a delay in declaring an heir to the farm or business postponed children's transition into their 'occupational and full social adulthood'.[22] With adulthood delayed, adult sons were often treated and referred to as 'boys', and emigration was often the only route by which to establish independence, turning rural Ireland into a gerontocracy.[23] Socio-economic developments in the 1960s would generate opportunities for an indigenous independence for young adults. Both the expansion of the industrial base and the introduction of free second-level education in 1966 provided greater opportunities for children who would have previously left school to work for their fathers or remained on family farms. A broadening of the industrial base also brought more opportunities, particularly for non-inheriting sons of farm households. Adult children earned an income which was independent of their parents and granted them more autonomy over the conduct of their lives. Young children, according to Zelizer, became sacred, occupying a 'special and separate world, regulated by affection and education, not work or profit'.[24] Tom Garvin also points to how the 'growth of a stratum of relatively moneyed and leisured youth in society shifted the relationships between generations' in Ireland in the 1960s.[25]

Consider my own father's story. Born in 1937 in rural Co. Tipperary, he left education after primary school to work with his father and contribute financially, aged 12, to a household of eight children. Even by 1964 only 36 per cent of 16-year-olds and 14 per cent of 18-year-olds were in full-time education.[26] Three of these children would emigrate permanently to Britain, with my father moving to London to work for three years. The Ireland he returned to in 1963 was different and the choices that his children, born in the 1960s and 1970s, would make reflected a greater opportunity in education, though not always greater economic opportunities.

This era of the 'prized child' has continued apace ever since. Children who are the product of expensive IVF treatment enter the world eagerly awaited by parents who are ready to lavish their attention and almost exclusive focus on them. For Ulrich Beck and Elizabeth Beck-Gernsheim, parents, specifically mothers, now come under increasing pressure to be regularly briefed by child-rearing experts who will compensate any potential deficiencies while encouraging language, music and sports skills.[27] Child rearing becomes a science in which parents must become proficient. Parents, again often mothers, who are under pressure from expert opinion dispensed in the mass media and advice columns sacrifice their own ambitions so that their child's 'needs' are met.[28] The relationship of the parents suffers because it takes a back seat as they struggle to implement the dictates of the child experts. Beck and Beck-Gernsheim support a view that the net result of expert intervention is to increase the level of surveillance over children, who are viewed as dependent and in need of parents to define and organize their more staged childhood.[29] For Viviana Zelizer this had more to do with childhood play moving off the 'dangerous' streets of the community and into the organized safe setting of the playroom.[30] For Henry A. Giroux too, public recreational space like youth centres, public parks or empty lots where children could play have disappeared, with the growth of a private sector to 'care' for children.[31]

It would be incorrect to view such a preoccupation with child rearing by parents and experts alike as being a product of the late twentieth century. Ann Hulbert traces the evolution of a century of expert commentary on raising children from the publication of L. Emmet Holt's best-selling *The Care and Feeding of Children* in 1894.[32] A science of childhood developed in order to deal with the challenges of child rearing in a rapidly changing society. It coincided with a more urban, educated America where fertility had dropped and women were freed from productive household labour.[33] As the century progressed, a trend towards encouraging parents to exercise greater patience and flexibility took hold among expert opinion, culminating in Benjamin Spock's best-selling book, *Baby and Child Care*, first published in 1946[34] in which Spock advised parents to take a child-centred approach by refusing to scold their children, whom they should be encouraging. As the political climate of the Cold War exerted its influence over public opinion, Spock's later work returned to being more 'parent centred', though he still advocated balancing the control and freedom of children while bringing them into the decision-making process.[35] As Spock turned from child-rearing expert to anti-Vietnam War activist in the 1960s, his style of permissive parenting that had influenced millions of mothers became associated with the decline in the respect for authority in homes and schools across the country.[36] Counter-expert opinion such as that of Bruno Bettelheim castigated child-rearing practices that had indulged a generation of more affluent post-war children deprived of strong father figures.[37] Child-rearing expert commentary could not be separated from the social and political context in which it was read.

CHALLENGING AUTHORITARIAN AND DISTANT FATHERS IN THE HOME

Letters to Angela Macnamara's column reveal that many Irish fathers were both a dominant presence in the family home and at the same time largely absent from the everyday lives of their children. Mothers and their children wrote to Macnamara to seek advice on how to deal with domineering husbands and how to persuade them to engage with their children. A young man writes in a letter of 21 December 1969 that his father had refused to allow his brother to marry a particular girl, which led him to emigrate to England after terrible rows in the family home. While the other family members missed him, their father's word remained final in this matter. This row had happened in the context of rising debts which the family were struggling to pay. Angela Macnamara advises that his father, like most men, wanted to 'feel that he is head of home, and respected as such' and that underneath this gruff exterior was probably a man who felt 'unloved and unsuccessful'. Another 16-year-old girl, in a letter of 8 August 1968, describes how her conservative father refuses her permission to go to dances and gets angry when she challenges his authority. Angela Macnamara recognizes that the existing gendered power relations within the family will lead to greater conflict as children strive towards independence. She advises:

> I get many letters like yours indicating mistaken attitudes on the part of parents. In some cases fathers have been domineering for so long and the mothers have grown to be submissive for the sake of peace. But children are facing adulthood, and want, quite naturally, to have an increasing amount of independence. The father finds it hard to give up being unquestioned dictator ... parents who are unreasonably domineering will be resisted all along the line by the young person with the emerging individuality.

Women wrote that they had often assumed both parenting roles in their families and struggled, particularly with boys, to impart sex education and religious education and to instil values of independence, consideration and respect for women. A letter of 2 February 1975 describes how a woman felt sad that there was no relationship between her husband and their teenage sons, which ensured that 'all the children come to me with their troubles and with the things they have to decide on'. Her husband, whom she describes as a good earner, spends most of his time watching television despite her efforts to get him to 'talk man-to-man with the boys'. Interestingly, it is not the fact that his leisure time entails watching television that is problematic but his neglect of a duty presumed to be his responsibility. In her reply Macnamara is slow to blame men for their lack of interest in their children, seeing this as a personality trait and recognizing that some men have difficulty in expressing themselves to others, but is in no doubt about the positive role fathers can play in their sons' lives, building them into 'men of real integrity and gentleness, capable and confident, courageous and loving'. For Angela Macnamara this positive paternal influence would only come through greater education which emphasized the role that men could play in child rearing.

In a letter of 6 February 1972 a woman describes how her husband has a 'terrible temper and for the least thing he would start shouting, cursing and swearing. It's hard for him to agree with anyone ... He even uses bad language with the children. I don't think he has any feeling for anyone at times. It's just hell to live with.' Macnamara responds that 'the first thing is to tell your husband that the home atmosphere must change, that if it doesn't you will have to seek outside help from a marriage counsellor, priest or social worker ... what is of first importance is that you provide your children with a happy home.' Angela Macnamara's tolerance for behaviour in the home that affects children is lower in comparison to relationship disputes between married couples. She also places the responsibility of creating a 'happy home' on women. In a reply to a letter of 3 September 1972 Macnamara advises a wife to seek professional help for her domineering and bullying husband. She continues:

> The 'father figure' in this country has not been good. In too many cases the father opts out of parenthood and leaves the responsibility of rearing the children almost entirely to the mother. She become [sic] the dominant one in the home. The sons suffer from a lack of positive influence a father should exert. In manhood they

exhibit their inner feelings of inferiority and inadequacy by bullying, over indulging in alcohol, temper tantrums, self-indulgence, 'jokes' at the expense of others and opting out of family responsibility.

In a letter of 2 February 1975 a woman writes that her husband 'comes back from his work and sits looking at television or going to an occasional film or bringing work home in the evenings and he spends little or no time actually doing things with the children or talking with them'. Similarly, on 28 November 1976 a woman complains that her husband

> is often out with his pals in the evening, likes football like all the men, and thinks that when he's in if there's a football match on the television, it's he who should be pleased and have the right to look at what he wants. He doesn't like the kids to disturb him too much and if they keep out of his way everything is OK.

In response Angela Macnamara argues that there are dire consequences for children of a neglectful father:

> His absence requires that the mother take a dominant role in family care, whereas the children do need an equal amount of care of differing kinds from both parents. So they suffer if the mother is forced to take over. Most delinquent boys, for example, are discovered to be the children of fathers who do not face up to their responsibilities. There can be serious results in children whose fathers are absent themselves regularly and show no interest in them. The boys have no male figure with whom to identify and can, as a result, be excessively shy and unsure of themselves. At a more serious level homosexuality is thought to develop where the role of father and mother are confused, and most particularly when a parent is seen to have no interest in or affection for the children. Daughters also suffer from deprivation if they cannot have the special affection and closeness of a father.

It is difficult to assess how this advice would have been received by deserted wives, widows and later lone parents. Richard Farson agrees that a dominant ideology that every child *should* have the complementary roles of a strong father and a soft mother has 'struck fear into the hearts of the 7 million single mothers in the US'.[38] Previous research on fathering clearly identifies the style of parenting described in the letters quoted above. Julia Brannen and Ann Nilsen developed a typology of fathering/hood based on their thirty-one interviews with fathers across four generations of families.[39] The 'work-focused' father whose identity was constructed around a work ethic and who had little involvement with his children was present, not just in the older cohort of men but across all generations and in all socio-economic groups. The second model includes the 'family men' who were the main breadwinners in their families but placed a great emphasis on 'being there' for their children.[40] The final group were termed 'hands-on' fathers who were only sporadically their children's main breadwinners and were heavily involved in their upbringing. Brannen and Nilsen point out that in some cases the level of fathers' involvement among the current generation had actually decreased over time, with younger generations working longer hours than their parents or grandparents.

The life history interviews I conducted also reveal high levels of involvement of some fathers with their children. Although the discourse of fatherhood had remained traditional in 1960s Ireland, a private masculinity was played out in the everyday life of families within the domestic sphere. The life histories reveal men reluctant to show in public their involvement in child rearing, having internalized a view of this labour as essentially 'women's work'. Brannen and Nilsen also recognize that the older men they interviewed did have greater difficulty in expressing themselves about areas of intimate life, which they saw as 'women's domains'.[41] While interviewing the men in this study, although there was some hesitancy in discussing certain topics I found that men were less than sure-footed when talking about the sequence of or dates of events, often telling me that their wives would be able to remember that better. Penny Mansfield and Jean Collard appear to be correct when they state that it is women who are 'the custodians of detail and so tend to be the biographers of relationships'.[42]

Joanna Bourke, in her study of British working-class communities from 1890 to 1960, stated that it is hard to reconcile this public dominant image of men as being essentially undomesticated; the qualitative data she analyzed did show considerable involvement of fathers in child care and domestic chores in the privacy of their own homes.[43] To start with, she argues that the home was increasingly located further from places of work and became a site of leisure with the availability of radios and, later, televisions. In large families, fathers took care of older children while mothers nursed young babies. As children stayed in school longer, fathers took over chores that were previously the responsibility of older children. Crucially, Bourke argues that of the

250 autobiographies that she analyzed during the period, for every one writer who described a father who didn't do housework, fourteen mentioned one who did.[44] Women who had accepted an image of their husbands as breadwinners rather than homemakers showed surprise at their husbands' domestic competence. Bourke retells a woman's story of teaching her husband in the 1920s how to change their baby's nappy and using the Vaseline and baby powder, only to feel piqued when the father could change the nappy as well as she could.[45]

My own mother reliably informs me that over three pregnancies in 1966, 1970 and 1972 my father changed not one nappy. She attributes this reluctance to the presence of my grandmother who acted as a third parent in my childhood home. Moving into our home shortly after the death of her husband and no longer in paid employment, my grandmother contributed financially to our household. She was also an extra pair of hands when household chores had to be done. She was the peacemaker in time of dispute. While always a hard worker, inside and outside of the home she remained, like many women of her generation, elegantly dressed and pristinely coiffed.

The potential to be a good father was also part of the mate-selection criteria increasingly used by some women. A woman writes in a letter of 1 March 1970 that while she enjoys her sociable, witty fiancé she has reservations about his suitability for fatherhood. In her reply, Macnamara reminds her:

> [many] a very happily married man was a 'gay bachelor' who showed no signs of fondness for children. Remember that women are born with an instinct for home-making and child-rearing. Men have to learn these arts by experience. A father's love for his child develops from the time he sees the child as a person ... Man is much more orientated towards social and business success and women must not make the mistake of thinking that their husbands are neglecting them when the husband places a natural importance on professional attainments.

Many of the life history interviewees in this study constructed their image of fatherhood in opposition to what they considered the distant or domineering style of their own fathers, although as the men grew older they were more likely to reappraise their relationships with their fathers in a more positive light.[46] Eddie Cullen (56) lamented his father's inflexible, domineering parenting style:

> He would have had his head down ... I have a role and this is the

way I am going to do it, he won't have really considered that I was also a human being, he would have considered – I am your father, I decide what you do and that was it ... I wouldn't condemn him now as an adult. I certainly wouldn't condemn him because he always provided the resources for me to get a good education.

Another quality Eddie believed he learned from his father was a belief in the need to teach his children to become independent. He believed that the first eight years of a child's life were the most important in terms of parental investment. He explained that 'I would always have taught my children to be independent of me, if they want to climb a tree I don't want to stop them doing it. If they want to do things, they can do them with my blessing provided it is within the boundaries of what I would consider to be reasonable.' He puts this parenting style down to his own parents' decision to send him to boarding school when he was 12, where he had to 'fend for myself ... I had to become independent and stand up for my rights ... I had to be able to find my feet and fend for myself from the age of 12.' The nurturing of independence in children has been identified as a key means by which fathers 'parent' differently from mothers. In Brandth and Kvande's study of Norwegian men who opted to share parental leave with their partners, a greater emphasis on *doing* activities with their children held greater importance in a form of intimacy identified as side by side rather than face to face.[47] Mothers in this study highly approved of their partners' involvement, placing a greater value on these activities than on their own activities with their children. Mothers often expressed regret that although they too would like more outdoor activities with their children they felt restrained by the need to 'make sure that everything is in order at home'.[48] Fathers in the study expressed the importance of children being taught to be independent of their parents and feared that theexcessive pampering and over-involvement of mothers in child rearing undermined this.[49]

For Patrick McGrath (75) it was also a *doing* activity that was important, with an interest in reading instilled by his own parents that acted not just as an educational tool but as a means of bonding with his children and now his grandchildren:

> My father would have been in the whole business of talking to the children and I'm constantly reminded of it now when my children bring along their children who are my grandchildren and they say

would you ever tell them the stories you told us when you put us to bed years ago and here am I repeating the same stories that I told them 40 years ago now and we are having a great time.

While Irish fathers were often conveyed in the pages of Angela Macnamara's column as being of a domineering temperament, it was Irish mothers who often enforced patriarchal decrees or assumed, as in life history interviewee James Kelly's (70) case, the role of head of the household. James explained that due to financial problems one of his two sisters was sent to live with his aunt and uncle in Co. Kilkenny. 'She went down for a holiday and never came back', he told me. His father was displeased but the family had little choice and he attributes much of the decision making to his mother:

> My father was twenty years older than my mother, a widower, a very gentle man and I would have thought the authority in the house was very definitely with my mother – a harsh woman would be too strong but a strong woman who would keep things on the road ... I loved my mother, I thought she was an extraordinary woman, got on well with people, people liked her ... My mother was the bastion of the house, she was the fulcrum, I thought she was an extraordinary woman and the sad thing is you become more aware of that as you grow older. She wasn't affectionate, we weren't an affectionate family, I kissed my mother for the first time the day I was getting married.

This quote reveals the complexity that lay behind the facade of Irish patriarchal family life. It reveals a married relationship based more on a shared understanding of the financial challenges that the family faced.

David Moloney's (63) description of his father's presence in the house was more reminiscent of the letters from children and wives to the Angela Macnamara column. He remembers tension in the house that was the result of his father's dominant position. He describes how his father 'would have been very strong about don't do this and be careful and make sure you do that and rules and regulations and whatever'. He believed, growing up, that such behaviour was normal until he 'met other people and then realised that there are different ways of living'.

While fathers may have held a dominant place at the heart of the family their role was often largely symbolic. Patrick McGrath (75) remembered his parents' relationship as warm but lacking physical expressions of affection. He continued:

They had very clearly defined roles, my father was the farmer, he
was the worker, my mother was the housekeeper and the manager
of things within the house. My father would have been designated
in an old fashioned way as being head of the household, he had a
special chair which he used and which everybody had to
vacate when he came into the place. He was the head of the household, he had his special chair and my mother had her special
duties and I remember a lovely thing, my father when he'd go to
town or when they would go to town he would always bring home
a present to my mother and I remember that quite well.

Damian Hannon and Louise Katsiaouni also revealed in their study of
the Irish family that there was a disparity in the amount of influence the
mother or father exercised over particular household decisions, with
the wife having a dominant influence over household and child-rearing
decisions while the husband retained control over financial management.[50] However, as I discussed in the previous chapter, women often
carried the full burden of financial budgeting in the home. In the life
histories too, Tony Fitzgerald (62) recalled that while his parents were
traditional, in that his father worked as a barber and his mother worked
full-time in the home, she paid all the bills and ran the house. In his
own marriage, circumstances intervened that dramatically increased his
role in the upbringing of his children:

I was a very active father, [a] participating father, and at times I
was their mother and their father when my wife was in ill health.
If she had normal health, how would I have been? I don't know.
I'm sure I would have been involved but not to the same extent as
I was. I was very heavily involved with the children. I'd get up, get
them ready for school, get them their breakfast, dress them. When
they were younger, nappies, fed them, I brought them to school,
then I went to work. I'd often, not often, plenty of times come
home and the breakfast dishes would still be in the sink and I'd
have to clear that up and then start cooking dinner. It was
because of her health. I'm not saying that in a complaining way,
sometimes I was pissed off, most times I understood.

Tony's description of his active fathering in these circumstances is
different from how other fathers have constructed masculine care-
giving identities. Brandth and Kvande's research on fathers shows that
mothering practices did not act as a role model for their care-giving;
they preferred to spend more time with their children in activities

outside the home.[51] These fathers did no more housework during their period of parental leave than they did when they worked full-time. Housework remained heavily gendered where there were 'no gains for masculinity' in its completion.[52] Within this understanding of constructing masculine care-giving, the household tasks and childcare identified by Tony Fitzgerald represent how fathers 'mothered' in times of familial crises. This underscores how important it is that research into practices of fathering should be relational and within an interactionist perspective. Christine Castelain-Meunier goes much further, arguing that 'fatherhood depends on the woman, including the ways in which the father will be able to fulfil his role'.[53]

CHILDREN'S QUEST FOR GREATER AUTONOMY

Many young people who wrote to Macnamara did so to complain how their personal freedom outside the house was curtailed and overly supervised. An 18-year-old, in a letter of 10 November 1963, explained that her parents continue to treat her like a child, bringing her and collecting her from parties. Other 18-year-olds were allowed a lot less freedom. In a letter of 2 January 1966 a young woman wrote that 'my mother does not allow me to go to dances, to the pictures or any other amusement', while in a letter of 6 August 1967 another woman complained that she was 'not allowed to date any local boys or participate in any amusements' and was therefore considered odd in her neighbourhood. She locates her mother's refusal to let her socialize in the fear that she will date a local boy of unsuitable class background. 'It is impossible to convince my mother that everyone is equal', she writes. In such cases Macnamara thinks it unreasonable that young people are not given the opportunity to socialize with a wide range of people, provided that they have been instructed in the facts of life and are willing to obey their parents' instructions about the time of their return. Even within the home young peoples' activities were restricted, with a young woman writing on 26 April 1964 that her mother reads her mail.[54] For other young people it was the changing tastes in fashion and music that caused arguments in the home:

> Q. I am 16 and my mother does not allow me wear lipstick. Some of the girls in my class wear eye make up and lipstick even to school. I don't want to wear it at school but just on special occasions ... Don't you think my mother is narrow minded about this?

A. Ask your mother if she will come with you to the cosmetics department of one of the big stores and hear what a beautician has to say about your skin. Then ask your mother to consider a pink lipstick – or a delicate one that would suit your colouring. If you take your mother into your confidence and discuss it with her as a friend, I am sure she will agree ...

Angela Macnamara's advice here, to disclose and include her mother in a discussion about her make-up, is significant. Telling the young girl to discuss make-up with her mother 'as her friend' lends weight to the argument that stricter and more hierarchical models of parenting were giving way to more democratic ones in which parent and adolescent child were conceived more as equals. In the Brannen et al. study of relationships between parents and children in the 1990s, mothers and daughters regularly drew from descriptive terms like 'friendship, trust, equality and sisterhood'.[55] While daughters did refer to their mothers as their 'best mate' they also chose to hold back certain information if they perceived that it would limit their autonomy in the home.

Another young girl wrote to Angela Macnamara in a letter of 11 December 1966 to complain that since John Lennon had said 'we are more popular than Jesus now', her mother had banned her from playing the Beatles's records in the house. In her reply, while Macnamara does not agree with her mother's actions, she said that 'it was an irresponsible comment to make ... the Beatles are not concerned with saving your soul. They can maintain their popularity and increase it by playing up to the side of man that loves the things of the world.' Other letters such as one published on 8 July 1979 reveal more complex family dynamics, where an adult daughter struggles to forgive her mother for the cruel things she has said about her. She explains that she 'was reared with my grandmother who was very strict and cruel at times ... I often worry about my mother and stepfather ... but my mother is always insulting me even in front of strangers.' Angela Macnamara advises the woman to 'forgive your mother unconditionally for the hurts of the past and visit her regularly'.

Relationships between fathers and their children were also the subject of research on the Irish family. Hugh Brody discusses how in farming families sons only start to spend considerable time with their fathers after confirmation. Now there is a transfer of supervision from the mother's intimate world of the home and schooling to a period of preparation for when the son would eventually take over his responsibilities on the farm.[56] The subservient role that the son takes up when he works on his father's farm ends only when he marries. Humphreys saw this as having a beneficial effect on the son's socialization into adulthood as he observes his father learning technical skills and also how to interact with other adults in places of work and recreation. This would remain beneficial only if the father was a suitable role model for his son.

Brody's study reveals that many fathers were often frustrated by the limitations of farm life themselves, while some harboured regret that they did not choose to emigrate as many of their peers and later their children were forced to do.[57] Stories of children returning home from England flush with success, promotion and increased spending power did little to comfort those who remained at home, often surrounded by ageing bachelors in isolated farmhouses. For married couples too, there was a great anxiety that if all their children rejected farm life and decided to leave they would be left alone; they often relied on the last child having a sufficient sense of duty or pity to remain at home to care for them. Daughters who had no part in the inheritance of the farm felt economically and emotionally freer to leave it, often with their mother's blessing. Non-inheriting sons faced a more uncertain outcome, often choosing emigration or the priesthood to establish independence from the family home.[58] Within the interviews I carried out, there were two farmers' sons, one of whom inherited the farm while the other found employment outside farming. Of all the men interviewed none had emigrated during the 1960s or 1970s, which would have been somewhat unusual at the time, influencing their access to information and sexual opportunity and perhaps shaping their conduct in intimate life.

RELIGION IN THE HOME

The letters reveal that the task of transmitting religious and moral values fell disproportionately on mothers, a situation for which many refused to accept exclusive responsibility. In a letter of 10 September 1967 a woman wrote that 'my husband and I disagree as to whether or not the children should be made to go to daily Mass during the holidays. They are aged 9, 11 and 14.' Macnamara replied: 'I consider any compulsion for adolescents an unwise approach. They are struggling towards independence and very much want to try planning their own lives.' She continued that parents 'will teach primarily by example and secondly they will ask the children's opinion when making the rules for the home'. We see here again Macnamara rejecting older concepts of parenting where children should be 'seen and not heard' in favour of opening a dialogue with children, canvassing their opinions and rejecting the imposition of rules, especially with regard to religious education. In her own home, Angela Macnamara's daughters at times disagreed with their mother on advice she had offered particular letter writers to the column.[59]

Parents were often divided in their approach to their children's religious education. In a letter of 19 March 1972 a woman wrote about her disappointment that she carried the sole responsibility of this education, describing how 'for several years now I have begged and pleaded with my husband to take the kids to Mass but always the answer was "No" [because] he didn't believe in religion. Time and again we ended up arguing about it.'

There is agreement that the Irish mother played a crucial role in the transmission of Catholic social teaching to her children in the home. Men's role in their children's religious education has remained unexplored. Tom Inglis describes how this construction of Irish motherhood had its roots in Catholic education in the nineteenth century which stressed the virtues of modesty, passive femininity and industriousness. It was an education that would leave a lasting legacy over women's lives. It facilitated priests and nuns to exercise control over women's lives and instilled ignorance, shame and guilt about their bodies.[60] The Irish mother provided an organizational link between the Catholic Church and the individual, ensuring that a range of practices learned in Church and the school classroom would also be carried into the home.[61] Children were reflections of their parents, but particularly their mothers, and were sent home from school if dirty or disobedient.[62] The practice of family prayer and the exercise of modesty, emotional and moral discipline also became the preserve of the Irish mother.

It was a role that mothers learned from their own mothers but it was a transmission that would be seriously disrupted in the 1960s and 1970s. Mothers resisted this exclusive responsibility in an era when their moral authority was being challenged inside and outside the home. Children increasingly resisted family prayer in the home and the regular observation of sacraments. In a letter of 16 November 1975 a young woman writes that she doesn't believe in religion and that her mother 'tries to force me to believe', to which Macnamara responded that no one can force another person to believe. Another mother wrote in a letter of 15 July 1979 that she would like to say the family rosary at home but 'our children look at me if I am out of the stone age'. While young people stopped believing, others became involved in other religious groups, to the disapproval of their parents. In a letter of 18 November 1979 a mother describes how her daughter had joined a religious sect to escape the rat race which Irish society had become and warned that the established churches must wake up to this danger.

Some letter writers, like one of 19 March 1972, were disappointed with Angela Macnamara for what they perceived as an unwillingness to support a more coercive attitude in ensuring that children participated in family prayer:

> Q. In your reply to the parent who wrote about the family rosary you said 'let it be clear to your children that there is no obligation to join in family prayer' ... firstly isn't there an obligation on children to respect their parents. If they do respect them they won't refuse to join them for ten minutes each evening for the family rosary ... I believe the family rosary should be said in every Catholic home daily.

> A. I certainly agree with you that from the earliest years families should pray together daily. But as children grow older I don't think that they should be forced on their knees and I do think that they should have an opportunity to discuss their feelings on the matter.

Other parents recognized that they should talk to their children about religious and moral concerns but felt inadequately equipped to do so, given the pace of change and the different moral challenges that young people now faced. The belief system which governed parents' lives now seemed more open to challenge and contestation in a more open society. In a letter of 9 December 1979 a woman wrote:

> I realise that we should be talking to the growing children about all the modern problems that we are faced with every day. But when I was young these problems didn't exist and we never talked to our parents like that ... I find it very hard to talk about them or to put up good reasons why certain behaviour is wrong or right. I know it is wrong or right but I can't explain why. Also, it's hard to put into words the reasons why we have the values we have.

Macnamara responds: 'Often we haven't worked out the "why" that is behind the value we hold. Then when we are asked "why not have divorce" or "why not have sex before marriage for people who are really in love" ... Our inability to explain sometimes causes the young person to feel confused or to assume that we have adopted our values unthinkingly.' Alexander J. Humphreys draws a distinction between rural and urban homes in this question of blindly accepting religious doctrine.[63] He concludes that by virtue of living in Dublin there has been no significant decline in Mass attendance or observation of sacraments but specific points of religious doctrine are subject to more discussion and scrutiny, while the clergy are criticized more and expected to justify Catholic social teaching. In Humphreys's case study of the Dunn family, religion played a central role in their lives.[64] Both parents were active in religious instruction and in setting out the obligations that were required of their children in the home. These obligations included morning and evening prayers, prayers before meals, confession and Mass and Holy Communion. The Dunns also believed that a 'good Catholic' went beyond the basic required of them and also became involved in religious organizations such as the Sodality and in visits to the Blessed Sacrament.[65] Both parents took an equal role in their children's religious instruction, with their father saying evening prayers with his children before bedtime.

Despite having both parents committed to religious instruction, older interviewees in Dorine Rohan's research remained pessimistic about the future of religion in Ireland.[66] They expressed distress at the attitudes of the younger generation and the changes introduced into the Church governing fasting and the use of the Latin Mass. There was an awareness of the changing attitudes to religion abroad and a realization that Ireland would soon succumb to the same changes.

Patrick McGrath (75), the oldest of my interviewees, grew up in a traditional farming household where family prayer would still have played a key role. He describes an 'important spiritual dimension – the rosary was said every night as well and we all had a round and we all had our decade and that was a big part of our lives'. While Patrick describes how as parents themselves he and his wife encouraged their children to go to Mass, practices such as the family rosary were in decline. He explained that 'it was part and parcel of our lives ... the rosary ... no, we wouldn't have been as consistent as that [i.e. his own parents] now but my wife Mary is very religious now, very into the church, more so than myself so she would have us all going to Mass and going to devotions and I think maybe our children maybe resented some of it'. As their children grew into adulthood the gap between Patrick and Mary's religious beliefs and that of their children widened further. He continued: 'when youngsters go to college they become their own bosses really, they do their own thing and wouldn't have the same feeling about [it] as [we do] ... it would upset Mary that they didn't have the same feeling about it. Times have changed and it has brought its change into thinking, youngsters don't go to church, they don't regard it as a must.' This belief that university proved detrimental to children's religious faith also found voice in the column. In a letter of 11 July 1976 a mother complained that she felt her son 'had fallen into bad company and has abandoned the practice of his religion'.

Tony Fitzgerald (62) played a greater role than his wife in ensuring his children attended Sunday Mass although his explanation that 'there was no question of you not going to Mass' applied to himself as much to his children: 'It was just ... you got up, that's what you did on a Sunday morning', he explained. William Moss (46) also described the central role of religion in his home:

> It [religion] was a big part of my life for as long as I can remember, it was big for my family especially my mother, she encouraged me to be an altar boy when I was eight I think, we had our Sunday clothes for Mass and freshly polished shoes and I remember my mother always debuted a new coat or dress on a Sunday. So I guess I was around church a lot, I was an altar boy for years.

In my own childhood home it was my mother who assumed the role of ensuring her three children were dispatched to Mass every Sunday morning. When I was a child, preparations for this would have started the night before. Shoes were polished, baths were had and new coats were debuted. Getting children out to Mass early on Sunday morning was quite an achievement, given that, as a result of living in a rural parish, the only Mass was held at 9.30 in the morning. When my oldest brother learned to drive this facilitated attendance at later Masses in a nearby town, but by then there was a greater resistance to attending Masses at any hour. My older brother, never an early riser in his childhood, either by accident or design even missed these later Masses. This was the minimum religious requirement in our family home. Both my parents were active in their local church throughout these years, my mother being a Eucharistic minister and my father being a church gate collector. The exception to this minimum requirement was attendance at the annual Holy Cross Novena. Again, this was a remarkable achievement as the Novena – with long sermons, choirs with compulsory singing and thousands of people in attendance – often lasted three hours. Thirty years later this novena remains just as popular.

SEX EDUCATION IN THE FAMILY

A similar pattern emerged with regard to sex education. Mothers wrote, unhappy that they had to be both mothers and fathers to children when instructing them about sexuality, a task many women felt they were ill-equipped or unwilling to undertake. A letter of 24 November 1963 asked 'why do so many husbands look on it as the mother's job to give the boys and girls of the family sex education?', to which Macnamara replied, quoting Pope Pius XII, that it was a father's duty to 'delicately reveal the truth' of sex to their sons. Others believed that it was the responsibility of primary schools to instruct in such matters.[67] A widow wrote, in a letter of 17 January 1965, that she had struggled to teach her son the facts of life, believing that it was the duty of the father to do so. Macnamara suggested asking a priest or layman she trusted to speak to her son on her behalf. In a letter of 2 March 1969 fathers were also blamed for not giving 'any sex education to their sons during the adolescent years'. The letter continued:

> Why do they run away from what is clearly their duty? Our boys were in their twenties when, on my insistence, their father told them a bit in an awkward round about way ... I'd like you to write a few words of advice to fathers. It's no use advising men to get books. They wouldn't admit to needing books to help them in rearing their children.

Angela Macnamara responds:

> I cannot help wondering why we do not give much greater care and attention to the training of parents for their most responsible duties. The thoughtful upbringing of children is not something that comes naturally to parents. We have certain basic instincts towards our children but we have a great deal to learn as well ... why is it so widely accepted that parents have nothing to learn? As you say, fathers are often too proud or too lazy to read anything about their responsibility as husbands and fathers. Many mothers say they have not time to delve into the wealth of most excellent literature available on child-rearing. They argue we 'don't need it' ... We are their primary and most important educators. We must admit to the necessity to study and learn so that we can face our responsibilities as parents fairly and squarely.

In recognizing that parenthood was not merely an intuitive practice but a skill to be learned through the consultation of experts Angela

Macnamara's advice confirmed the emergence of child rearing as a science identified by, among others, Beck and Beck-Gernsheim. A letter of 21 September 1980 also asks why fathers are so reluctant to talk to their boys about the 'facts of life and about the physical feelings that go with growing up', to which Macnamara responds that men never spoke openly about these issues with anyone before but that is not an excuse for the mother to take over the responsibility.

Other potential fathers were more honest about their desire – or lack of it – to have children in the first place. In a letter of 6 May 1979 a woman describes how she has been married for three years and is on the pill but is anxious to have a child, although her husband 'doesn't seem to be interested and puts it off from one month to the next'. In her reply, Macnamara blames a contraceptive culture that has enabled husbands to delay having children. She states that 'men very often do not feel the same longing for a child as a woman feels. Fatherly instincts are very often not aroused until the child is actually born while the instinct to conceive and give birth is very primitive and strong in most women. In our affluent success oriented society men are often unaware that they are being driven to achieve and possess almost to the exclusion of truly human considerations.' Angela Macnamara's reliance on an essentialist understanding of parenthood may have reflected a widely accepted belief about men at the time, but disguised a real love and wonder for fatherhood expressed through the life history interviews. It also disguised a deep public versus private understanding of the roles of men and women within the home, certainly reflecting the historical ethos of the Irish Press Group of newspapers.

Humphreys's case study of John and Joan Dunn's family revealed that while they were anxious to have children, unrestricted by family planning, they both entered marriage in remarkable ignorance, having received no sex education from their own parents.[68] They gathered pieces of information mainly through contemporaries at work, and, when Joan was pregnant, from female relatives and friends. As parents they remained crippled by embarrassment when speaking of sexuality and had refused to give their children any instruction, allowing them 'to find out for themselves just as our parents did'.[69]

The life histories revealed that the men often had difficulties in speaking emotionally with their children about sex and relationships – difficulties which they had inherited from their parents. James Kelly (70) explained how he opted out of discussing the facts of life with his sons, leaving the task to their mother, whom he described as a 'fantastic

woman' who was their children's educator in sexuality and their disciplinarian. He expressed regret that this lack of an emotional bond continued throughout their adult lives, although he struggled to repair it.
He explained:

> I have a son in the States ... and we talk on the phone but our
> conversations are purely practical, my wife usually talks about
> their children and all that. It's interesting, I get to talk about the
> practical things, work, how he's managing. Recently he had diffi-
> culty in his marriage [recording unclear] and we had a very good
> heart to heart and that was the first time we spoke about emotional
> issues.

David Moloney (63) recalled that the first time his father spoke to him
about sex was when he told him he had just become engaged. His
father said 'I hope you know what you are doing and be careful and
whatever.' He does recall being in school and a Christian Brother
taking him aside to explain 'this is what a boy and this is what a girl,
and this is what happens or whatever'. He similarly describes how his
children's questions about sex were dealt with by his wife, purely
because she was spending more time with them during the day while
he was at work, and how this didn't reflect his unwillingness to have
those conversations.

Farson states that children have a right to information about sex.[70]
He believes that this was hampered in school by a pressure to place this
knowledge within a context of maturity, marriage, moderation and
heterosexuality, and that in the home it was hampered by the sexual
ignorance of adults which was widespread in the United States, claiming that 'having performed sex acts hardly provides the necessary
information to teach others'.[71] This was part of a wider cultural strategy,
Farson argues, that denied children sexual knowledge and was
epitomized most starkly in the manufacture of children's dolls with no
genitalia, and in the parental obsession with preventing their child
masturbating. The lesson that children learned was that 'adults do not
want them to look at, touch or think about genitalia or their
functions'.[72] John Holt agrees that even among liberal parents there is
a belief that they need to keep their children 'innocent' and 'pure'.[73]
Holt claims that it was easier for parents to ignore their children's
sexual impulses if they denied the existence of such feelings altogether.
'Ignorance is not a blessing', Holt writes.[74]

Shulamith Firestone also argues that the myth of childhood that stresses innocence and purity is as powerful as the myth of femininity is in subjugating women.[75] Both women and children are designated as asexual and thus 'purer' than men, contributing to a second-class citizenship thinly disguised as respect. Adults deny the sexuality of children, forcing them to lead a 'sexless – or secretive – life not even admitting any sexual needs'.[76] Firestone believes that both women and children were set apart, often in impractical clothing, and given tasks of housework and homework, while both were seen as mentally less proficient than men. Like Holt and Farson, Firestone believes that concepts of cuteness and adoration mask the true and natural behaviour of women and children, making them feel shy and ill at ease in adult or male company. These concepts make it more difficult to escape the underlying oppression. Children, Firestone argues, must become 'living embodiments of happiness'.[77] Sulky children are not liked. Childhood is constructed as the happy, golden age of the life cycle, which has more to do with fulfilling an adult need for at least one carefree period of life before the drudgery of adulthood overwhelmed them. Firestone also points to the growing belief that children are now too pampered and too indulged, a development present in the Macnamara column to which I return later.[78]

The myth of childhood that emphasized the innocence and purity of children and the interventionist measures to maintain it had its roots in the mid-nineteenth century. Danielle Egan and Gail Hawkes claim that contributions by American health reformer John Harvey Kellogg stressed that although children were born pure they were highly susceptible to corrupting influences.[79] Other theorists such as Albert Moll argued that sexuality was an active part of a child's life from birth onwards. Michel Foucault identified four strategies which emerged since the eighteenth century and which 'formed specific mechanisms of knowledge and power centering on sex', one of which was the pedagogization of children's sex.[80] This strategy understood that all children were likely to indulge in sexual activity and that this behaviour posed specific dangers to individuals and wider society. Foucault argued that parents, teachers and doctors would intervene to manage and direct this sexual potential, particularly against masturbation.

Macnamara received many letters from young men who were distressed by their practice of masturbation. Masturbation had been a long-standing concern to educationalists and religious leaders who sought to eliminate the practice by instilling fears of both eternal damnation and physical deformity.[81] Jeffrey Weeks suggests that British nineteenth-century educators had long believed that masturbation was the gateway to homosexuality and a range of other sexual vices and condemned it relentlessly.[82] This belief was grounded in the denial of childhood sexuality, seeing masturbation as a bridge to further sexual exploration. Jonathan Gathorne-Hardy argues that there was no doubt that medical advances, better housing and an awareness of nutrition did lower the age of puberty in the twentieth century, increasing the risk of adolescent sexuality.[83] Headmasters in Britain's public schools became agents of surveillance, seeking out and extracting confessions from those who had sexually transgressed. Sermons were devoted to masturbation and prayers said for its suppression within the school walls. Trouser pockets were sewn up and lavatory doors removed. With school libraries censored and stewards patrolling dormitories at night the repression seemed to generate the adolescent sexual behaviour that such measures were designed to eradicate.[84] Michel Foucault suggested that this pursuit of adolescent masturbation was in itself designed to fail, serving only to bolster the power of those who initiated it through increased means of surveillance.[85]

The level of misinformation and ignorance about masturbation revealed in Macnamara's column is astonishing, as was the needless anxiety which young men endured. Numerous letters to the column reflected this concern. The majority of letter writers were worried that they had contracted venereal disease through masturbation. Central to these letters is the hope that Macnamara will confirm their 'normality' to them. 'I think I may have venereal disease or some other illness', wrote the author of a letter published on 7 June 1970. 'I don't think I'm physically the same as others. I do actions alone which have caused the symptoms I have described.' Macnamara responded that 'Venereal disease is spread almost exclusively through intimate contact with others during sexual relations. The habit of self-abuse is unlikely to cause physically abnormality.' Macnamara reassured readers that there was no connection between venereal disease and masturbation, but her use of the word 'unlikely' did little to dispel the belief that masturbation could be physically harmful. Other letter writers believed that masturbation caused syphilis, nervous tension and homosexuality and had destroyed their chances of gaining entry to heaven.[86] 'Yours is the habit of self-abuse', she told one man on 10 December 1972. 'This is a normal impulse but must be controlled and disciplined. So the way to overcome self-indulgence is to set our minds to doing good for others.' In a letter of 27 January 1974 a man challenges Angela Macnamara's previous reply on masturbation. This is significant. Given the wider range of publications available to people, Macnamara now had to defend her – and her religion's – version of their 'truth' of sexuality. The man writes: 'I enclose a cutting from an English magazine, it is about masturbation. I compared it to your article on the subject and found it confusing that one problem page condemns it and another one says it is an essential part of sexual development.' Angela Macnamara replies: 'The truth is that masturbation is a natural inclination and like other natural inclinations it must be controlled and disciplined. I have been assured by two priests at least that my original statement on the matter is correct.'

The issue of childhood sexuality is more a feature of the life histories of the gay men I interviewed, which I discuss in the next chapter.[87] Six out of the eight men I interviewed had some sexual encounter with other boys their age. What is significant about the descriptions of these encounters is that they are not viewed as transgressions. With the denial of childhood sexuality and the subsequent absence of any condemnation, these experiences are interpreted as a normal childhood occurrence. My own close childhood friendship was cast as problematic by my parents long before I had understood the nature of the objection. For the interviewees too, their childhood sexual activities remained free from guilt and sexual categorization. It was later in secondary school that they learned the penalties associated with their previously carefree childhood behaviour. William Moss (46) described such an encounter: 'I suppose the most important sexual encounter I can remember was with my cousin Brian, we were eleven or twelve on a beach at the time. It was just mutual masturbation and messing around. It happened and I had no language to contextual it all, it was strange, exciting, pleasant and something I wanted to repeat.'

Even in the Christian Brothers' secondary school that William Moss (46) attended there was a silence around masturbation except during the twice-yearly retreats with the Holy Ghost fathers who spoke of 'the evils of masturbation'. Kieran Slattery remained unsure why the students involved in mutual masturbation and oral sex in his intermediate year were never disciplined even though their behaviour was known to the school authorities. He explained that 'Everybody knew about it, it was bizarre ... the Brothers knew but nobody was expelled from school, maybe because nobody was caught. I've always expected that it was because two of them were very bright academically and sporting. Mind you how could they have expelled these lads without talking about the sexual acts they were engaged in? Emer O'Kelly's inclusion of Fergus's story in her book, *The Permissive Society in Ireland?*, also conveys the impact of a Catholic education on the lives of young men. Fergus explains:[88]

> I was perfectly conscious of being homosexual by the time I was twelve. But I suppose the one thing I do resent is that around that age I got one of those old hell fire sermons about eternal damnation and the unnatural abomination of it all. It had me shaking in my shoes for the rest of my teens. Which means that in terms of trying to develop relationships, my teens were a total write off. I regret that.

Of course, not all countries left their children in such sexual ignorance or fear. In Sweden, sexual education was recommended for secondary school pupils in 1921, becoming compulsory in 1956 and low rates of teen pregnancy, abortion and sexual transmitted disease are attributed to this .[89]

It may appear surprising that Macnamara was in agreement with these liberal leaders of the children's rights movement in the United States, but she believed that children should be taught the proper names of the sexual organs and be given the facts of life. It was a position that led to accusations by some letter writers that she was destroying the innocence of children. These responses illustrate divergent views on sex education in Ireland at the time. Many parents, teachers and the clergy believed that ignorance of sex was a successful strategy that would instil fear in young people and so would prevent sexual experimentation.

Angela Macnamara warned parents in her pamphlet *When to Give Sex Instruction* in 1968 that if we 'neglect to explain procreation to our children, we may be fully sure that someone outside will be willing and ready to do so'.[90] She continued: 'if we insist on burying our heads in the sand and talking about "the wrongs of contaminating innocent minds" we are risking that our children view life through the distorted window presented readily to them outside their homes'. Macnamara was right. She knew there were alternative explanations, that challenged the Catholic Church's view of sexuality, available to children through the wider media and believed that such education should be placed within a moral context at the earliest opportunity. She was damning of parents who refused to do this, writing that it is 'essential that parents get rid of their selfish inhibitions and work together in the interest of the child'.[91] In hindsight we know that better sex education would have made children less vulnerable to the child sexual abuse that thousands suffered at the hands of their family relatives in their homes and by priests and religious orders. Not one letter to the column I examined referred to sexual abuse. 'Child sex abuse did not enter the picture', Macnamara explains. 'It wasn't written about in those days so I did not have to deal with it.' Indeed, it would have been difficult to write about an experience which children would have struggled to find words to communicate. Macnamara had experienced this danger first-hand. As a 10-year-old, she and her family went to visit a married couple who were friends of her parents in a seaside hotel. When the husband asked Angela to come and see the couple's bedroom, she agreed; however, she describes how while they were alone in the room together his behaviour changed. 'He was exposing himself and showing me what happens to men when aroused', Macnamara explained. She continued: 'I was horrified. I felt breathless and sat in terror. I had no idea what was happening. He didn't touch me, but asked me a couple of questions ... Back home I felt that I couldn't tell anyone. I didn't have any words for the situation.'[92] Thousands of other children did not have such a lucky escape. The Ryan Report commissioned by the Irish government and published in 2009 revealed the shocking catalogue of child abuse in sixty residential homes for children run by Catholic religious orders since 1936. The first residential home closed was in 1969. The Murphy Report examined allegations of child sex abuse in the Dublin Archdiocese from 1975 to 2004, revealing how church authorities had actively concealed their knowledge of their priests' prior sexual abuse.[93]

For Angela Macnamara to encourage that children should have sex education was certainly progressive in the Ireland of 1963. She and other more unlikely allies believed that giving children information about sex was more likely to encourage responsible and appropriate sexual behaviour. The context remained traditional, however. Macnamara wrote that while giving sex education, parents should 'point out that boys usually have bigger bones, stronger muscles and are braver than girls as God intends men to protect and look after women ... Parents must instil in their children the Christian attitudes of manliness and womanliness if, as teenagers, they are to have a noble understanding and unselfish approach to one another.'[94] Her position on subjects such as sex education and corporal punishment shows that Angela Macnamara's actual views were a nuanced mix of modern and traditional characteristics, in contrast to her more strictly conservative caricature.

CORPORAL PUNISHMENT IN THE HOME

Young people were often beaten by their parents when their authority was defied or when children broke established rules of behaviour. A letter of 30 January 1966 from a 15-year-old girl told how she was 'strapped when I was found smoking for the second time'; she believed such punishment to be 'brutal and degrading' for a girl of her age. In reply Macnamara said that she did not 'agree with corporal punishment for girls' but could sympathize with the girl's parents, who feared that their daughter's experimentation would develop beyond smoking. Other times it was children who wrote after witnessing their mother being assaulted by their father.[95] A parent wondered in a letter of 24 November 1963 whether they should slap their son for using 'vulgar phrases' among his friends, to which Macnamara replied that the boy may not know what those phrases mean but should be punished for disobedience if he was to continue to use them after being instructed not to. The use of physical force in the home was not confined to the very young. A 19-year-old woman wrote to Macnamara in a letter of 23 May 1965 to seek advice on how to deal with her father, who beat her:

Q. I am a 19 year old girl in a good job that I like. My trouble is that my father is very strict and beats me for the smallest thing. I don't mind the beatings so much, but one evening a girl I know called unexpectedly and saw me being beaten. I'm sure she told others where I work as remarks have been passed since. Do you consider this punishment too severe? Should I leave home? Do other girls get this type of punishment? I need your help and advice.

A. I seem to have received quite a number of letters like this in recent weeks. I consider it undignified and unnecessarily severe to punish a teenage girl in this way. Most young people striving towards independence give their parents anxious and aggravating moments. They need discipline and self control but these should be exercised with love and understanding. Most of the girls who are being beaten like this are asking me would it be right for them to leave home. Such ignominious punishment neither helps a girl to respect herself or her parents

> ... I think teenagers who are being punished this way should on a calm happy moment endeavour to discuss it with their parents. Tell them that you will do your best to keep the rules if they will agree to punish you by some deprivation.

Boys also experienced violence in the home. In a letter of 5 August 1973 a mother describes how her eldest son, who has now left school to work with his father, is subject to beatings from him if he does not observe a midnight curfew. She describes her husband as believing that 'boys only respect one thing and that is punishment and that talking to them or reasoning with them, which I suggest, is a waste of time'. She asks Macnamara how 'can I convince my husband that the boys are too old for this form of punishment. Sticks and belts went out with our generation.' Angela Macnamara agrees that this is a completely disproportionate and inappropriate form of discipline and welcomes that the son in question refuses to obey the curfew, given that most dances and pictures are not over by then. She advises that 'boys need to discuss authority problems with their father. In life they will find that it is with men that they have to solve most authority problems and the problems are not solved in life by beatings ... often beatings are only a way out of honest discussion and forming of true and worthwhile values'.

Angela Macnamara's views on corporal punishment were not shared by all her readers. In a letter of 31 July 1966 a father wrote that he thought Macnamara's views 'were far too lenient' and he had 'always administered the cane to my children for their more serious misdemeanours up to the age of 17. I have not found them hostile or resentful until they started reading your column. Now my 15 year old daughter defies me and makes out it is old fashioned to use the rod even though she deserves it.' Macnamara in her reply focuses on the root of his daughter's defiance of authority and wonders whether an earlier intervention in childhood would have prevented the use of corporal punishment as a teenager. Crucially, Macnamara states that she is 'not saying that you are wrong or right' to this parent, believing that ultimately he must decide on how best to raise and discipline his children.

Young children were also subject to discipline. In a letter of 23 March 1975 a woman wrote believing her husband to be 'disciplining the children too much in my opinion ... when we are at Mass whoever is beside him gets rapped on the shoulder or arm for turning around or doing the ordinary little childish movements ... he feels that children have to be very strongly disciplined nowadays or else they'll go wrong'.

Humphreys saw discipline exercised by the father as more a feature of rural Ireland, wheras in urban families the mother occupied a role that offered both warmth and affection but also authority and discipline in the home.[96] Unlike in rural areas, urban fathers no longer exercised a regular supervision and discipline over their children and were more likely to have a more relaxed attitude towards them. Humphreys identified a greater equality among urban married couples which contributed to a changed relationship with their children, based on less fear and domination and an earlier emancipation from parental control.[97] His case study of the urban Dunn family revealed a changed attitude towards the disciplining of their children with a decline in corporal punishment; a rod was kept in the house but seldom if ever used.[98] The family explained how the rod would usually be used as firewood and that reasoning had largely replaced physical discipline in the house. They spoke of a generational shift in the punishment of children; it was the father in their parents' generation who would have been the almost exclusive disciplinarian. Now, as Joan Dunn explained, it was almost impossible to get her husband to discipline the children, a role that she was expected to fulfil, and she believed this to be a common feature of family life.

Patrick McGrath (75) grew up with his family in rural Co. Cork. He attributes the clear delineation of tasks between his parents as influencing his own approach to marriage. With regard to discipline he described how his father 'would come and would lay down the law in the old fashioned corporal punishment way that it was done, he was the one who would have the final say and the final power in the thing as far as I was concerned as well. So there is no doubt that I grew up, and I can only talk for myself rather than talking for other members of the family, I grew up with a very clear understanding of the role thing in the family.' Eddie Cullen (56) had a similarly strict father, which was a source of conflict at the time although his attitude towards his father mellowed throughout the years with a belief that 'he would have provided the resources for me to get a good education and I think that was his primary motive'. Eddie describes his relationship with his father as 'difficult, I think we just clashed. My father was a very strict man and he saw things in black and white and he would have been in the whole mould of corporal punishment and I was quite a wild young fellow, to be honest.'

David Moloney (63) described how, as a couple, he and his wife largely rejected any form of corporal punishment with their children. 'Mary had a philosophy', David explained. She said that they should 'treat our children as people, they are small people so you treat them with dignity and respect ... we might have smacked them once or twice but there was never ... smacking as such wasn't on our agenda, it was more negotiating'. Declan Staunton (62) also described his approach to discipline with his children:

> I wouldn't have said I was restrictive of their freedom although I would have been keen that they go to Mass, that they were mannerly, that when they were younger that they obey their parents, that they weren't bold. But I wouldn't have described myself as strict, maybe others would. Not strict as in Victorian strict, I certainly wouldn't have been like that ... I would have tried to instil in them a certain amount of discipline and work ethic ... I wouldn't have been dead casual but I wouldn't have seen it as being inhibiting.

Children were often not safe from beatings in school, either, and such behaviour continued after the close of the Macnamara column in 1980. In my final two years in a Catholic primary school, the principal, ominously referred to as 'the Master', regularly beat children in our class. This was despite corporal punishment having being made illegal in Irish schools in 1982. The regulation issued by the Minister of Education John Boland stated that teachers who were found to be in breach of it would be 'guilty of conduct unbefitting a teacher and will be subject to severe disciplinary action'.[99] This wasn't the case in Co. Tipperary.

My Achilles heel would prove to be a mediocre ability in maths which exposed me to being pushed, thumped, slapped and often dragged out of my chair. While the principal's behaviour was well known among parents, including my own, and the wider community a deafening silence surrounded it. This was all the more unusual because any form of physical discipline was almost unknown in our family home. Only one mother in our school was indignant at the corporal punishment to which her daughter was subjected. She would arrive before school, often without taking the time to put her shoes on, standing in the school foyer in pink fluffy mules with four-inch heels as she argued with 'the Master' about her daughter's treatment. It worked. My principal would regularly joke that he couldn't lay a hand on the girl for fear that 'your mother would have me in the High Court'. His other students, including myself, didn't find it quite so funny, given that we possessed no such immunity. Interestingly, such defiance of the school principal by this mother was not greeted with any great community support. In fact, such public confrontation was deemed by many to border on the 'common'. The principal eventually recognized that he did not possess a suitable temperament to be an educator and resigned, leaving to establish a business venture.

The reluctance to challenge the authority of the school principal in a rural community has been previously identified by J.C. Messenger in his study in the west of Ireland between the years 1959 and 1966. Here parents would have little or no contact with the headmaster regarding their children's education.[100] Nor did they contest the severe discipline to which their children were subjected by the principal and two other teachers in the school.[101] This violence was actually used by parents as a threat to ensure the children's compliance and obedience in the home. The use of violence in a Catholic school or home should come as no surprise to those familiar with the Bible. Richard Farson reminds readers that passages from Proverbs (22:15) and Deuteronomy (21:18) encourage the use of corporal punishment on a wayward son, even to the point of death.[102] The Book of Proverbs (23:13, 14) states: 'withhold not correction from the child, for if thou beatest him with the rod he shall not die. Thou shalt beat him with a rod and deliver his soul from hell.'

Sometimes it wasn't violence in school but other forms of humiliating behaviour that children wrote to Macnamara about. In a letter of 13 April 1980 a girl at secondary school complained that a teacher 'humiliated me in front of the whole class by calling me names'. Getting to and from school was also upsetting for some children. In a letter of 27 January 1974 a 14-year-old girl described how she and other girls were being bullied by boys on the school bus. The authoritarianism of the school system caused one 15-year-old boy to question, in a letter of 22 September 1974, how useful the whole education system was and whether 'instead of having all those teachers shouting at us, they should be teaching us how to live more fulfilled lives'.

Firestone argues that an overlapping ideology of school and childhood isolated children from adults and other children who were not the same age, and designated that they should be treated in a 'special' way, often requiring discipline.[103] All the naturalness of children's play is restrained in a desire for supervised play that best helps to socialize or repress children. Children spend most of their time in this coercive, heavily structured environment or doing homework for it outside school hours. Free time is often spent being forced to attend religious services with their parents or smiling inanely at distant relatives.[104]

Stephen Lassonde reflects on this transition in how authority was presented to children and how they perceived it in the United States in the twentieth century.[105] He locates this transition in the context of a number of cultural shifts which had occurred in America after the Second World War, particularly the Civil Rights movement, the women's movement and protests against the Vietnam War. He argues that organizations that exercised influence over how children thought, specifically schooling and religion, underwent profound change during this era. Political conservatives blamed a rise in 'permissive parenting' for contributing to the perceived anti-patriotic student demonstrations that marked American involvement in Vietnam. Lassonde points to arguments by Richard Brodhead to suggest that these different parenting norms had their origins long before the cultural politics of the 1960s.[106] Brodhead argued that in the mid-nineteenth century, middle-class mothers had began to instil a means by which children would discipline their inner selves, in contrast to the external forms of physical punishment to which they were subjected in schools and the home.

Lassonde suggests that the Catholic Church in the United States also revised its teachings in the 1960s with respect to the levels of authority, obedience and autonomy which children were expected to observe.[107] Prior to the 1960s there had been a divergence between Catholic and Protestant Churches in regard to child obedience, with the latter valuing a greater autonomy in children. The Catholic Church, by contrast, had continued to stress obedience to both Church and family authority. Indeed, Lassonde explains that the Catholic Church regarded the family as a 'domestic church' based on authority – where a wife should obey her husband and children should obey their parents. With the advent of the 1960s the divergence between the Churches with regard to child obedience narrowed, with a slow and growing trend toward autonomy being identified in the Catholic Church.

GROWING WEALTH AND LEVELS OF EXPECTATIONS

There was a similar concern in Ireland that there had been a decline in respect for authority in homes, schools and everyday life. The 1960s brought increased wealth into Irish households. Parents who had experienced the unemployment, poverty and associated frugality of the previous decade now had increased disposable income, much of which was spent on their children. The result was a growing perception, conveyed in the column, that children and adolescents were overly indulged, spoiled and inactive and had little respect for their parents, teachers or other elders. Parents who as children themselves contributed economically to their households now seemed to have mixed feelings about what Viviana Zelizer describes as the arrival of the 'economically useless child'. Children's work was now educational or instructional, rather than instrumental in teaching them 'the proper values and attitudes towards work and spending'.[108] This perception of the inactive pampered child was offset, for most, by a gradual but corresponding rise in the 'emotionally priceless child'. Zelizer argues that during the twentieth century both the 'surrender' cash value of children at death and their 'exchange' value through adoption dramatically increased while their economic value disappeared.[109]

Letters to the Angela Macnamara column suggest that readers remained unconvinced. A 40-year-old man wrote in a letter of 9 August 1964 that he was 'shocked at the way young boys are being reared. Pampered and petted by their mothers, taught no self control or self-discipline.' Angela Macnamara replied that she did 'think that the rearing of boys is left too much to mothers. They need their father's firm hand and a man's mentality to turn them into the right kind of men.' In another reply of 2 February 1969 Macnamara comments on the state of Irish childhood and the confused messages which parents give their children:

> Many children nowadays are hopelessly spoilt; they do not respect authority, they are not taught to do without, self-sacrifice is never mentioned at home. They are quietened by promises of sweets one moment and with threats of the wooden spoon the next moment. They are alternatively bribed, nagged, shown off or ignored. Money spells success to them because they see their parents' attitude to money. The rules made in many a household are broken more often than they are kept. Insecurity surrounds them even though their material needs are over supplied. Spiritually they are left quite infantile and under-developed.

Other letter writers agreed with Angela Macnamara's assessment that children were spoiled. A letter of 25 January 1970 from a shopkeeper complains that 'The parents of today are ruining the kids. I see it everyday. The youngsters whine and nag and get what they want. The mothers have no time for training them; one minute they are hitting them, then when the child roars and kicks and slaps the mother, he is given sweets to quieten him.' It was the effect of fatty foods on adolescents that also created concern in a letter of 10 September 1967, with a mother describing how her 15-year-old daughter eats far too much, encouraged by her husband.

This view of children as being overly indulged and showing little respect for their elders had been a concern since the turn of the nineteenth century in both Britain and the United States, reaching fever pitch during the 1950s and 1960s. Joanna Bourke's study of working-class communities in Britain quotes the words of the American Howard Association in 1898: 'the tendencies of modern life incline more and more to ignore or disparage social distinctions which formerly did much to encourage respect for others and habits of obedience and discipline ... the manners of children are deteriorating ... the child of today is coarser, more vulgar, less refined than his parents were'.[110] This refusal to accept social distinctions would continue throughout the next century and contribute to an informalization process that would see the gaps between social groupings narrow, including parents and their children. In Michael Schofield's study in 1965 he reported that 'there are clear signs of alienation between the young people of today and the adult generations'.[111]

A letter of 10 January 1971 from the wealthy parents of an only child of 15, who are able to 'give her anything she wants in the way of modern clothes and shoes and such things', expresses worry about how this might spoil her in the future. Angela Macnamara agrees that irrespective of wealth all parents should exercise 'moderation and charity' with their children, encouraging them to give to those who are less well off. Other less well-off parents also wrote of pressure to keep up with their neighbours. A letter of 1 August 1971 from a parent explained that 'lots of girls in class with our daughter (aged 16) go on holiday on the Continent for summer holidays. We feel we cannot afford such a family holiday for one member of the family when we have a family of five children to do our best to give a good summer to. But we are told that it's part of their education nowadays.' Macnamara replies: 'I think that there is much travelling done for no better reason than to have it to boast about! Some people feel ashamed to say they spent holidays at home and have never been abroad ... don't go into debt or feel that you are not doing your best for her.' Increased incomes had led to the expansion of foreign travel, with package holidays to Europe, introduced in 1960, resulting in the numbers of Irish people holidaying abroad rising to 110,000 by the early 1970s. Domestic tourism had also expanded, as working-class families now holidayed in seaside resorts that were once the preserve of the middle classes.[112]

Patrick Baggot also recognized that parents, particularly fathers, were struggling to compete for financial reward and social prestige in a more affluent society, leaving men alienated from their children:[113]

> In Ireland and elsewhere with economic development there are many men who after a struggle have become big socially, financially and professionally, who are well placed in knowing the right people but who are also deeply aware of an inner emptiness and are ill at ease about it and always at pains to cover it up in company. Their feelings have never been given a chance to develop and though perhaps able to number acquaintances by the score they have never succeeded in establishing warm personal relationships with anyone, wife and children included.

Another letter of 31 May 1970 refers to an article in the newspaper that described how children didn't see their fathers because they had 'to work overtime to keep up with the demands at work and the material demands at home'. Historically it was industrialization that separated paid labour from the home, thus separating fathers from their children. Peter Stearns argued that there was a simultaneous development of an expanding literature which endorsed women as children's exclusive carers.[114] These processes of industrialization came later in Ireland. The stage was set for newer work practices and longer hours as families worked and struggled to pay mortgage repayments at exorbitant interest rates during the 1960s.

The rise in consumer durables, and particularly the trend for having a number of television sets throughout the house, altered the experience of child rearing for parents, a development not welcomed by all readers. A letter of 31 May 1970 was from a grandmother upset at her daughter's use of the television as a babysitter:

> Q. My daughter has four young children under nine years of age. They seem to spend all their free time from early afternoon sitting in front of the television. She uses the TV as a babysitter, and, indeed, as a parent for them. No matter what programme is on she leaves it on and goes off doing other things ... I'm heart broken seeing my own grandchildren so neglected. The house and clothes and so on get all the attention.

Another woman in a letter of 7 May 1972 described how her husband's only interest on getting home from work was to 'settle down to TV until the TV stations close' – behaviour which she said would drive her into the arms of another man.

Increased wealth and opportunity also altered young people's perception of work, fulfilment and marriage. A letter of 19 August 1979 from parents concerned that their daughter has unrealistic expectation of work revealed how many young people were unwilling to work purely for financial reward:

> [She] has not done well in her Leaving Certificate ... She has her mind set on a particular kind of work and is very choosy. She says she won't take up anything if she can't get a job that gives her 'job satisfaction'. Why are we feeding young people today with all this 'job satisfaction' business? Long ago we worked because we had to earn money to live. Nowadays they feel they have to enjoy everything.

Angela Macnamara recognizes that there is a 'great deal of talk about "job satisfaction" at the present time' but urged the parents to tell their daughter that it was the value she placed on the work that in fact made it worthwhile. She also advised that the parents should stop supporting her at home and encourage her to take a job, even if it was not her ideal. Ironically, Emer O'Kelly suggests that it was this older generation that had taught their children to expect and demand more in their work and home lives.[115] This generation had responded to deprivation with a stoicism that produced no tangible improvement in their lives, an attitude they would be reluctant to see their children take. The children of this post-war era rose to the challenge of heightened expectations, O'Kelly argues; they 'questioned the working economic norm adhered to by their parents, which was one of gratitude for a barely living wage'.[116] The younger generation had placed a concept of self to the fore of their identities, setting them on a path of self-discovery which often questioned formal religion.

The life histories also revealed tension between parents' expectations and their children's desire to break free of the more limited opportunities that often governed their parents' lives. In many cases these men were the first generation of their families to attend third-level education. Some parents were more encouraging than others about this mobility. Tony Fitzgerald (62) described the tension in his relationship with his father when he refused to leave school after his inter cert to become a barber, which was the tradition in his family:

> He didn't impact on my life because he went out in the morning and worked 'til 7 in the evening you know so ... he wasn't ... as I grew into a teenager he wanted me to become a barber as well because my two older brothers were. But I didn't want to. I

wanted to go on in school, he was happy for me to go on and do my inter cert but wasn't happy for me to do my leaving cert so I had a few run-ins with him about that and I had another sister in America and herself and her husband paid for my school fees to do fifth and sixth year in school ... I understand that he was doing what he believed to be right because his father was a barber and all his brothers were barbers and that was the change in recognising the need for education and all that.

Young women especially had higher expectations of marriage than their parents. In a letter of 15 April 1973 a 16-year-old girl described how she was considering giving up the idea of marriage completely as she would 'hate the idea of endless nappy washing, cleaning, cooking and all those household things unless I had a really happy family life and a husband who continued to love me'. Macnamara responds:

> living in a materialistic pleasure seeking society people tend to look on hard work and suffering as evils to be avoided at all costs ... hard work and suffering are only as unbearable as we allow them be for ourselves and for each other ... when we are not-seeking our own happiness but concentrating on making others feel good then the happiness comes to us. The pessimism such as it is that some young people feel about marriage is, I think, the fruit of an affluent society where too many individuals want to be free to 'do their own thing'. And not hampered by having to suit other people.

Letters from Frankie Byrne's radio show also revealed higher expectations among those choosing to marry. A 35-year-old professional man looking to 'marry and settle down with a nice sensible settled wife' received a sharp rebuke from Byrne, who replied:[117]

> This may come as a shock but women are actually human beings and very few of us, if any, would be particularly pleased to find ourselves scrutinised like items in a Christmas catalogue in your search for the most trouble-free model of the current trend in nice settled wives ... A professional housekeeper might not object – if the salary and the home comforts were acceptable – but I suspect that the man who says he's looking for a nice, settled, sensible wife means that he's really searching for an unpaid housekeeper with a civil tongue in her head. I'm afraid women are more demanding and difficult to please nowadays than they used to be.

CONCLUSION

This chapter has explored the changing relationships between parents and their children. A process of informalization was identified through the pages of the problem page, where children challenged corporal punishment and fought for greater freedom to socialize and date outside the home. Mothers also sought change. Letters revealed that they felt they carried a disproportionate burden of child-rearing practices, especially in the areas of sex education and religious education. The letters showed that where parents did not give such education, children were now open to more information from various media, including Angela Macnamara's column, with which to challenge their parents.

The life history interviews revealed a more complex distribution of power in the home than was reflected in the column's letters. Some of the interviewees rejected corporal punishment because it had been used in their own homes when they were children. Others saw their father's power as being largely symbolic, while the real power lay with their mothers. In the upbringing of their own children, the interviews show a high degree of involvement with their children. This does bring the concept of the 'participant father' as a product of late modernity into dispute. Indeed, the historical evidence suggests a much greater domestic involvement from men than is widely understood. With the advent of television, the home became more a site of leisure, with fathers spending more time at home than socializing outside, as reflected in work by J.C. Messenger.[118]

Angela Macnamara, while operating within a Catholic ethos, rejected keeping children ignorant about the basic facts of sexuality and believed that when children were informed they could make better, responsible choices. She recognized that power in the family was changing, between often dictatorial fathers who were slow to relinquish power, mothers who for too long had assumed a submissive role, and children who were more vocal in demanding greater autonomy. She remained highly critical of volatile family situations where children were exposed to emotional or physical distress and encouraged mothers to threaten outside involvement through a priest, counsellor or social worker to resolve it. This advice was more interventionist compared with how Angela Macnamara advised couples on exclusively relationship problems. She encouraged parents to read an expanding expert literature of child rearing to enable them better to face the challenges of bringing up children in a society which was radically different from their own.

NOTES

1. C. Wouters, *Informalization: Manners and Emotions since 1890* (London: Sage, 2007), pp.3–4.
2. A. Giddens, *The Transformation of Intimacy: Sexuality, Love and Eroticism in Modern Societies* (Stanford, CA: Stanford University Press, 1992), pp.136–40.
3. Ibid., p.182.
4. A. Giddens, *The Third Way: The Renewal of Social Democracy* (Cambridge: Polity Press, 1998), pp.93–4.
5. Giddens, *Transformation of Intimacy*, p.92.
6. Ibid., p.191.
7. J. Brannen, K. Dodd, A. Oakley and P. Storey, *Young People, Health and Family Life* (Buckingham: Open University Press, 1994), p.181.
8. Ibid., p.182.
9. Ibid., p.184.
10. Ibid., p.187.
11. Y. Solomon, J. Warin, C. Lewis and W. Langford, 'Intimate Talk between Parents and their Teenage Children: Democratic Openness or Covert Control?', *Sociology*, 36, 4 (2002), p.970.
12. Ibid., pp.971–2.
13. Ibid., p.973.
14. Ibid., p.976.
15. Ibid., p.977.
16. U. Beck, *Risk Society: Towards a New Modernity* (London: Routledge, 1992), p.118.
17. Giddens, *Third Way*, p.92.
18. V. Zelizer, *Pricing the Priceless Child* (Princeton, NJ: Princeton University Press, 1985), p.3.
19. Ibid., p.5.
20. Ibid., p.6.
21. A.J. Humphreys, *Urbanization and the Irish Family* (London: Routledge & Kegan Paul, 1966). p.12.
22. Ibid., p.19.
23. Ibid., pp.20, 22.
24. Zelizer, *Pricing the Priceless Child*, p.209.
25. T. Garvin, *Preventing the Future: Why Was Ireland So Poor For So Long?* (Dublin: Gill & Macmillan, 2004), p.252.
26. D. Ferriter, *The Transformation of Ireland, 1900–2000* (London: Profile Books, 2004), p.597.
27. U. Beck and E. Beck-Gernsheim, *The Normal Chaos of Love* (Cambridge: Polity Press, 1995), p.129.
28. Ibid., p.133.
29. Ibid., p.137.
30. Zelizer, *Pricing the Priceless Child*, p.49.
31. H.A. Giroux, *Stealing Innocence: Youth, Corporate Power, and the Politics of Culture* (New York: St Martin's Press, 2000), pp.10–11.
32. A. Hulbert, *Raising America: Experts, Parents and a Century of Advice about Children* (New York: Alfred A. Knopf, 2003), p.21.
33. Ibid., p.35.
34. Ibid., p.241.
35. Ibid., p.250.
36. Ibid., p.258.
37. Ibid., p.260.
38. R. Farson, *Birthrights* (Harmondsworth: Penguin, 1974), p.140.
39. J. Brannen and A. Nilsen, 'From Fatherhood to Fathering: Transmission and Change among British Fathers in Four-Generational Families', *Sociology*, 40, 2 (2006), p.340.
40. Ibid, p.340.
41. Brannen and Nilson, 'From Fatherhood to Fathering', p.344.
42. P. Mansfield and J. Collard, *The Beginning of the Rest of your Life? A Portrait of Newly-Wed Marriage* (Basingstoke: Macmillan, 1988), p.71.
43. J. Bourke, *Working-Class Cultures in Britain, 1890–1960: Gender, Class and Ethnicity* (London: Routledge 1994), p.81.

44. Ibid., p.83.
45. Ibid., p.93.
46. I discuss the life history component of the study in Chapter 1.
47. B. Brandth and E. Kvande, 'Masculinity and Child Care: The Reconstruction of Fathering', *Sociological Review*, 46, 2 (1998), p.301.
48. Ibid., p.302.
49. Ibid., p.303.
50. D.F. Hannon and L. Katsiaouni, *Traditional Families? From Culturally Prescribed to Negotiated Roles in Farm Families* (Dublin: ESRI, 1997), p.115.
51. Brandth and Kvande, 'Masculinity and Child Care', p.303–4.
52. Ibid., p.307.
53. C. Castellain-Meunier, 'The Place of Fatherhood and the Parental Role: Tensions, Ambivalence and Contradictions', *Current Sociology*, 50, 2, (2002), p.190.
54. 26 April 1964.
55. Brannen et al., *Young People*, p.192.
56. H. Brody, *Inishkillane: Change and Decline in the West of Ireland* (Harmondsworth: Penguin, 1973), p.110.
57. Ibid., pp.120–1.
58. In 1966, 819 Irish men entered religious life (Diocesan clergy, clerical religious orders or Brothers). This figure fell to ninety-two men in 1996. Research and Development Commission, *Irish Priest and Religious 1970–1975*; Research and Development Commission, *Vocation Returns 1996*, cited in T. Inglis, *Moral Monopoly: The Rise and Fall of the Catholic Church in Modern Ireland* (Dublin: University College Dublin Press, 1998), p.212.
59. A. Macnamara, *Yours Sincerely* (Dublin: Veritas, 2003), p.65.
60. Brody, *Inishkillane*, p.188.
61. Inglis, *Moral Monopoly*, p.179.
62. Ibid., p.191.
63. Humphreys, *Urbanization and the Irish Family*, p.38.
64. Ibid., pp.104–7.
65. Ibid., p.105.
66. D. Rohan, *Marriage Irish Style* (Cork: Mercier Press, 1969), p.88.
67. 12 November 1967.
68. Humphreys, *Urbanization and the Irish Family*, p.119.
69. Ibid., p.120.
70. Farson, *Birthrights*, p.130.
71. Ibid., p.132.
72. Ibid., p.134.
73. J. Holt, *Escape from Childhood: The Needs and Rights of Children* (Harmondsworth: Penguin, 1974), p.206.
74. Ibid., pp.207, 89.
75. S. Firestone, *The Dialectic of Sex: The Case for Feminist Revolution* (London: Women's Press, 1979), p.87.
76. Ibid., p.96.
77. Ibid., p.91.
78. Ibid., p.91.
79. R.D. Egan and G.L. Hawkes, 'Imperiled and Perilous: Exploring the History of Childhood Sexuality', *Journal of Historical Sociology*, 21, 4 (2008), p.355.
80. M. Foucault, *The History of Sexuality, Volume 1: An Introduction* (London: Allen Lane, 1979), p.103.
81. A. Warren, 'Popular Manliness: Baden Powell, Scouting and the Development of Manly character', in J.A. Mangan and J. Walvin (eds), *Manliness and Morality: Middle Class Masculinity in Britain and America, 1800–1940* (Manchester: Manchester University Press, 1987); J. Gathorne-Hardy, *The Public School Phenomenon 597–1977* (London: Hodder & Stoughton, 1977).
82. J. Weeks, *Coming Out: Homosexual Politics in Britain from the Nineteenth Century to the Present* (London: Quartet, 1977), p.25.
83. Gathorne-Hardy, *Public School Phenomenon*, p.357.
84. Ibid., p.91.
85. Foucault, *History of Sexuality*, p.28.

86. 24 March 1974; 28 July 1974; 19 February 1978 and 24 October 1976. This attitude is a legacy from Victorian sexology, which associated masturbation with an array of physical ailments. Fears that masturbation weakened the body, enfeebled the mind and damaged the moral will of the afflicted were widespread; see Weeks, *Coming Out*, pp.24–5; and R.A. Posner, *Sex and Reason* (Cambridge, MA: Harvard University Press, 1992), pp.16–7.
87. I interviewed eight gay men as part of a life history study of men coming out in Ireland in the 1970s. This research was the basis of my PhD thesis: P. Ryan, *Strangers In Their Own Land: The Everyday Lives of Irish Gay Men and Irish Society* (unpublished doctoral thesis, University College Dublin, 2005). It was these men who alerted me to the Angela Macnamara column, which they all had read and to which they attributed feeling less isolated, knowing that there were men similar to themselves.
88. E. O'Kelly, *The Permissive Society in Ireland?* (Cork: Mercier Press, 1974), p.30.
89. T. Inglis, *Lessons in Irish Sexuality* (Dublin: University College Dublin Press, 1998), p.82.
90. A. Macnamara, *When to Give Sex Instruction* (Dublin: Redemptorist Publications, 1968), p.7.
91. Ibid., p.8.
92. Macnamara, *Yours Sincerely*, pp.20–1.
93. The full report can be read at http://www.justice.ie/en/JELR/Pages/PB09000504.
94. Macnamara, *When to Give Sex Instruction*, p.12.
95. 31 January 1971.
96. Humphreys, *Urbanization and the Irish Family*, p.34.
97. Ibid., p.37.
98. Ibid., p.122.
99. The regulation against corporal punishment was included in Department Circulars 9/82 and 5/82. Teachers' immunity from criminal prosecution was later removed in section 24 of the Offences Against the Person (Non Fatal) Act 1997.
100. J.C. Messenger, *Inis Beag: Isle of Ireland* (Prospect Heights, IL: Waveland Press, 1969), p.63.
101. R. Farson suggests a link between corporal punishment and the sexual gratification of those who implemented it on partially undressed children. See Farson, *Birthrights*, p.126.
102. Ibid., p.114.
103. Firestone, *Dialectic of Sex*, p.86.
104. Ibid., p.98.
105. S. Lassonde, 'Age and Authority: Adult–Child relations during the Twentieth Century in the United States', *Journal of the History of Childhood and Youth*, 1, 1 (2008), p.95.
106. Ibid., p.97.
107. Ibid., p.99.
108. Zelizer, *Pricing the Priceless Child*, p.212.
109. Ibid., p.210.
110. Bourke, *Working-Class Cultures*, p.28.
111. Ibid., p.46.
112. Ferriter, *Transformation of Ireland*, p.543.
113. P.A. Baggot, *Unspoken Problems of Married Life* (Dublin: Irish Messenger Office, 1965), pp.34–5.
114. P.N. Stearns, 'Fatherhood in Historical Perspective: The Role of Social Change', in F.W. Bozett and S.M.H. Hanson (eds), *Fatherhood and Families in Cultural Context* (New York: Springer, 1991), p.40.
115. O'Kelly, *Permissive Society*, pp.xi–xii.
116. Ibid., p.xi.
117. P. O'Dea, *Dear Frankie* (Dublin: Mentor, 1998), pp.92–3.
118. Messenger, *Inis Beag*, pp.68–9.

CHAPTER SIX

Emerging Gay Voices

INTRODUCTION

The first letter on the subject of homosexuality appeared in the Angela Macnamara column in 1966. The column had received similar letters since 1963 but the editor, Francis Carty, had refused to publish them. It was perhaps not surprising, given the legacy of censorship in the Irish press. The Censorship of Films Act (1923) and the Censorship of Publications Act (1929) had placed legislative boundaries on how Irish people could experience sexuality through film and print. This regime of censorship was coming to an end, with the film board reconstituted in 1964 and an Act, two years later, that led to the unbanning of 5,000 books. This first letter, dated 18 December 1966, was from an engaged woman who had discovered that her fiancé had had relationships with men. Macnamara reassured her that it should be an automatic impediment to their marriage, in what would be a precursor to the tone of her advice on homosexuality in the future.

It became more difficult for newspapers such as *The Sunday Press* to ignore homosexuality. In Britain, Parliament had passed the Sexual Offences Reform Act in 1967 which decriminalized private homosexual acts where both men were over 21 years of age.[1] Some areas of Ireland, mostly on the east coast, had access to BBC television, and British newspapers were widely available in Ireland. The policy of the political and cultural elite in acknowledging homosexuality while not speaking of it, most conspicuously in fêting the relationship of Dublin's Gate theatre founders Micheál Mac Liammóir and Hilton Edwards, slowly came under pressure. Homosexuality remained illegal and hundreds of men were prosecuted under legislation that criminalized what were known as 'gross indecencies' between men.[2] By publishing letters from gay men in her column Angela Macnamara gave voice to the fears and anxieties of ordinary men and women who lived lives that were barely understood outside the language of religious and legal condemnation. Terms such as 'intrinsically disordered' and 'gross indecency' masked the reality of often confused men and women who were struggling to reconcile their sexuality with their religious faith, fears of mental illness and alienation from Irish society. Often these terms were the only means through which gay men understood themselves, and the letters to Macnamara are couched in such religious and medical language. It was a terminology that would increasingly be contested and rejected. As a variety of different media became available a new voice emerged which spoke about homosexuality in a context of human rights, relationships and fulfilled lives.

Everyone who read the Angela Macnamara column learned more about homosexuality. This included Macnamara herself. In my interview with her she suggested that at the time she was 'frightened by it [homosexuality] and frightened by the moral implications and felt a little bit horrified by it', but through private correspondence with members of the Irish Gay Rights Movements (IGRM) and letters from ordinary gay men she acknowledged that she 'began to talk with them and became more informed myself'. She described her replies to gay men in the final years of the column as 'compassionate'. Gay men also learned from the column. The men that I interviewed learned that they were not alone. The column was read by all of them and they recognized in these pages others like themselves who did not fit the camp stereotypes of media portrayal. Others wrote too. Women wrote that they suspected their boyfriends to be gay. Parents wrote distressed about what the future would hold for their gay sons.

In this chapter I trace the rise and fall of two expert voices on homosexuality – religion and psychiatry – both heavily used by Angela Macnamara in her replies. Readers were often displeased when Macnamara relied too heavily on one as opposed to the other. Both would be challenged during the duration of the column. Influences from abroad, such as the decision by the American Psychiatric Association to remove homosexuality from its register of psychopathology in 1973, and the rise of second-wave feminism that challenged the link between sex and reproduction and freed sex from the confines of the marital bed paved a new path for people to understand sexuality as individual matters of conscience.

'CONDEMNED BY THE CHURCH?': HOMOSEXUALITY AND SIN

The publication by the Vatican of *Humanae Vitae* and *Persona Humana* provided the framework within which Macnamara mediated advice to her readers. The documents were a resource with which to guide the faithful and denounce the sexual transgressor. In the previous chapters we saw how Angela Macnamara drew heavily on a language of self-control and discipline popular in Catholic dating guides of the day. *Humanae Vitae* provided the column with this language of self-restraint, advocating chastity and the discipline of sexual drives within and outside marriage. It states: 'We take this opportunity to address those who are engaged in education and all those whose right and duty it is to provide for the common good of society. We would call their attention to the need to create an atmosphere favourable to the growth of chastity so that true liberty may prevail over license and the norms of the moral law may be fully safeguarded.' Angela Macnamara certainly saw it as her duty to create this chaste atmosphere, believing that her column had a duty to tackle human problems on both practical and spiritual levels.

The publication of *Persona Humana* in 1975 reaffirmed Catholic teaching on sexual morality, including masturbation and homosexuality. In the previous chapter I discussed the fears expressed by readers about the side effects of masturbation – one of which was thought to be homosexuality. Here letter writers confuse both activities in their attempt to understand their sexuality. The publication of the document came two years after the founding of the Irish Gay Rights Movement (IGRM) and received widespread coverage in *The Sunday Press*, where the text was reproduced in full on 25 January 1976. The document recognized that some people were homosexual, not by choice but by an innate disposition. It advised those in the pastoral field to treat homosexuals with understanding but to offer no moral justification for these acts. This distinction would provide the framework through which Angela Macnamara provided her advice, but it began to change as she came into contact with gay people through her column.

The publication of *Persona Humana* gave merely an illusion of uniformity on the issue of homosexuality. Behind it lay tension and disagreement. Crucially, the document relied heavily on scientific notions of homosexuality and (re)introduced the concept of sexual pathology at a time when campaigns within professional bodies in psychiatry were seeking successfully to remove it. With regard to homosexuality, *Persona Humana*'s condemnation is uncompromising:

> For according to the objective moral order, homosexual relations are acts which lack an essential and indispensable finality. In Sacred Scripture they are condemned as a serious depravity and even presented as the sad consequence of rejecting God. This judgment

of Scripture does not of course permit us to conclude that all those who suffer from this anomaly are personally responsible for it, but it does attest to the fact that homosexual acts are intrinsically disordered and can in no case be approved of.

Persona Humana also placed the blame for the questioning of Church teaching among the young on the 'unrestrained licentiousness of so many public entertainments and publications, as well as with the neglect of modesty'. In an article in *The Sunday Press* on 19 March 1978, Angela Macnamara also laid the blame for the growth of the permissive society firmly on the media and on intellectuals. 'Our young people are under vicious attack,' she wrote, 'bombarded by a dizzying kaleidoscope of pop culture, misinformation about the basic nature of human beings, encouragement through permissive magazines, newspapers, TV and books to "live it up," treacherously influenced by nihilist intellectuals who are attacking what is most valid and enriching in human experience.' Macnamara's husband, Peter, had also been critical of the role that intellectuals played in criticizing his wife's column. In a television documentary on her life, Peter Macnamara suggested that 'criticism generally [came] from people who would regard themselves as intellectuals, they are perfectly able of dealing with their own problems and wouldn't need any help from someone without a university qualification'.[3]

Humanae Vitae and *Persona Humana* emanated from the Vatican and were dispensed downwards through bishops, priests, religious orders and lay organizations. They were interpreted by the bishops who issued pastorals and joint statements to their congregations more frequently in the 1970s.[4] There was often a disparity between discourse and practice. Tony Fahey argues that new forms of sexual behaviour had spread since the 1960s without a dramatic decline in religious observance, suggesting that the implementation of these documents on the ground was sporadic while it adapted to the new realities of modern Ireland.[5] The Church was changing too. Mary Kenny argues that *Humanae Vitae* represented a softening of the Church's position on the role of women and was, in general, less authoritarian in tone.[6]

While the potential sinfulness of sexuality occupied the minds of many of Angela Macnamara's letter writers it was gay men who were often the most distressed. I have argued elsewhere that many Irish gay men struggled to reconcile their obligations to their families and their faith while remaining true to their sexual selves.[7] One letter from 26

June 1977 exemplifies this conflict between a strong religious faith and a newly discovered homosexual identity but without shame or any desire to change: 'I am seventeen and a Catholic, a practising homosexual for the past fifteen months. I do not want to be cured but I want to be a Catholic. I do not feel dirty but am worried and puzzled that my state is condemned by the Church. Did Christ actually condemn homosexuality?' Macnamara replied that 'First of all, Jesus did not condemn homosexuality ... There is nothing morally wrong in having homosexual tendencies, or even in being so constituted that you have no interest whatsoever in the opposite sex, but the question of moral responsibility arises when you decide what you are going to do about this, how you will cope with it.' Others wrote expressing concern that their behaviour was both sinful and immoral. In a letter of 13 March 1977 a letter writer asked: 'is it abnormal for a person to be homosexual? Is it morally wrong?', to which Angela Macnamara responds:

> Right through the animal kingdom the norm is that male and female be attracted to one another, unite and reproduce their kind. However that does not mean that people with homosexual tendencies are abnormal as people. It simply means that their tendencies are not the norm. It is not morally wrong to have inclinations that are not according to the norm. It would be wrong to encourage such tendencies at their onset rather than to endeavour to adjust to the normal pattern. Some people go through homosexual phases in their lives but with counselling discover themselves to be heterosexual.

Angela Macnamara took on the role of mediator in deciding whether Catholics should be counselled to seek the sacrament of confession. The column becomes, in effect, a confessional space itself, where the truth of Irish sexuality was exposed and transformed into discourse. Macnamara's columns allowed readers to confess their sexual deviations in greater detail than they would be likely to do in the sacrament of confession. For example, a young man who received money for having sex with a homosexual man explained to Macnamara in a letter of 29 January 1978 that he had been unable to tell this sin in confession and subsequently was unable to receive Holy Communion. Here, she coached the man as to a possible wording that would minimize his embarrassment when speaking to a priest. With 66 per cent of Irish Catholics attending confession at least once a month in this period, the column played a crucial role in enabling letter writers to return to the sacrament once Macnamara had adjudicated the potential sinfulness of the act and suggested a solution.[8]

The column served as an expert forum wherein Macnamara presided over the sexually naive, the confused, and the sexually transgressive in a manner entirely reminiscent of Michel Foucault's description of the purpose of the official sacrament of confession: 'It is a ritual that unfolds within a power relationship, for one does not confess without the presence (or virtual presence) of a partner who is not simply the interlocutor but the authority that requires the confession, prescribes and appreciates it, and intervenes in order to judge, punish, forgive, console and reconcile.'[9] The tone of Macnamara's advice itself demonstrates how much she saw her role as a pastoral one not unlike that of a priest to a confessor. Accordingly, although the teachings of the Catholic Church influenced Macnamara's advice on homosexuality, the biblical condemnations in Leviticus (18:22) and Romans (1:27) did not find a place in the language of her column.

Angela Macnamara's column did not rely on a legal discourse either when answering readers' letters. This was most unusual. Gay men lived their lives under the shadow of criminalization and were subject to harassment, arrest and prosecution in Ireland during the 1960s and 1970s. Chrystal Hug writes that between 1962 and 1972 there were 455 convictions for acts of gross indecency under the Labouchere amendment to the Criminal Law Amendment Act 1885.[10] Men were humiliated by the State and the judiciary, with the publication of the names of those convicted in newspapers; this led predictably to job losses and alienation from family and friends. The IGRM sought to defend the men accused but also to refute the legislation itself. Following the lead of American organizations, the IGRM arranged sympathetic solicitors to support its members in gross indecency cases, motivated by the belief that it was the stigma associated with court appearance that led mostto plead guilty to the charges, allowing the legislation to remain uncontested.

'IT'S ONLY A PHASE': HOMOSEXUALITY AS A TRANSITION

The extent to which the homosexual was culpable for his condition formed an important feature of Angela Macnamara's advice. *Persona Humana*'s distinction between homosexuality deemed to be transitory or curable and homosexuality deemed to be innate became the basis for her evaluation of the letters from her sexually confused readership and thus influenced the course of action she recommended. *Persona Humana* stated: 'A distinction is drawn ... between homosexuals whose tendency comes from false education, from their lack of normal sexual development, from habit, from bad example, or from other similar causes and is transitory or at least not incurable; and homosexuals who are definitively such because of some kind of innate instinct or a pathological constitution judged to be incurable.'[11] Following this distinction, Angela Macnamara categorized the majority of the letters she received as 'transitory' even when faced with compelling evidence to the contrary. By contrast, Christine Brinkgreve and Michel Korzec's analysis of Dutch advice columns from the same era revealed a willingness to confirm an individual's homosexuality, as in the reply to a mother about her son: 'You know it, we know it and your son has known it for a long time: he is most probably homosexual.'[12]

In her response to a letter of 6 May 1979, for example, Macnamara suggested that it was the public speech about homosexuality itself that was causing much of the confusion among the otherwise heterosexual people who wrote to her. In doing so she inadvertently recognized the success of the IGRM participation in a debate throughout the decade. She writes how 'In the last few years homosexual groups have become much more outspoken about their way of life. But it does seem that this outspokenness may also have caused increased anxiety amongst people who are in fact quite heterosexual. Don't rush into any quick decisions about whether you are homosexual or not. Get good professional help and advice first.'

Angela Macnamara received many letters from individuals who thought of themselves as homosexual, such as this one from 'George' on 23 September 1973:

> Q. I'm a 16 year old boy and feel that I'm not like other boys at all. I'm homosexual. I know this is often a passing phase, I feel I am quite well developed and now this attraction has not gone. I am quite intelligent and quite popular with girls in school but I'm in no way attracted to them. Please tell me if I have a chance of becoming normal. I also have the habit of masturbation, I wonder if both these plagues are connected though I understand that many young men indulge in this selfishness. I want to improve, believe me. I want to drop this habit ... Please try to set me at ease.

> A. It is understandable that a young man of your age would feel

as you do for a while. This may be due to various influences
in your life about which I know nothing. In order to find the
reason for your tendencies you would need to have a confidential chat with someone who could help you sort it all out
and assess your position ... Many young people go through
emotionally mixed up phases and the majority of them are
perfectly normal and just need a little sympathetic help in
their adjustment to adult life. Do not look on the two big
worries you have as being plagues. As you say, masturbation
is a tendency which is experienced by the majority of young
men and some girls. It is something that we learn to control
in the course of learning to use our sexuality in a proper
human way.

While Angela Macnamara devotes the majority of her reply to 'George'
on how masturbation is a natural inclination and can be controlled, she
will not countenance the possibility that the young man is indeed gay.
It is unlikely that the confidential person she recommended would do
so either. One of the consequences of this advice was that the men
continued to embark on heterosexual relationships which were doomed
to failure and caused further distress. A woman wrote to Angela
Macnamara on 26 October 1975 after a serious chat with her boyfriend
who told her he thought he was gay. Her reply is compassionate but still
clings to the concept of a transitory phase:

Q. A couple of nights ago my boyfriend and I had a serious talk.
   He had been worried for some time and I knew about the
   worry but didn't know what it was. The other night he told
   me that his worry is that he fears he is homosexual. Angela, I
   don't know anything about homosexuality. I don't know
   whether it is a sin or what I should do about it in this situation
   ... we are both in our early twenties.

A. It is important to point out that a young man or woman who
   feels an attraction to their own sex is not necessarily homosexual ... A great deal of harm can be done if a shy, sensitive
   boy is cruelly labelled homosexual by his classmates. Perhaps
   your boyfriend has had feelings of attraction toward other
   boys, been shocked by these feelings and told himself or
   has been told by others that he is homosexual ... Of itself

homosexuality is not a sin. One does not choose to be this way but discovers these traits in oneself. Just as the heterosexual person can abuse himself and exploit others which would be sinful so also can the homosexual. But of itself, homosexuality is not sinful ... Since your boyfriend is upset and worried about his present feelings it is essential that he knows that you accept him as a person and would like to see him helped.

The life histories also revealed other choices made by men who had failed to accept themselves as gay. William Moss (46) abandoned college after one year to join the seminary. He explains that 'I didn't admit it to myself at the time but the seminary offered me an escape from questions about me and girls and offered me a way out of having sex with women which I knew I didn't want to but what I didn't realise was that it would bring my attraction to men so in my face that I just couldn't ignore it any longer.' Kieran Slattery (49) continued to have a series of failed relationships with women. Much of his energy went into avoiding sexual situations, particularly with his last girlfriend, a woman from Belfast, whom he describes as having little of the sexual restraint associated with her southern counterparts. He describes that he 'avoided all occasions where I thought I'd end up in her flat' although he noted that he didn't think his reluctance 'raised any questions in her head, she certainly wouldn't have jumped to the conclusion that I was gay, not then. But it was an unhappy time.'[13]

Other men wrote in far greater despair because they suspected, rightly or wrongly, that they themselves might be gay. 'I enclose a cutting from one of the Catholic newspapers which describes a film now on show in Dublin', wrote one person on 20 June 1971. 'Many of the symptoms described in the article coincide with my own feelings. It has so upset me that I have quit my job and cannot sleep.' Heterosexual people also wrote in, curious to understand this new sexual species that was finding a new voice in Ireland. One letter published on 4 January 1970 asked 'What is a homosexual? There have been films and plays and things in the newspapers etc about people called homosexual, and I don't know what it means. I hear the other fellows talking about it.' In her reply Angela Macnamara explains what homosexuality is and continues:

Most young people go through a phase when their sexual emotions are developing and they have not mixed much with the opposite

sex and they may feel an interest in and admiration for a member
of their own sex. This is sometimes called a 'crush' and is quite a
normal phase of development but not a phase to encourage or get
stuck in. The average young person moves from the 'crush' into
perfectly normal mixed friendships. Compassion must mark our
attitudes towards people who are going through difficult
phases or who have abnormal tendencies.

Central to Macnamara's advice, however, was the distinction
between homosexual tendencies and individual homosexual acts.
Persona Humana argued that while the homosexual person must be
treated 'with understanding', the homosexual act is to be viewed as
'intrinsically disordered'.[14] Unlike heterosexual couples, however, whose
sexual activity would find an approved outlet in marriage, no such
scenario existed for gay men. For Angela Macnamara, her gay
letter writers would remain free from sin as long as they didn't engage in
any sexual activity with other men – ever. Angela Macnamara did avoid
any direct condemnation of individual people yet consistently viewed
sexual anxiety as a phase and seemed reluctant to confirm any reader's
concern about his or her sexuality. 'Some people believe themselves to be
homosexual when in fact they may only have tendencies that way', she
wrote on 8 February 1970. 'People can certainly be helped to overcome
tendencies of this kind and if not curable they can be helped to cope.'

Angela Macnamara reassured readers whom she deemed to be in
this transitory stage of homosexuality that these tendencies were
indeed a normal feature of sexual development. To overcome these
inclinations the readers should not obsess about their feelings or even
talk about them, and should concentrate on other pursuits in their lives.
A 15-year-old boy wrote in a letter of 15 March 1970: 'I don't find
myself sexually attracted to girls. For the last eight months I have
behaved badly with boys ... am I homosexual?' Macnamara responded:
'It seems highly unlikely that you are homosexual.' She continued: 'I do
hope you enjoy sport, football, swimming, etc., indeed any outdoor
activity is essential for a young man.' She offered this advice to another
man on 3 September 1972 who was attracted to his best friend's next-
door neighbour and believed it to be unnatural:

> One can experience a disordered emotion like this without it being
> an indication of any deep personality upset. Stop talking about it
> and building it up as a tragedy. Instead continue in your ordinary
> friendships. A phase like this is not all that unusual but talking

about it and thinking continually about or acting out your feelings will prolong the phase.

Men wrote to Angela Macnamara in doubt that their same-sex attraction was transitory. In a letter of 12 August 1979 a 25-year-old man described how 'I feel I am becoming a homosexual or have become one. I have always thought it was just a passing thing but lately I have become very worried about myself.' Again Angela Macnamara advised that it was his isolation and the worry itself that was distorting the man's sexuality so that the 'tendency grows and develops'. In a letter of 19 February 1978 a woman wrote asking advice on behalf of her friend whose 'life is crippled by the fear that she is a lesbian'. Letters from women who feared they were lesbian are conspicuous by their absence in the Macnamara column.

There was a contradiction in Angela Macnamara's advice on homosexuality in that she was encouraging young men to see these feelings as a natural transitory phase which they should not overly think or talk about while at the same time the column was providing one of an increasing number of forums where discussion was taking place. Indeed, many of the life history interviewees clearly remembered Angela Macnamara's column and saw it as a forum reducing their isolation regarding their sexuality and offering stories from letter writers that they could identify with. Chris Moore (47) spoke of the difference between gay stereotypes on the television and his search for more 'factual information', discovering that the 'Angela Macnamara column in the Press did have stories of ordinary Dublin lads, carpenters, bus drivers, whatever, who happened to be gay'. Similarly, Emer O'Kelly's inclusion of the story of Fergus in her book, *The Permissive Society in Ireland?*, mentions that he is a gay man whom she describes as 'extremely good looking ... and [he] does not mince'.[15] Fergus is a teacher and feels compelled to hide his sexuality, knowing that 'even the most liberal of parents would object to him as a teacher for their child'.[16] Unlike the men who wrote to the Macnamara column about their experiences, Fergus has not been, as O'Kelly suggests, 'torn by guilt complexes, unable to accept what they are'.

In the previous chapters, interviewees spoke of a lack of information about sexuality while they were dating or married, with Tony Fitzgerald describing the sex manual which he and his wife consulted during their honeymoon. There were no manuals available for the gay men I interviewed and the consequences were devastating. Tim McDonnell (50) spoke of finding the section on sexual reproduction on page 138 of his science text, pages never dealt with by his teacher: 'I read the pages over and over and I guess I understood but it wasn't me, what I was thinking or feeling', he explained.[17] He continued:

> I was nineteen before I discovered that there was something called 'gay sex', as a teenager I thought the only way I could ever have sex was if I had a sex change so I thought it was just masturbation for the rest of your life and then I had the Catholic Church telling me that even that solitary pleasure was a mortal sin.

Tim wanted to speak about his sexual attractions in an effort to understand them but was worried by a fear of disclosure. The diaries he wrote over a three-year period in secondary school can only be understood through an elaborate code devised by Tim to avoid disclosure about his difficult school life and his emerging gay sexuality. Here, certain keywords unlock the true meaning of his experience. The secrecy was inspired by his mother's reaction to the discovery of drawings of men that Tim had made at the age of 11, which reinforced his belief that 'nothing could be written down in case it could be used as evidence against you'. It was a caution that continued into adult life. As a student on a return trip home from New York, Tim feared the discovery of some gay publications he had purchased, deciding to leave them 'in the seat pocket in the plane, I was actually embarrassed that they might be seen or be taken by the customs people'. He continued: 'There was nothing here [in Ireland], nothing, my parents bought *The Sunday Press* and I can remember reading Angela Macnamara's column first before anything else, it was really the only place to read about sex, about menstruation, puberty ... and ordinary gay men like me, all as lonely and confused as I was then, it made me hope that I wasn't alone.' The column provided some little comfort in a society in which Tim explained that he 'thought it would be easier to admit to having being an IRA bomber than admit to being gay in Ireland in the seventies; at least they'd say "he was doing it for Ireland" '.

For Macnamara, sport particularly seemed to offer young men confused about their sexual orientation an immunization against homosexuality. J.A. Mangan and James Walvin argue that equating sport and the disciplining of the body with moral self-restraint had been a feature of a nineteenth-century scientific and educational tradition that blurred the boundaries between muscle power and willpower.[18] It was a tradition continued in the Macnamara column. Sport acted as a repressive mechanism on a boy's impulses, guarding him against sexually deviant adolescent ailments. Similarly, the sexual discipline that sport was believed to possess contributed to his future increased productivity and labour power.[19] For Michel Foucault too, sport is an arena where the body is disciplined and trained.[20] The suggestion to pursue sports and outdoor activities perpetuated the belief that the physical and emotional contact that happened through sport was essentially asexual.

The life history interviewees expressed little interest in the limited range of sports on offer in the Christian Brothers' schools in which they were educated – usually Gaelic football or hurling. The Christian Brothers, like other religious orders, had since the mid-nineteenth century consolidated their control of the education of Irish Catholic boys. Daire Keogh sees the Christian Brothers as being part of a modernizing process that swept Ireland in the early nineteenth century, playing a crucial role in the modern church.[21] As part of a modern civilizing process the Christian Brothers became responsible for the educational and moral needs of the unruly children of the working classes.[22] The virtues of discipline, chastity and cleanliness were instilled and reinforced through a system of surveillance by the Brothers themselves and through the guilt and shame the boys carried internally.

Sean Thornton (48) described how school authorities were usually only concerned with the illusion of taking part, describing how 'being seen to be taking part was all they [the Christian Brothers] were interested in, so you would have to tog out in all weathers but I would spend most of my time standing around maybe chatting to some guy, supposedly marking him, who had as little enthusiasm for it as I did'. Others like Tony Kennedy (50) spoke of the humiliating ritual of being forced to take part in sport where team captains would select those they wanted for their team, describing how he had a 'feeling of being completely worthless, this person that no team wanted and desperately tried to avoid getting you and these captains who were put in this position could make you feel that way'. His reluctance and inability to play sport was confirmation to others of his homosexuality and he was bullied as a result, but Tony Kennedy also spoke of other young men who he was certain were straight but who were also bullied and labelled as gay by some of their classmates.

My own experience of sport in secondary school was not dissimilar. Playing either hurling or Gaelic football was a compulsory element though its enforcement declined throughout my time in this Christian Brothers' school. So ingrained was this sporting culture that a refusal to participate was genuinely seen as odd, hence the name-calling or bullying described by the interviewees quoted above.

As we saw in the previous chapters, in Angela Macnamara's column sex was viewed as external to human control, requiring its repression as well as guidance and strategies to overcome it. A letter of 15 November 1970 from a young man reveals this struggle: 'I am a young Kerry man who came over to London last month to find work. But I find it quite impossible to avoid occasions of sin. Would it help me to wear a miraculous medal?' Readers relied heavily on concepts of instinct, drive and impulse, demanding what Jeffrey Weeks describes as social prescriptions to rein them in.[23] In Macnamara's column these prescriptions were most often hobbies, charity work and sport.

Towards the close of the column in 1980 Angela Macnamara still relied on the possibility of a reader's fear about homosexuality being transitory but a greater realism had entered the column as well. Macnamara believed that talk about homosexuality had increased so much that heterosexual men now doubted their sexuality. To those who thought they were homosexual, like the writer of this letter of 9 May 1979, 'a distressed 21-year-old', the advice focuses on appropriate levels of sexual restraint, whether homosexual or heterosexual. Angela Macnamara writes:

> remember that no matter what your sexual tendencies may be there are standards which all of us must follow. There is a danger for all of us that we concentrate so much on the sexual area that we forget each of us is first and foremost a person. Sex is an important element in life but it is not all of it. Have you tried to develop other areas in your life?

PATHOLOGIZING HOMOSEXUALITY: CAN IT BE CURED?

As the column progressed into the 1970s, Angela Macnamara gave advice to gay men that was increasingly derived from a medical discourse, primarily the psychiatric profession. This distinction is by no means clear-cut, and both the religious and the medical often coexisted in her columns. The gay men who wrote to the Angela Macnamara column understood their sexuality in a similar language to that created by the medical profession. Terms like 'intrinsically disordered', used by the Catholic Church and others, located homosexuality within a field of psychopathology. During the late nineteenth century, sexuality came increasingly came under the remit of the medical profession, as part of a wider social restructuring of sexuality that had taken place throughout the century. Jeffrey Weeks argues there was an increased emphasis within bourgeois society on the importance of the family to the stability of social life.[24] Women became increasingly more economically dependent on men within the monogamous heterosexual family. Perceived threats to the family were removed from respectable society. Jane Ussher argues that the dangerous sexuality of the prostitute, the mistress and the rape survivor would be held responsible for inciting men's uncontrollable sexual drives and be pathologized by the newly acquired power of the medical profession.[25] The scope of this medical power went further. For Michel Foucault it involved an examination, a confession, a personal history and recognizable signs and symptoms with which to track down the 'truth' about sexuality.[26] A range of sexual practices were now medicalized including masturbation, childbirth outside marriage, frigidity, promiscuity, nymphomania and homosexuality. The treatment of these sexual perversions also lay in the hands of male medical experts. The 1845 Lunatics Act and an amendment of 1867 consolidated medical power over the use of asylums. Mark Finnane argued that, unlike the situation in England, in Ireland it would be men who would account for the greatest number of admissions to asylums.[27] According to Pauline Prior, the 1901 census identified four categories of insanity, with 12 per cent of cases classified as 'moral or mental causes'.[28]

Following the criminalization of homosexuality in the nineteenth century the medical profession was increasingly called upon to determine the newly 'discovered' homosexual's culpability before the law. The profession was divided as to the cause. Whether it was a congenital defect or mental illness that brought about what was widely perceived as moral depravity, the medical profession's stature in society ensured its judgment would be binding.[29] Jonathan Gathorne-Hardy argues that medical discourse had previously been called upon to support the moral prohibition of sexual practices such as masturbation with 'scientific' evidence to prove it to be physically damaging.[30]

In Ireland this medical discourse would remain associated with – but subservient to – religious control over how sexuality should be understood solely in the context of Catholic social teaching. Ruth Barrington argues that since Catholic emancipation in 1829, Ireland had a growing Catholic bourgeoisie of doctors and religious nursing orders that led to the establishment of hospitals like St Vincent's (1835) in Dublin and the Mercy (1857) in Cork.[31] After independence the Catholic domination of hospitals strengthened. Teaching hospitals too would become imbued with a Catholic code of ethics that cared for both the moral and physical welfare of the patient. Doctors from these hospitals would take a leading role in the formation of the Irish Medical Association (IMA) in the 1830s. The development of the medical profession as a powerful interest group in society was bolstered by its close links to the Catholic Church. Both were united in limited State interference in the physical and moral health of Irish families.[32] It was the dramatic increase in venereal diseases such as syphilis that brought sexuality into the public domain as a serious medical issue for much of the twentieth century. Diarmaid Ferriter argues that despite the overwhelming evidence, early Free State governments were reluctant to accept venereal disease as a real public health issue.[33] It was women's sexuality that was identified as responsible.

The power that religious and medical discourses held over homosexuality was revealed in 1983 when the Supreme Court judgment upholding the criminalization became known. It centred on four principle arguments.[34] The Chief Justice claimed that homosexual acts were unnatural through the use of sexual organs for non-reproductive pleasure. The Court deemed homosexuality to be sinful as defined in the Judeo-Christian tradition on which the Irish State rested, locating the legitimate practice of sexuality solely within the context of married love. Sexuality outside this context was judged to be an affront to the natural order and a contributing factor to a perceived permissiveness sweeping Ireland that brought moral decay to the nation. The Supreme Court further claimed that homosexuality should be regarded as a criminal behaviour as its promiscuity contributed to the spread of venereal disease and was an issue of public health. For the Supreme Court, homosexuality was a physical and moral contagion understood as a series of casual sexual behaviours where the possibility of men forming stable, monogamous relationships was not considered. In its attempt to plot and construct the rights and boundaries of the homosexual it neglected the human elements of love, loyalty and companionship. The final ground on which the Supreme Court rejected the challenge to the constitutionality of the criminalization lay on a belief that homosexuality was an individual disorder. Here the court saw itself protecting homosexuals from themselves. Whether congenital or acquired, it led to unhappiness, despair, loneliness and suicide. The minority judgment of the Court correctly observed that it was perhaps the very legal regime to which homosexuals were subject that was the root cause of much of that despair.[35]

The belief that homosexuality was a sexual pathology remained unquestioned within the political establishment. In the Dáil (Irish Parliament) in 1977, former Minister of Health Noel Browne questioned the Minister of Justice, Gerry Collins, on whether the government had any intention of re-examining the law against gross indecency. Noel Browne argued that it was not homosexuality that was disordered, but rather society's reaction that caused disorder. Browne, described by the *Irish Independent* in an article of 14 December 1977 as 'one of the country's top psychiatrists', cited the mental health consequences of the criminalization of homosexuality. He argued that 'Irish society creates formidable emotional problems for homosexuals. It ridicules them, calls them names and is suspicious that they might seduce children.' Browne claimed to have seen the psychological consequences of this stigma in his own practice. The questions he posed to the minister were part of a strategy to gain the support of six Dáil deputies so as to underwrite his private members' bill to decriminalize homosexuality. No deputies on the government or opposition benches were willing to do so.

It is significant that although the IGRM was founded in 1974, Macnamara only once recommended the organization, and then only as a source of advice after psychiatric help had been sought, in a 15 May 1977 reply to a reader who had speculated about whether the organization could be helpful:

Q. I am a 19 year old boy and I have never told anybody about my problem. I am a homosexual. This is the first time I have ever expressed this. I have been aware of it for about 5 years. I never engaged in any sexual acts with anyone yet. I saw a TV programme about it and I saw how the Gay Rights Movement helps people like me. What would you advise me to do?

A. Some experts claim a person cannot be definitely classed as a homosexual before the early twenties. I think you would benefit from a talk with a counsellor or psychiatrist who would help you discover your basic orientation. It would be premature to consider that you are definitely homosexual and then concentrate on the homosexual community for most of your friendships. Many members of the Gay Rights Movement are conscientious in helping others to discover their true sexual orientation and direct them to counsellors who are qualified.

Macnamara's personal views on homosexuality also changed over the duration of the column. In the following letters, for example, we see

Macnamara advising both psychiatric and spiritual direction, but in my interview she stated that she was often reluctant to do so because people were 'quite anxious about psychiatry ... it just meant the same thing: they weren't normal, [and] that was frightening.' Letter writers were also anxious about the crossover between religion and psychiatry in their search for solutions. A 20-year-old man wrote in a letter of 8 February 1978: 'My problems are that I blush a lot ... I also masturbate ... I am worried as to whether I'm homosexual. If I go to a psychiatrist should I tell him of my sinful deeds?' Angela Macnamara believed that this young man's problems stemmed from 'an absence of positive and clear sex education' and told him that 'it seems unlikely that you are homosexual'. For another letter writer on 6 October 1974 blushing was also a reason to suspect homosexuality, but Angela Macnamara declared that 'your letter gives me absolutely no reason to believe that you have homosexual tendencies'.

On 8 February 1970 she wrote: 'A person who is worried about this [homosexuality] should consult a doctor, who will refer him to a psychiatrist if that is found to be necessary ... In all cases medical and spiritual help should be sought.' On 4 April 1971 she wrote: 'It is essential that you talk to a doctor, a spiritual director or a prudent coun-sellor ... It is difficult to help an adult who is deeply homosexual, but even he can be helped to cope with his own condition and to find some degree of happiness.' And on 13 March 1977 she wrote that 'some people go through homosexual phases in their lives but with counselling discover themselves to be heterosexual'. The relationship between Macnamara and the psychiatric profession was at times uneasy. In the Radharc documentary, when asked about the criticism levelled against her by members of the counselling profession who had undergone years of professional training and who deemed her unqualified, Macnamara was equally critical of the profession, describing them as 'clinicians' rather than motivated by humanity and care for others.[36]

Macnamara's column was not the only Irish problem page in the decade suggesting referrals to the psychiatric profession. In 1973 the tabloid *Sunday World* was launched, and its 'Dear Linda' column penned by Valerie McGrath was even more explicit about what course of action to take – as, for example, on 2 February 1975, when advising a 21-year-old man claiming to have got himself into 'a type of homo-sexual habit'.[37] 'Dear Linda' tells the man:

> Psychiatric help is what you need for a problem of this sort. Don't shy away from the word. There will be a psychiatric department

attached to most of the hospitals in and around Cork. Be sure to keep your appointment and don't let cold feet stop you at the last minute. And remember for any bad habit that you get into use the AA motto – 'A Day at a time.'

The *Sunday World* also ran a series of articles on homosexuality in October 1973 that generated letters both from men anxious about their sexuality and from organizations suggesting help and counselling for them. In a letter to the paper of 21 October 1973 the Legion of Mary, a lay Catholic organization, announced the start of discussion groups in Dublin for those believing themselves to be homosexual and 'anxious to discuss their problem in an informal, understanding and constructive atmosphere', assuring readers that the meetings were 'nondenominational and strictly confidential'. For some men, encountering similar men at these meetings only confirmed their homosexuality, and so they rejected the notion that such discussion would be helpful. 'Trevor', in a letter of 28 October 1973 to the paper, explained his position:

> I developed tendencies towards my own sex and even at this stage in my life (32) I am still trying to fight it. Thank God I have tried to stay on the straight road. I have never had any relations with or met another homosexual. I have tried retreats, novenas and [a pilgrimage to] Lourdes, asking God to show me some light for the future. I feel for me it [the Legion of Mary meetings] would be like asking an alcoholic in for a jar [of beer], nevertheless good luck to them in their work.

Similarly, Angela Macnamara recommended that her readers who thought they might be homosexuals should contact what she called the 'Thursday Discussion Group', although she gave no further details about the group's aims or affiliation. For other men there appeared to be no hope, no cure and no recovery from their homosexuality, as this extraordinary letter of 23 April 1978 to Angela Macnamara suggests:

> Q. I'm a young man, homosexual and completely alone with no friends or social life. My life has been a misery, I can no longer face each day. I intend to take my life. The purpose of this suicide letter is to say I'm sorry to everyone.

> A. I wish I had your name and address. If you see this would you please write to me privately enclosing a stamped addressed envelope and I shall put you in touch with a caring and concerned person.

The fate of this young man remains unknown, but Macnamara most often recommended private correspondence when there was a need for urgency, as above, or when letters were deemed too explicit for publication.

TALKING BACK: DISSENTING GAY VOICES

By the mid-1970s the Catholic Church and the psychiatric profession's views on homosexuality were being challenged on several fronts. This challenge would come from the mobilization of New Social Movements (NSM) such as the IGRM and organizations affiliated to a second wave of feminist activism in Ireland. I have argued elsewhere that founding members of the IGRM David Norris and Edmund Lynch were inspired by a climate of student and worker unrest that had erupted in Paris and throughout Europe in 1968, and by Stonewall riots in New York the following year, while the American civil rights movement had inspired the Catholic community to resist the Stormont government's abuse of power in Northern Ireland.[38] The reluctance of some in the women's movement and the broader campaign for sexual liberation to pursue the legitimate issue of gay rights made the argument for the formation of a movement all the more convincing.[39] Questions remain about whether the conditions were present in Ireland that existed in other affluent liberal democracies of Western Europe. Dennis Altman suggests that for a homosexual identity to develop, a society must be urban, secular and affluent.[40] He draws distinctions between countries of southern Europe such as Italy, Spain and Greece, where homosexual practice was widespread, but which had yet to reach the economic conditions of their northern neighbours. Several factors militated against the development of a widespread identity in Ireland. The affluence that Ireland experienced in the late 1960s and early 1970s was short-lived as worldwide recession plunged Ireland into economic freefall from which it was slow to recover. These economic conditions were not conducive to the extension of the gay scene so vital for the increased visibility that would help foster the development of a collective gay identity. The inclusion of the gay commercial world into mainstream consumerist society, that Altman suggests occurred in North America and Western Europe in the 1970s, would not become a reality in Ireland for another twenty years.[41]

Lay experts such as Angela Macnamara, who had carved a niche for herself as an authority on sexuality, would also be increasingly challenged both by their readership and by these new actors mobilizing in NSMs.

The resistance to this power, spawned in NSMs and universities, challenged the knowledge and competence of others designated as experts in a specific field. New experts on homosexuality were about to emerge in Ireland at this time. Alberto Melucci argues that it was the 'new' middle classes – those working in public sector occupations such as education, health and media, or students waiting to join these professions – who were most visible in NSMs.[42] This was certainly the case in the emergence of public figures who voiced a new truth about homosexuality in Ireland.

Todd Gitlin argued that it was the ability of those in the gay movement to communicate their message to the public through the mass media which was critical, often turning leadership into celebrity overnight.[43] The IGRM needed more than a public face to succeed; it needed to develop strategies to maintain a high media profile for its activities. Founding member of the IGRM, Edmund Lynch, had joined RTÉ in 1969 and developed a key role in alerting journalists to the newsworthiness of an emerging gay movement story:[44]

> I didn't do newspaper interviews. I knew that was David's [Norris] thing not mine. My job was [to], I wouldn't say manipulate the media, but to inform the media whether it was a good story, whether there was a good spin on things. Knowing the content and format of what constitutes a good news story was really helpful in getting our message across.

The relationship with and knowledge of the media would provide a tactical advantage throughout the decade. Lynch's knowledge of new organizations enabled the subsequent Campaign for Homosexual Law Reform to shape their press releases to ensure that they were newsworthy and released to meet the demands of news routines. Lynch continues:[45]

> Our access to journalists was really based on our individual relationships with them, but it did help that a lot of journalists who were writing about us had been students of English and David Norris had taught a lot of them, and certainly that had a great effect. But one phone call could have a huge effect. Like the time I remember being sent down to a USI [Union of Students in Ireland] meeting in Wexford to speak about gay rights, and being refused the first night and talking to a journalist friend of mine who ran an article the following day: 'GAY ACTIVIST REFUSED' [laughs]. Not surprisingly, they let me speak the next night.

RTÉ also took up the gay movement story. Cathal O'Shannon's documentary on homosexuality, shown in July 1977, beamed footage from an IGRM disco in Parnell Square, showing happy, dancing (albeit almost in the dark) homosexuals, into the nation's living rooms.[46] An 'Insights' documentary, *Patrick Pearse 1879–1916* by Ruth Dudley Edwards, shown in November 1979, concluded that patriot Patrick Pearse was a latent homosexual. This was challenging material, undermining a vision of Irishness that had been carefully crafted long before the birth of the nation in 1922. R.J Savage argues that the very establishment of RTÉ in 1961 had been greeted with some trepidation by Ireland's political and cultural elite.[47] The decision had been postponed by previous governments for fear of offending the Catholic Church, the Gaelic Athletic Association (GAA) and various Irish-language groups who had expressed reservations about its cultural impact on Irish society. A decade later that impact was undeniable. It also represented the further erosion of the Catholic Church's control over Irish civil society and the nature of the debate now conducted in the public sphere. There remained limits to what could be broadcast. In 1976, an RTÉ interview with David Norris caused public disquiet, leading to a ruling by the Complaints Advisory Committee that the station had broken its broadcasting code in the production of the programme by violating its social mores.[48] Nor was all media coverage favourable. A Dublin City councillor writing in the *Evening Press* in February 1977 stated: 'If people want to indulge in homosexuality then they should keep quiet about it. In my opinion these people are not only weak but sick and they should not be permitted to contaminate others, especially the young.'[49]

Tom Inglis argued that the discourse and language of the public sphere was dominated by the Catholic Church where sympathetic intellectuals put forward arguments supportive of the Church's view of social life that rested on its control over the discourse and language with which it operated but also the manner in which it was mediated to audiences by intellectuals and public figures who supported the Church's view of social life.[50] The media facilitated a new debate and discussion on non-traditional alternatives to Catholic family life and, crucially for Inglis, in the expression and fulfilment of the self.'[51] Social movements like the IGRM proved considerably more adept at mastering the new realities of debate in the public sphere than their competitors.

SEXUAL STORYTELLING

We saw earlier in this chapter how Angela Macnamara had advised men who suspected they were gay against talking about these feelings. The era of *not* talking about your sexual desire was over in Ireland. Tom Inglis describes this sharp contradiction between the Catholic Church and a new, more open society: one an 'institution based on silence, repressed egos and one based on self-revelation, debate and discussion'.[52] I discussed in Chapter 4 how Angela Macnamara remained suspicious of any trend towards self-development at the expense of another person. In an era where television, radio and the media, according to Inglis, encouraged 'self-realisation and self-expression while the Church was essentially of self-abnegation or denial', it became increasingly implausible for Macnamara to offer such advice.[53] Part of this self-expression was telling stories. Richard Kearney argues that narratives 'provide the most viable forms of self-identity', both individual and communal, and they are used as a bridge between the individual experience and the broader cultural practices at work in Ireland.[54] Long before the advent of radio and television, the retelling of religious stories, folktales, prayers and proverbs in the family home was commonplace in Ireland, passed down through a rich oral heritage.[55]

In the late twentieth century a new type of story was being told in Ireland. Ken Plummer identifies stories in which sexual suffering, endurance and an ultimate transformation of the individual take place.[56] These stories are part of a broader process in which individuals have sought to bring their private sexual lives into the public area, where they are constructed into narratives for public consumption. Angela Macnamara's column contributed to this desire for sexual stories. The gay stories told there were often radically different from the growing body of coming-out literature that had emerged on both sides of the Atlantic since the late 1960s.[57] In Ireland the stories would follow the somewhat uneven contours of Irish modernization, with schooling and religious practice playing key roles in men's developing sexual identity. Kevin Porter and Jeffrey Weeks describe the complexity of stories in their own collection, claiming that such stories were 'insights into the complex, varied and uneven fashion by which homosexually inclined people made sense of their needs and desires and fashioned for themselves manageable, social and sexual ways of life'.[58] The stories told in Ireland had a similar complexity. Kieran Rose describes the evolution of the gay movement as being the 'polar opposite' of the emergence of similar movements in other Western societies, since our absence of modern, industrial ways of life would seem to condemn us to a profound sexual silence.[59] Both Rose and Linda Connolly reject this view of the Irish as backward in matters of sexual morality, a view which ignores the networks men and women had created for themselves in the early twentieth century. The details of the homosexual scandals which beset the Dublin Castle administration in 1884 confirm the existence of these networks.[60]

While the American pre-Stonewall stories fit neatly into a modernist narrative whereby the spread of capitalism, urbanization and family change facilitated the growth of this storytelling genre, similar developments in Ireland failed to achieve the same results. Clodagh Boyd's landmark text did tell the stories of Irish gay men and women, some twelve years after the founding of the IGRM. The stories present the successful coming out of people who would take a leading role in the movement that was just two years away from David Norris' victory in the European Court of Human Rights.[61] But the story of ordinary gay men remained untold. The most recent contribution to this genre has been *Coming Out*, edited by Glen O'Brien – not the editor's real name but a pseudonym, an ironic twist in the Irish coming-out story.[62] The book gives some fascinating insights into lesbian and gay lives. There is a promise of diversity in the stories because they address issues of disability and sexuality but they are dominated by the role that Christianity has played in the contributors' lives. The subjects range from a victim of clerical child sex abuse to Dublin gay Christian groups and three chapters written by Catholic priests. The real insights come from the fragments of their ordinary lives. One story recalls desperate letters written to Angela Macnamara, confirming her role as the leading lay experts on sexuality in the country.[63] 'Sean' describes the letter and the advice he received, allowing a rare insight into how those who wrote interpreted and acted upon the advice they received from Macnamara:

> At eighteen, in desperation, I wrote to Angela McNamara [sic] who had a 'Problem Page' in *The Sunday Press* newspaper. She put me in touch with a very understanding Redemptorist priest. It was a great relief to talk to someone face to face. But the 'problem' remained. I went to dances – danced with girls and looked at the men. I dated some girls. The prohibition of any kind of genital contact was a great cover … At twenty-two I made contact again with this Redemptorist priest … He advised me to stop trying to have relationships with girls … Aged twenty-three I write my pain

[to] Angela McNamara [sic] again. By return of post she tells me of a day retreat for gay men and lesbians. The following Sunday, 1 October 1978, I lie to my mother, telling her I am going to a trade union meeting in Dublin ... People listen and share experiences and stories. They are so ordinary really.

The media would intervene again in Sean's life when his mother was prompted by a news feature on the Gay Byrne radio show about the opening of the Hirschfeld Centre to ask whether he was gay or not.[64]

In the first chapter of this book, I outlined the socio-economic changes which Ireland underwent in the 1960s and 1970s. It would be tempting to place the stories of gay men in this modernization framework of changing patterns of kinship and family, education and growing secularization. This would underestimate the variations that continued to exist within Irish family life. I agree with Tony Fahey that these variations, such as the importance of older-kinships networks in large industrial cities, illustrate the limitations of the traditional–modern dichotomy. Similarly, the life histories in this study do not follow a linear, one-dimensional line of development. Nor are they presented as a form of gay victimhood in which gay sexuality is seen to be always problematic. The life histories reveal stories from a particular historical time in Ireland when people adapted to the sociocultural change that swept the county during that period. This would seem part of the modernist promise. Marshall Berman argues that urbanization, particularly, provided people with the necessary anonymity so that they were 'free to act' and free from the surveillance of neighbours, family and priests to grow and develop.[65] Within this environment individuals can recreate themselves within what Berman describes as a process of 'perpetual disintegration and renewal, of struggle and contradiction'.[66] This more accurately reflects the plight of those gay men who wrote to Macnamara's column and of the men who were interviewed for the life histories in this study. It recognizes the existing social and sexual networks constructed prior to their coming out. The extent to which modernity would allow gay men to reconstruct their biographical narratives was limited within the urban areas where they lived, as Berman's promise of anonymity and the removal of surveillance often went unfulfilled. Their own self-surveillance of the potential sinfulness of their sexuality would exist still whether they enjoyed the anonymity of Limerick or Leeds.

In Chapter 1 I described how, for Anthony Giddens, social life becomes characterized by modernity's reflexivity, with the self becoming part of this project where it must be reflected upon, constructed and changed by the individual throughout their life course.[67] Individuals are faced with a multitude of choices from which one must negotiate and choose. The Angela Macnamara column becomes part of this rise of expert systems, deploying knowledge to the 'intimacies of self' through counsellors and therapists. The problem page becomes part of this ongoing reflexivity of the self as people construct and reconstruct the narrative of their lives.

The methods employed by women's groups in harnessing the power of the media to garner publicity provided a blueprint for IGRM campaigns. Women were the first to tell alternative stories of their lives in the public sphere. The appearance of the Irish Women's Liberation Movement (IWLM) on 'The Late Late Show' in 1971 marked a shift in how sexuality was spoken about and brought previously private decisions about marital sexuality into the public domain. Crucially, women themselves were now talking about their own bodies in defiance of the religious and legislative discourses that had previously claimed jurisdiction over them. In the same year the IWLM's importation of contraceptives into the Irish Republic from Northern Ireland in defiance of the 1935 legislation banning the sale and importation of contraceptives generated international media coverage.

In my interview with Angela Macnamara she revealed how her own views on contraception had also changed. Though believing that the introduction of contraception would bring increased exploitation of some women, she recognized that for married couples, the issue was a source of conflict and unhappiness. She explained:

> I began to think that in some way this must be regulated so that only married people could avail [themselves] of contraception and I was sure that I was accepting eventually of the need for it, and you know my own life showed that too it was extremely difficult to show your full affection in a marriage ... without its arguments in that whole area.

The campaign for the legalization of contraception challenged a deeply held belief that saw sex purely as an instrument of procreation. Only after this change had been achieved could a discourse of sexual pleasure and non-reproductive relationships be validated. More radical organizations such as Irish Women United (IWU), founded in 1975, became the springboard for the formation of single-issue campaigning organizations like the Rape Crisis Centre (1977), the Contraception

Action Programme (1976), and Women's Right to Choose (1979). Irish lesbians, who first began to press for rights through the women's movement, broke away from the movement to form the Liberation of Irish Lesbians in 1978. Media coverage of the development of the incipient gay movements in Britain and the United States and the work of the fledging IGRM called into question Catholic teaching on a range of non-procreative sexual practices. This coverage alerted Catholics to arguments contradictory to the position laid out by the Catholic Church and communicated by columns such as Angela Macnamara's.

In Ireland the Catholic Church's teachings on sexuality had long remained unchallenged as the undisputed 'truth' about sexual deviation. One letter writer criticized Macnamara for advocating psychiatry. This letter of 10 January 1971 illustrates the conflict between traditional Catholic teachings and the rising power of the psychiatric profession in the field of sexual ethics:

> In your suggestion that a person suffering from depression see a doctor, I take it you have in mind a psychiatrist? I dispute that such a person has a role to play in a Christian community. It strikes me that psychiatrics set themselves up as purveyors of happiness and usurp, to some extent, the confessor. Perhaps it would be best to suggest a saintly priest be sought out. I'm inclined to think that what nowadays we like to call an illness is really a spiritual malaise.

There is also evidence that loved ones close to the person concerned about homosexuality were reluctant to accept the Catholic or psychiatric definition of them as disordered. Perhaps Irish gay men and their friends and family did not accept this advice passively but actively resisted efforts to promote psychiatric treatment. In one letter of 26 October 1975 a girlfriend grapples with reconciling the revelation of her boyfriend's homosexuality and her religious faith: 'I don't know whether it is a sin or not or what I should do in this situation ... He is good at his work and very kind to his people at home. I can't believe that he is a bad person.'

Sometimes the precise nature of the sexual problem referred to in the column is unclear. The effect is that Macnamara seemed to be speaking directly to an individual through the column and ignoring the wider readership. One letter writer wrote to Macnamara on 10 December 1972: 'For as long as I can remember I have had this habit ... I read in an American magazine that a woman had the same habit and she did really bad things ... I'm 15, please tell me if my problem can be cured.' Sometimes the problem was deemed too explicit to be discussed openly in the column. Macnamara's response to one letter on 2 April 1971 was as follows: 'Intimate problems like yours are quite unsuitable for publication. Please write privately.' At other times the nature of the problem is perhaps assumed to be understood by the broader readership. A letter of 21 January 1972 read: 'I am a man in my middle thirties who everybody might think is living an ordinary happy life. But secretly my life is most unhappy. I have suffered for years. Please ask some kind priest of your acquaintance to say a Mass for me that I may soon be living a holy, happy and normal life.'

Homosexuality would also benefit from the growth in a more liberal Irish sexual culture. Angela Macnamara's tone grew steadily more conciliatory in the late 1970s, especially when compared to the more uncompromising message that she had communicated to her readers in the 1960s and in the early 1970s. Her reply of 2 April 1978 to a mother distressed at the news of her son's homosexuality illustrates this message but also the strength of patriarchy in the Irish home and the genuine surprise that her gay son isn't lonely, unhappy, or crippled by guilt:

> Q. Our son is twenty one years of age and has just informed us that he is homosexual. We are horrified, I feel absolutely numb. His father's reaction was to tell him to leave home immediately. He has done this. I feel that it would have been impossible for us to go on having him at home and knowing this about him. At the same time I wonder if his father may have been too harsh. We've had quite a bit of trouble with this boy as he never settled to any one job since he left school. He seems quite happy in himself, knows other homosexual people and leads what seems to be an enjoyable social life. I'm so afraid he is doing wrong. What could we have done that caused this?

> A. In telling you that he has homosexual tendencies your son has been honest and has shared something that is very important in his life. For too long we have condemned out of hand the person whose sexual tendencies are not the norm ... However, the fact remains that there are many people who are this way and who lead lives of great integrity, responsibility and love ... I do hope now that you have had time to think about it you

will contact your son and assure him that your love for him is not conditional and you want him to know that home will always be home for him. You may feel that it is necessary to apologise for rejecting him in the way you did. It would be good to have a chat with your son. He may be unhappy with his situation and benefit from discussion with a counsellor. On the other hand he may have already discussed his situation, have accepted it and adjusted his life accordingly ... Hopefully accepting himself and with your acceptance he will now be able to put his mind to establishing himself in a career.

Inadvertently, Angela Macnamara's column had become a force for sexual change in Ireland. By refuting articles published by British magazines that spoke of a different truth about sexuality, Macnamara was responsible for new language that was incorporated into the debate taking place within the public sphere in Ireland. This discussion would also take place against a backdrop of creeping secularization in Ireland.

Liam Ryan, writing in 1983, stated that new Catholics had emerged 'who wish to remain within the Church, who are weekly Church goers but who question the Church's authority over their private lives'.[68] The human resources of the Church, so vital for its continued influence in education, health and other areas, would begin a steady decline. Between 1970 and 1995, Christian Brothers would suffer a decline in membership of 58 per cent, followed by Sisters at 35 per cent and Diocesan clergy falling by 7.2 per cent.[69] The political deference shown to the Catholic Church would also decline, facilitating the waning of a monopoly it once held over how sexuality was understood in Ireland.

CONCLUSION

Angela Macnamara's column represented a unique space within which to speak publicly about sexuality in Ireland in the 1960s and 1970s. The initial success of the column can be attributed to the changing media landscape throughout the 1960s, which recognized women as a specific constituency within the traditional Irish newspaper. Men also wrote to Macnamara, however, confused about their sexuality. Yet while Macnamara and *The Sunday Press* articulated a predictable reverence for the pronouncements of the Catholic Church and its bishops, it would be incorrect to view the column merely as a mouthpiece for Catholic social teaching. The language used by letter writers and by Macnamara herself revealed a combination of expert teaching on sexuality from both clergymen and psychiatrists, often competing with and contradicting each other in the search for the truth about homosexuality. There is no doubt that readers of the column used her advice in a similar way. The column gave men and women access to a language of sexuality that was not otherwise freely available in Ireland. The language of these 'experts' on sexuality eventually filtered back into lay discourse, transforming it and ultimately modernizing it. Readers of the column became as knowledgeable as these experts, lay or religious. They became more critical too, demanding advice that ran contrary to the Catholic social teaching upon which Macnamara had originally based the column. Macnamara also changed. Her replies on moral issues such as homosexuality and contraception changed, not as a result of any attempt to become as 'modern' as the Ireland around her but due to the exposure of debates within her family, the column, and wider media discussion of new social movements in Ireland.

NOTES

1. J. Weeks, *Coming Out: Homosexual Politics in Britain, from the Nineteenth Century to the Present* (London: Quartet Books, 1977), p.176.
2. Homosexuality was illegal under Sections 61 and 62 of the Offences Against the Persons Act 1861 and Section 11 of the Criminal Law Amendment Act 1885 which criminalized not just sodomy but a range of physical intimacies or 'gross indecencies' conducted exclusively between men. Ibid., pp.14–16.
3. 'Dear Angela', Radharc documentary first broadcast on 24 April 1975.
4. T. Inglis, *Moral Monopoly: The Rise and Fall of the Catholic Church in Modern Ireland* (Dublin: University College Dublin Press, 1998), p.43.
5. T. Fahey, 'Religion and Sexual Culture in Ireland', in F.X. Eder, L.A. Lally and G. Hekma, *Sexual Cultures in Europe: National Histories* (Manchester: Manchester University Press, 1999), pp.53–4.
6. M. Kenny, *Goodbye to Catholic Ireland* (Dublin: New Island Press, 2000), pp.236–7.
7. P. Ryan, 'Coming Out, Staying In: The Personal Narratives of Some Irish Gay Men', *Irish Journal of Sociology*, 12, 2 (2003), pp.68–85.
8. M. Nic Ghiolla Phádraig, 'Religion in Ireland: Preliminary Analysis', *Social Studies*, 5, 2 (1976), p.144.
9. M. Foucault, *The History of Sexuality: Volume 1: An Introduction* (London: Allen Lane, 1979), pp.61–2.
10. C. Hug, *The Politics of Sexual Morality in Ireland* (Basingstoke: Macmillan, 1999), p.207.
11. Sacred Congregation, *Persona Humana*, sec. 8.
12. C. Brinkgreve and M. Korzec, 'Feelings, Behaviour, Morals in the Netherlands, 1938–78: Analysis and Interpretation of an Advice Column', *The Netherlands Journal of Sociology*, 15, 2 (1979), p.125.
13. Ryan, *Coming Out, Staying In*, p.80.
14. Sacred Congregation, *Persona Humana*, sec. 8.
15. E. O'Kelly, *The Permissive Society in Ireland?* (Cork: Mercier Press, 1974), p.27.
16. Ibid., p.29.
17. Ryan, *Coming Out, Staying In*, p.77.
18. J.A. Mangan and J. Walvin, *Manliness and Morality: Middle Class Masculinity in Britain and America 1800–1940* (Manchester: Manchester University Press, 1987), p.14.

19. See J.M. Brohm, *Sport: A Prison of Measured Time* (London: Ink Links, 1978).
20. Foucault, *History of Sexuality*, p.5.
21. D. Keogh, *Edmund Rice 1762–1844* (Dublin: Four Courts Press, 1996), pp.97–8.
22. Inglis, *Moral Monopoly*, p.151.
23. J. Weeks, *Sexuality and its Discontents: Meanings, Myths and Modern Sexualities* (London: Routledge, 1985), p.84.
24. J. Weeks, 'Capitalism and the Organisation of Sex', in Gay Left Collective (ed.), *Homosexuality: Power and Politics* (London: Allison & Busby, 1988), p.15.
25. J. Ussher, *Women's Madness: Misogyny or Mental Illness?* (London: Harvester Wheatsheaf, 1991), p.74.
26. Foucault, *History of Sexuality, Volume 1*, p.65.
27. M. Finnane, 'Law and the Social uses of Asylum in Nineteenth Century Ireland', in D. Tomlinson and J. Carrier (eds), *Asylum in the Community* (London: Routledge, 1996), p.101.
28. P. Prior, 'The Appeal to Madness in Ireland', in Tomlinson and Carrier (eds), *Asylum in the Community*, p.83.
29. J. Weeks, 'The Construction of Homosexuality', in S. Seidman (ed.), *Queer Theory/Sociology* (Cambridge: Blackwell, 1996), p.51.
30. J. Gathorne-Hardy, *The Public School Phenomenon 597–1977* (London: Hodder & Stoughton, 1977), pp.88–9.
31. R. Barrington, *Health, Medicine and Politics in Ireland 1900–1970* (Dublin: Institute of Public Administration, 1987), p.15.
32. Ibid., p.148.
33. D. Ferriter, *The Transformation of Ireland, 1900–2000* (London: Profile Books, 2004), p.321.
34. L. Flynn, 'The Irish Supreme Court and the Constitution of Male Homosexuality', in D. Herman and C. Stychin (eds), *Legal Inversions: Lesbians, Gay Men and the Politics of the Law* (Philadelphia, PA: Temple University Press, 1995), pp.37–42.
35. Ibid., p.41.
36. 'Dear Angela'.
37. See M. O'Brien, *De Valera, Fianna Fáil and the Irish Press* (Dublin: Irish Academic Press, 2001), pp.87, 132.
38. P. Ryan, 'Coming Out of the Dark: A Decade of Gay Mobilisation in Ireland, 1970–80', in L. Connolly and N. Hourigan (eds), *Social Movements and Ireland* (Manchester University Press, 2006), p.89. See C. Harman, *The Fire Last Time: 1968 and After* (London: Bookmarks, 1998), pp.92–6, on European social unrest.
39. L. Connolly, *The Irish Women's Movement: From Revolution to Devolution* (Dublin: Lilliput Press, 2003), p.122.
40. D. Altman, 'What Changed in the Seventies?', in Gay Left Collective (ed.), *Homosexuality: Power and Politics* (London: Allison & Busby, 1980), p.54.
41. Ibid., p.57.
42. A. Melucci, *Challenging Codes: Collective Action in the Information Age* (Cambridge: Cambridge University Press, 1996), pp.298–9.
43. T. Gitlin, *The Whole World is Watching: Mass Media and the Making and Unmaking of the New Left* (Berkeley, CA: University of California Press, 1980).
44. Ryan, *Coming Out of the Dark*, p.94.
45. Ibid., p.95.
46. Ibid., p.95.
47. R.J. Savage, Jr, *Irish Television: The Political and Social Origins* (Cork: Cork University Press, 1996), p.xiii.
48. V. Freedman, *The Cities of David: The Life of David Norris* (Dublin: Basement Press, 1995), p.81.
49. P. Ryan, *Strangers In Their Own Land: The Everyday Lives of Irish Gay Men and Irish Society* (unpublished doctoral thesis, University College Dublin, 2005).
50. T. Inglis, 'Irish Civil Society: From Church to Media Domination', in T. Inglis, Z. Mach and R. Mazanek (eds), *Religion and Politics: East–West Contrasts from Contemporary Europe* (Dublin: University College Dublin Press, 2000), p.55.
51. Ibid., p.57.
52. T. Inglis, *Moral Monopoly: The Rise and Fall of the Catholic Church in Modern Ireland* (Dublin: University College Dublin Press, 1998), p.214.
53. Ibid., p.232.

54. R. Kearney, *On Stories* (London: Routledge, 2002), p.4.
55. S. O'Suilleabhain, *Storytelling in Irish Tradition* (Cork: Mercier Press, 1973).
56. K. Plummer, *Telling Sexual Stories: Power, Change and Social Worlds* (London: Routledge, 1995), p.54.
57. For examples of these stories, see Hall Carpenter Archives, *Walking after Midnight: Gay Men's Life Stories* (London: Routledge, 1989); J.P. Preston, *Hometowns: Gay Men Write About Where They Belong* (New York: Dutton, 1991); P.M. Nardi, D. Sanders and J. Marmor (eds), *Growing Up Before Stonewall: Life Stories of Some Gay Men* (London: Routledge, 1994).
58. K. Porter and J. Weeks, *Between the Acts: Lives of Homosexual Men 1885–1967* (London: Routledge, 1991), p.viii.
59. K. Rose, 'The Tenderness of the Peoples', in I. O'Carroll and E. Collins (eds), *Lesbian and Gay Visions of Ireland* (London: Cassell, 1995), p.72.
60. Dublin Castle was the seat of British administrative power in Ireland prior to independence in 1922. It was brought into disrepute in 1884 when James Ellis French, the chief of the Constabulary Detective Department, was dismissed for having sexual relationships with several junior male officers in the force. He was tried, along with the Secretary of Dublin Post Office, on indecent offences charges. The nationalist press, most notably the *United Ireland* newspaper, made much political capital through their misfortune, onto which it projected the corruption and immorality of the entire colonial presence in Ireland.
61. The European Court ruled in 1988 that Ireland, by refusing to recognize a right to homosexual privacy, was in contravention of the Convention on Human Rights that specifies that an individual's sexual life is part of private life under article 8. See C. Hug, *The Politics of Sexual Morality in Ireland* (Basingstoke: Macmillan, 1999), p.217.
62. G. O'Brien, *Coming Out: Irish Gay Experiences* (Dublin: Curragh Press, 2003).
63. Ibid., p.112.
64. Ibid., p.113. The Hirschfeld Centre was the headquarters of the National Gay Federation which was opened in Dublin in 1978.
65. M. Berman, *All That Is Solid Melts Into Air: The Experience of Modernity* (New York: Penguin, 1988), p.66.
66. Ibid., p.15.
67. A. Giddens, *Modernity and Self-Identity: Self and Society in the Late Modern Age* (Cambridge: Polity Press, 1991), p.5.
68. L. Ryan, 'Faith Under Survey' *The Furrow*, 34, 1 (1983), p.6.
69. Inglis, *Moral Monopoly*, p.212.

CHAPTER SEVEN

Writing our own Intimate Biographies

Rosanna Davison is an agony aunt. This young Irish woman won the Miss World competition in the Chinese city of Sanya in 2003. She was also, coincidentally, a student of mine when I lectured in University College Dublin (UCD). The daughter of singer Chris de Burgh, Davison has never left the tabloid headlines since becoming a regular feature on Dublin's social scene along with her long-term boyfriend, Wesley Quirke, heir to a fortune built upon slot machines and gaming arcades. Interestingly, in a radio interview Davison credits her sociology degree with bolstering her credentials as she imparts advice to the readers of her column in the *Evening Press* newspaper. 'I'm approaching it from an academic and a personal point of view', she explains in a radio interview.[1] 'My degree is in sociology from UCD so we studied what people do and why they do them.' Davison is an intelligent woman. But it is not her sociological insights on intimate life that her readers look forward to reading every Wednesday. She is a new kind of agony aunt who trades in celebrity. Readers want not her expert opinion or information that they themselves can't access by a click of a mouse; they want advice from someone they 'know' – this 'personal point of view'. What readers know of Davison is filtered through tabloid stories of her fast life as a model; of cavorting with property developers; of midnight trips to Marrakesh by private jet. The letters she receives are very symptomatic of twenty-first-century society. A young woman writes, worried that her boyfriend has become addicted to internet pornography, while another woman is pestered by her date from an online internet dating site, who turned out to be much older than he had previously admitted.[2] A 23-year-old woman writes that she is being pressurized to have Botox; another young woman feels pressure to make a sex tape with her boyfriend.[3]

The era of the agony aunt as personified by someone like Angela Macnamara is over. Macnamara's power lay in the monopoly of information about sex that she held over a section of the population, particularly in 1960's Ireland. The prevalence of ignorance about often the most basic facts of life, upon which this monopoly was based, had declined. Macnamara can certainly take some credit for the decline. The lens through which Angela Macnamara viewed her readers' problems – the social teaching of the Catholic Church – had similarly lost much of its power over how its members conducted their intimate lives. It was this recognition that led her editor, Vincent Jennings, to cancel the column in 1980. The creeping individualization that Macnamara had warned her readers against embracing had arrived. Decisions governing personal life were increasingly motivated by the search for self-fulfilment and less by the obligations of families, communities or religions. This development was encouraged by the greater proliferation of magazines and newspapers that further redefined the priorities within relationships. There was a concentration on individual fulfilment within relationships and a search for an elusive balance between love, intimacy and sex. Crucially, it is difficult to assess whether this increasing 'talk' about fulfilment translated into relationships that were actually happier. Did greater discussion about techniques promising heightened sexual pleasure deliver the orgasms for women in the 1980s that proved so elusive for women a decade before? My analysis of the letters to Macnamara does not allow an insight into how people acted upon the information they received. The analysis of the men's stories in the book does reveal that greater discussion of sexuality did improve marital relationships but only when the information was available to them from the beginning of the courtship. All the men agreed that once a pattern of sexual behaviour had become established, it was almost impossible to change it, no matter what new information became available to the couple on how to maximize their sexual pleasure.

THE LAYPERSON AS EXPERT

While Angela Macnamara understood the demise of her column in 1980 as evidence of a greater secularization, I argue that it was also the result of the declining power of 'expert' voices, a by-product of infor-malization within society. For Cas Wouters a consequence of informal-ization is a declining gap between leaders and the led, between experts and lay audiences.[4] Armed with greater information acquired through an expanding education system, once the preserve of the middle classes, or through reading a wider range of publications now available in Ireland, more laypeople were now ready to challenge authority. It was a challenge that would manifest itself in several ways. Parents stopped their deferential behaviour to the schoolmaster that I discussed in Chapter 5.

The priest's opinion, while often sought on matters of sexual intimacy, was now just one opinion among many. People became more confident in devising a more individualized code of moral ethics which was further negotiated within dating and married relationships. People became their own experts. Ironically, the column contributed to a collective sense of identity – as people recognized that their unconventional doubts, feelings and desires were held by others – and emboldened some to embrace that individuality. It was an individuality that was fostered by a changing social environment where more private transport and holidays facilitated greater privacy, where relationships were freer from familial surveillance. The growing informality between couples encouraged the adoption of a new language of intimacy based on self-disclosure of sexual and emotional wants and needs. The wider availability of contraception enabled them to enjoy a new intimacy too, that of physical touch. No longer was Ireland a nation deprived of this physical intimacy, a nation where couples, principally women, withdrew from their partners, fearing that touch would be interpreted as a sexual invitation that held the potential consequence of an unwanted pregnancy. This opened up a different intimate experience from that charted by Wouters in his study of four European countries where legislative measures in the fields of contraception, homosexuality and divorce contributed to different stories being told. It was not just within sexually intimate relationships that there was an absence of physical touch. The life history interviews recall men who grew up within families devoid of physical intimacy. No hugs and no kisses goodbye as they headed off to school. For James Kelly (70), kissing his mother for the first time on the day he got married was not an unusual occurrence in 1960's Ireland. Nor was it much different a decade later. As a child growing up in a loving family in the 1970s and 1980s, physical displays of affection were conspicuous by their absence.

The 1980s did not herald a period of emotional enlightenment. Macnamara's hope, when embarking upon her column, was that a generation of young people would enter adolescence and adulthood armed with greater knowledge about sexuality. It was a mission that was largely unfulfilled when the column came to a close in 1980. There would also be stark reminders of times past. Teenager Ann Lovett's death in 1984 as she gave birth to a child she had concealed, alone in the Church grounds in Granard, Co. Longford, revealed the continued existence of a society starved of both sexual education and the ability to exercise compassion to those deemed to have sexually transgressed.

The forensic investigation of Joanne Hayes's sexual life, the same year as Lovett's death, as part of a tribunal established to investigate allegations of false arrest for the murder of her baby and police brutality continued this tradition. In Ireland, as Tom Inglis starkly points out, 'the discovery of dead, new-born babies is a frequent occurrence'.[5] These events were preceded by a divisive campaign to place a ban on abortion within the Irish constitution; although passed, its ambiguous wording led to four further constitutional amendments.

TELLING ALTERNATIVE STORIES

The men's life stories in this book constitute a significant contribution to telling alternative stories about intimate life in Ireland. They represent a missing piece in our understanding. There has been, quite rightly, a concentration on the stories of women or those men marginalized by their location within a subordinate masculinity. My previous work has contributed to these stories, in telling the complexity within the coming-out stories of Irish gay men in the 1970s.[6] These stories struggled to be told within a dominant narrative of sexual repression in Ireland. There is also complexity within men's stories of what Raewyn Connell identifies as hegemonic masculinity.[7] These stories have similarly been subsumed under this narrative that has contributed to an understanding of Irish masculinity as emotionally distant, unromantic and lacking in physical intimacy. The understanding has been bolstered by an essentialism that went unchallenged at the time. It wasn't challenged in the column where Angela Macnamara warns newly-wed brides to expect an end to the attentive behaviour that marked their husbands' often romantic courtships. Catholic dating advice concurred. Men by their *nature* felt restless in the home and needed diversions offered by the worlds of work and homo-social entertainment – diversions women should not compete with. This sowed the seeds of anger among many women who felt misled, overworked and unloved. It was, however, behaviour that many women, revealed in the men's stories, would not countenance accepting in their marriages.

This book complicates stories that have been previously thought of as uncomplicated within this narrative of repression. It facilitates a gaze inside the relationships of observant Catholics who held the teachings and leaders of their Church in high esteem. It allows us to understand the ways in which these 'trend followers' did not passively follow the teachings of their Church without a process of contestation and negotiation that drew information from wider debates within the public sphere. The book inserts this dimension of agency into our understanding of intimate lives and shows greater creativity in the face of a seemingly overwhelming bulwark of religious and State repression of desire.

Angela Macnamara was a case in point. Behind a public facade of unquestioning loyalty to the teaching of the Catholic Church, she too, like many Catholics, had questions and doubts about the Church's ability to guide a generation of the faithful through a period of tumultuous change in Ireland. The impact of the Catholic Church's continued prohibition on contraception, particularly for married couples, contributed to a weakening of the Church's authority over the intimate lives of their flock, accelerating a process of individualization that facilitated the emergence of what Liam Ryan, quoted in Chapter 6, described as a 'new Catholic'.[8]

Ireland was in the midst of an intimate flux: a nation in transition. This book allows us to see these processes acted out within intimate relationships over a seventeen-year period. In conjunction with the life histories it offers a more multidimensional understanding of what was happening within intimate life in Ireland. It is an understanding that illustrates a relational dimension of sex roles within the kitchen and the bedroom. These insights have been all too rare in the field of intimate life. The life histories are not presented as an antidote to the stories written in the column. Documentary research is not merely the sanitized official account that requires interviews to *really* understand what went on within relationships so that this account can be disproved. This has not been my approach in the book. The men's stories that have been included represent readers of the Angela Macnamara column who shared similar religious beliefs and often experienced the same anxiety as letter writers to the column as they managed their intimate relationships while dating, within marriage or as parents. They often show, for example, an abdication of responsibility in the areas of family planning and in early child rearing similar to the complaints of women published in *The Sunday Press*. The stories reveal men who were simultaneously attentive, aloof, romantic, emotional, distant, intimate, feckless, strategic, oversexed and kind. The stories are a somewhat 'open, messy and fragmented' representation of intimate life and I believe they are a more accurate reflection of the complex, uneven and often irrational intimate biographies we construct for ourselves over a lifetime.[9] Significantly, they illustrate alternative understandings of what constituted romance and intimacy in the 1960's. When we privilege this diversity in emotional experience, men cease to be prisoners of the past and can recast their own emotional biographies into the future.

ALTERNATIVE UNDERSTANDINGS OF ROMANCE

The life histories revealed that men rejected what was often described by them as 'hallmark romance' which was to become prevalent in contemporary Irish society. Patrick McGrath (75) told me a story about his parents' marriage. It at first appeared to be a story straight out of Arensberg and Kimball's rural Ireland of the 1930s. In public, the couple appeared to be physically distant from each other, occupying different spheres of the house and farm, exercising a jurisdiction over distinct worlds. Yet each week, as Patrick's father made his way to town for the mart, he would return with a small gift or token for his wife. A scarf, a pair of gloves or a small piece of jewellery was purchased. This was romance. It wasn't romance unfettered, though. The life history stories revealed how their romance was reined in by economics, dampened down by family approval and accelerated by fears of loneliness and growing older.[10] Romance was understood by some in this study as a form of chivalry. Romance was respect or kindness. Importantly, romance was something that was *done*, not *spoken*. Modern society was increasingly demanding that emotional life, like romance, should be spoken. It was premised upon a requirement of mutual self-disclosure within relationships and the men in this book struggled with these new conventions of intimate life. Recall the story of James Kelly (70) in Chapter 5, whose conversations with his son, now living in the United States, were restricted to the instrumental – his son's work, his job – and then the phone was passed to his wife who did the 'emotion' work. It was only upon the break-up of his son's marriage that father and son, for the first time, spoke about affairs of the heart. It is often in times of great trauma that we are forced to give voice to our needs and fears. This brings me back to the first chapter and my own difficulty in speaking emotionally about my illness. Throughout my recuperation and recovery I continued to struggle to find this voice. Those of us who lack the fluency to speak openly of love communicate by other means. During my own recuperation it was often spoken through time spent, meals cooked or dogs walked.

WHAT DO STORIES OF THE PAST TELL US ABOUT THE PRESENT?

The analysis of the letters written to Angela Macnamara contributes knowledge to an overall story we have as yet only partial knowledge of or access to. It fits into a tapestry of knowledge to which others, including sociologists, historians and political scientists have contributed. Each generation believes itself to be more sexually progressive than the last. To fully understand intimate life in contemporary Ireland we must look to the stories of the past or we remain destined to repeat the same mistakes, perpetuating the same anxieties within intergenerational conflict. Nowhere is that conflict more keenly felt that in the realm of intimate life. The analysis of the column reveals families grappling with some very familiar problems of modern life. Parents are outraged by their daughters heading out to dances in clothes they deem to be too revealing. Parents negotiate greater autonomy with their adolescent children as they become more economically independent, making choices in education, careers and relationships that will shape their lives. Parents struggle to accept that their values and life choices may not be embraced by their children. The personal problems that are told in the column also provide a mirror in which to examine the wider structural changes that were occurring in Irish society at the time. We learn much about the rise and fall of the institutional power of the Catholic Church. We learn about urbanization and family structure. We learn about increasing levels of wealth and the culture of consumerism. I have argued that while individuals were attempting to solve their private problems in a public forum such as Angela Macnamara's column, they were shaping the context in which those problems were being discussed. The discussion within the Macnamara column reflected a broader contestation of values right across Irish society. Those like Macnamara saw it as their duty to defend society against what she deemed as 'convention breakers' within intimate life, and to robustly defend the traditional Catholic values of 'trend followers'. It is here we see the dual purpose of the Angela Macnamara column. It operated at an individual level, educating the sexually ignorant and guiding back the faithful who had sexually transgressed to a more righteous path, often through mediation with a member of the clergy or psychiatric profession. The column also operated at a larger societal level. It represented a general deterrence perspective to the readership of *The Sunday Press*, full of cautionary tales about the perils of the permissive society. Britain, particularly, was held as an example of such a society that had lost its moral compass through its embrace of abortion, legalized homosexuality and the availability of contraception for single people. Such a deterrence approach was similar to Catholic dating advice in the US. When deterrence proved unsuccessful, the column and Christian Counsel were part of a network of lay Catholic organizations that offered advice and referrals to like-minded bodies. Pregnant unmarried women were referred by Macnamara to the Catholic Protection and Rescue Society, for example, and advised against travelling to England to seek help on adoption or abortion. It was advice and information that most observant Catholics who wrote to Macnamara would have wished to receive. We learned in Chapter 6 from the story of 'Sean', sent to a Redemptorist priest to discuss his homosexuality, that he viewed the advice he received to be compassionate and wise.

It is again within these 'private' exchanges that we glimpse Ireland's structural transformation from a traditional, Catholic, rural society to a modern, secular, urban one. It is within the life history stories that we better understand how men, particularly, often exhibited characteristics of both societies in transition. Macnamara herself is a perfect example of how the lived experiences of one's own life and the exposure to the lives of others can alter the way in which the institutional teaching of the Catholic Church is understood. The stories of gays and lesbians, for example, emerged from behind religious and medical categories of condemnation and pathology to reveal ordinary sons or daughters often struggling with guilt, confusion or familial rejection.

It is this more nuanced understanding of Angela Macnamara, in both her column and her private life, that emerges from this book. She is easily dismissed as a conservative firebrand, upholding a regime of Catholic dating advice under siege from alternative messages that placed a premium on the individual pursuit of pleasure, happiness and consumption. When describing her views in a newspaper interview as 'middle of the road', she was correct.[11] There was a large body of Catholic opinion at the time of the column's publication on the political right, which was uncompromising in its enforcement of Catholic social teaching regardless of the pain or suffering its followers endured. It was this same strand of Catholic thinking that had remained suspicious of the Macnamara column for allowing people to speak for themselves on matters of sexuality and its intersection with their religious faith.

Ultimately, Angela Macnamara's column will be remembered for being one of the few sources of sexual information in Ireland, especially during the 1960s. It provided both information and titillation to an audience eager to read of the sexual and emotional lives of others. Her contribution to how sexuality was spoken about, and the religious framework within which it should be understood, has contributed to her status as one of the most influential lay Catholics of her generation. Her legacy also has had unintended consequences. The discussion of sexuality within her column may have educated some, but it also mobilized and angered others, those who felt that their beliefs, experiences and feelings were marginalized within a narrow conception of what it was to be Catholic and sexual in Ireland. The column entered the mix of what would become an increasingly crowded terrain of competing explanations on how to live an intimate life that was emotional, moral and sexually fulfilled. By speaking openly of sexuality, Angela Macnamara's column has become part of the tapestry that is the history of Irish sexuality and, curiously perhaps, part of its modernization.

NOTES

1. Hear the full interview at http://www.rte.ie/radio1/thejohnmurrayshow/2010-10-13.html.
2. *Evening Herald*, 9 February 2011; 13 March 2011.
3. *Evening Herald*, 23 March 2011; 3 November 2011.
4. C. Wouters, *Sex and Manners: Female Emancipation in the West 1890–2000* (London: Sage, 2004), pp.1–2.
5. T. Inglis, *Lessons in Irish Sexuality* (Dublin: University College Dublin Press, 1998), p.1.
6. P. Ryan, 'Coming Out, Staying In: The Personal Narratives of Some Irish Gay Men', *Irish Journal of Sociology*, 12, 2 (2003), pp.68–85.
7. R.W. Connell, *Masculinities* (Cambridge: Polity Press, 1995), pp.78–9.
8. L. Ryan, 'Faith Under Survey', *The Furrow*, 34, 1 (1983), p.6.
9. The calls for more 'messy' representations are reviewed in A. Coffey, B. Holbrook and P. Atkinson, 'Qualitative Data Analysis: Technologies and Representations', *Sociological Research Online*, 1, 1, (1996), at http://www.socresonline.org.uk/1/1/4.html.
10. I presented a paper at the Sociological Association of Ireland Annual Conference in 2011 on the decision-making process men engaged in whilst considering marriage during the 1960s and 1970s. Read about the paper in the *Irish Times*, 10 May 2011, at http://www.irishtimes.com/newspaper/health/2011/0510/1224296591347.html.
11. *Sunday Press*, 24 January 1971.

References

Allen, K., *Fianna Fáil and Irish Labour* (London: Pluto Press, 1997).

Altman, D., 'What Changed in the Seventies?', in Gay Left Collective (ed.), *Homosexuality: Power and Politics* (London: Allison & Busby, 1980), pp.52–63.

Arensberg, C.M. and Kimball, S.T., *Family and Community in Ireland* (Cambridge, MA: Harvard University Press, 1968).

Atkinson, P. and Coffey, A., 'Analysing Documentary Realities', in D. Silverman (ed.), *Qualitative Research: Theory, Method and Practice* (London: Sage, 2004), pp.56–75.

Baggot, P.A., *Unspoken Problems of Married Life* (Dublin: Irish Messenger Office, 1965).

Barrington, R., *Health, Medicine and Politics in Ireland 1900–1970* (Dublin: Institute of Public Administration, 1987).

Bauman, Z., *The Individualized Society* (Cambridge: Polity Press, 2001).

Beck, U., *Risk Society: Towards a New Modernity* (London: Routledge, 1992).

Beck, U. and Beck-Gernsheim, E., *The Normal Chaos of Love* (Cambridge: Polity Press, 1995).

Beck-Gernsheim, E., *Reinventing the Family: In Search of New Lifestyles* (Cambridge: Polity Press, 2002).

Berman, M., *All That Is Solid Melts Into Air: The Experience of Modernity* (New York: Penguin, 1988).

Bourke, J., *Working-Class Cultures in Britain, 1890–1960: Gender, Class and Ethnicity* (London: Routledge, 1994).

Brandth, B. and Kvande, E., 'Masculinity and Child Care: The Reconstruction of Fathering', *Sociological Review*, 46, 2 (1998), pp.293–313.

Brannen, J. and Nilsen, A., 'From Fatherhood to Fathering: Transmission and Change among British Fathers in Four-Generational Families', *Sociology*, 40, 2 (2006), pp.335–52.

Brannen, J., Dodd, K., Oakley, A. and Storey, P., *Young People, Health and Family Life* (Buckingham: Open University Press, 1994).

Breen, R., Hannan, D.F., Rottman, D.B. and Whelan, C.T.,

Understanding Contemporary Ireland: State, Class and Development in the Republic of Ireland (Dublin: Gill & Macmillan, 1990).

Brinkgreve, C. and Korzec, M., 'Feelings, Behaviours, Morals in the Netherlands, 1938–78: Analysis and Interpretation of an Advice Column', *The Netherlands Journal of Sociology*, 15, 2 (1979), pp.123–40.

Brody, H., *Inishkillane: Change and Decline in the West of Ireland* (Harmondsworth: Penguin, 1973).

Brohm, J.M., *Sport: A Prison of Measured Time* (London: Ink Links, 1978).

Brown, T., *Ireland: A Social and Cultural History* (London: Harper Perennial, 2004).

Browne, B., *Against the Tide* (Dublin: Gill & Macmillan, 1986).

Bulcroft, K., Bulcroft, R., Smeins, L. and Cranage, H., 'The Social Construction of the North American Honeymoon, 1880–1995', *Journal of Family History*, 22, 4 (1997), pp.462–90.

Burgess, E.W. and Locke, H.L., *The Family: From Institution to Companionship* (New York: American Book Company, 1945).

Cancian, F.M., *Love in America: Gender and Self-Development* (Cambridge: Cambridge University Press, 1987).

Cancian, F.M. and Gordon, S.L., 'Changing Emotion Norms in Marriage: Love and Anger in US Women's Magazines since 1900', *Gender and Society*, 2, 3 (1998), pp.308–42.

Castellain-Meunier, C., 'The Place of Fatherhood and the Parental Role: Tensions, Ambivalence and Contradictions', *Current Sociology*, 50, 2, (2002), pp.185–201.

Clancy, P., 'Education in the Republic of Ireland: The Project of Modernity', in P. Clancy, S. Drudy, K. Lynch and L. O'Dowd (eds), *Irish Society: Sociological Perspectives* (Dublin: Institute of Public Administration, 1995), pp.467–94.

Clear, C., 'Women in de Valera's Ireland 1932–48: A Reappraisal', in G. Doherty and D. Keogh (eds), *De Valera's Irelands* (Cork: Mercier Press, 2003), pp.104–31.

Coffey, A., Holbrook, B. and Atkinson, P., 'Qualitative Data Analysis: Technologies and Representations', *Sociological Research Online*, 1, 1 (1996), at http://www.socresonline.org.uk/1/1/4.html.

Connell, R.W., *Masculinities* (Cambridge: Polity Press, 1995).

Connery, D.S., *The Irish* (London: Eyre & Spottiswoode, 1968).

Connolly, L., *The Irish Women's Movement: From Revolution to Devolution* (Dublin: Lilliput Press, 2003).

Connolly, L. and Hourigan, N. (eds), *Social Movements and Ireland* (Manchester: Manchester University Press, 2006).

Dennis, N., Henriques, F. and Slaughter, C., *Coal is our Life: An Analysis of a Yorkshire Mining Community* (London: Eyre & Spottiswoode, 1956).

Doherty, E., *Matt Talbot* (Combermere: Madonna House Publications, 2001).

Dufoyer, P., *Building a Happy Marriage* (London: Burns & Oats, 1962).

Dufoyer, P., *Marriage: A Word to Young Men* (New York: P.J. Kennedy & Sons, 1963).

Egan, R.D. and Hawkes, G.L., 'Imperiled and Perilous: Exploring the History of Childhood Sexuality', *Journal of Historical Sociology*, 21, 4 (2008), pp.355–67.

Elias, N., *The Civilizing Process: The History of Manners and State Formation and Civilization* (Oxford: Blackwell, 1994).

Encyclical of Pope Paul VI on the Regulation of the Faith, *Humanae Vitae* (Vatican City: Tipografia Poliglotta Vaticana, 1968).

Evans, M., *Love: An Unromantic Discussion* (Cambridge: Polity Press, 2003).

Fahey, T., 'Religion and Sexual Culture in Ireland', in F.X. Eder, L.A. Lally and G. Hekma (eds), *Sexual Cultures in Europe: National Histories* (Manchester: Manchester University Press, 1999), pp.53–70.

Farson, R., *Birthrights* (Harmondsworth: Penguin, 1974).

Fennell, N., *Irish Marriage How Are You?* (Cork: Mercier Press, 1974).

Ferriter, D., *A Nation of Extremes: The Pioneers in Twentieth-Century Ireland* (Dublin: Irish Academic Press, 1999).

Ferriter, D., *The Transformation of Ireland, 1900–2000* (London: Profile Books, 2004).

Ferriter, D., *Occasions of Sin: Sex and Society in Modern Ireland* (London: Profile Books, 2009).

Finnane, M., 'Law and the Social Uses of Asylum in Nineteenth Century Ireland', in D. Tomlinson and J. Carrier (eds), *Asylum in the Community* (London: Routledge, 1996), pp.91–110.

Firestone, S., *The Dialectic of Sex: The Case for Feminist Revolution* (London: Women's Press, 1979).

Flynn, L., 'The Irish Supreme Court and the Constitution of Male Homosexuality', in D. Herman and C. Stychin (eds), *Legal Inversions: Lesbians, Gay Men and the Politics of the Law* (Philadelphia, PA: Temple University Press, 1995), pp.29–45.

Foster, R.K., *Modern Ireland 1600–1972* (London: Penguin, 1988).

Foucault, M., *The History of Sexuality, Volume 1: An Introduction* (London: Allen Lane, 1979).

Freedman, V., *The Cities of David: The Life of David Norris* (Dublin: Basement Press, 1995).

Fuller, L., *Irish Catholicism since 1950: The Undoing of a Culture* (Dublin: Gill & Macmillan, 2002).

Garvin, T., *Preventing the Future: Why Was Ireland So Poor For So Long?* (Dublin: Gill & Macmillan, 2004).

Gathorne-Hardy, J., *The Public School Phenomenon 597–1977* (London: Hodder & Stoughton, 1977).

Gibbons, L., 'From Kitchen Sink to Soap', in M. Mcloone and J. MacMahon (eds), *Television and Irish Society: 21 years of Irish Television* (Dublin: RTÉ/IFI, 1984), pp.21–51.

Giddens, A., *Modernity and Self-Identity: Self and Society in the Late Modern Age* (Cambridge: Polity Press, 1991).

Giddens, A., *The Transformation of Intimacy: Sexuality, Love and Eroticism in Modern Societies* (Stanford, CA: Stanford University Press, 1992).

Giddens, A., *The Third Way: The Renewal of Social Democracy* (Cambridge: Polity Press, 1998).

Giroux, H.A., *Stealing Innocence: Youth, Corporate Power, and the Politics of Culture* (New York: St Martin's Press, 2000).

Gitlin, T., *The Whole World is Watching: Mass Media and the Making and Unmaking of the New Left* (Berkeley, CA: University of California Press, 1980).

Gross, N., 'The Detraditionalization of Intimacy Reconsidered', *Sociological Theory*, 23, 3 (2005), pp.286–311.

Hall Carpenter Archives, *Walking after Midnight: Gay Men's Life Stories* (London: Routledge, 1989).

Hannon, D.F. and Katsiaouni, L., *Traditional Families? From Culturally Prescribed to Negotiated Roles in Farm Families* (Dublin: ESRI, 1997).

Harman, C., *The Fire Last Time: 1968 and After* (London: Bookmarks, 1998).

Hesketh, T., *The Second Partitioning of Ireland: The Abortion Referendum of 1983* (Dublin: Brandsma Books, 1990).

Hilliard, B., 'The Catholic Church and Married Women's Sexuality: Habitus Change in Late 20th Century Ireland', *Irish Journal of Sociology*, 12, 2 (2003), pp.28–49.

Hilliard, B., 'Motherhood, Sexuality and the Catholic Church', in P. Kennedy (ed.), *Motherhood in Ireland* (Cork: Mercier Press, 2004), pp.64–76.

Hilliard, B., *Micro-Processes of Social Change: Aspects of Family Life in Late Twentieth Century Ireland* (unpublished doctoral thesis, University College Dublin, 2010).

Holt, J., *Escape from Childhood: The Needs and Rights of Children* (Harmondsworth: Penguin, 1974).

Horgan, J., *Sean Lemass: The Enigmatic Patriot* (Dublin: Gill & Macmillan, 1997).

Hug, C., *The Politics of Sexual Morality in Ireland* (Basingstoke: Macmillan, 1999).

Hulbert, A., *Raising America: Experts, Parents and a Century of Advice about Children* (New York: Alfred A. Knopf, 2003).

Humphreys, A.J., *Urbanization and the Irish Family* (London: Routledge & Kegan Paul, 1966).

Inglis, T., *Lessons in Irish Sexuality* (Dublin: University College Dublin Press, 1998).

Inglis, T., *Moral Monopoly: The Rise and Fall of the Catholic Church in Modern Ireland* (Dublin: University College Dublin Press, 1998).

Inglis, T., 'Irish Civil Society: From Church to Media Domination', in T. Inglis, Z. Mach and R. Mazanek (eds), *Religion and Politics: East–West Contrasts from Contemporary Europe* (Dublin: University College Dublin Press, 2000), pp.49–67.

Inglis, T., *Truth, Power and Lies: Irish Society and the Case of the Kerry Babies* (Dublin: University College Dublin Press, 2004).

Jamieson, L., *Intimacy: Personal Relationships in Modern Societies* (Cambridge: Polity Press, 1998).

Jamieson, L., 'Intimacy Transformed? A Critical look at the "Pure Relationship"', *Sociology*, 33, 3 (1999), pp.479–81.

Kanin, E.J. and Howard, D.H., 'Postmarital Consequences of Premarital Sex Adjustments', *American Sociological Review*, 23, 5 (1958), pp.556–62.

Kearney, R., *On Stories* (London: Routledge, 2002).

Kelly, G.A., *Dating for Young Catholics* (London: Robert Hale, 1963).

Kenny, M., *Goodbye to Catholic Ireland* (Dublin: New Island Press, 2000).

Kent, R., *Aunt Agony Advises: Problem Pages through the Ages* (London: W.H. Allen, 1987).

Keogh, D., *Edmund Rice 1762–1844* (Dublin: Four Courts Press, 1996).

Lassonde, S., 'Age and Authority: Adult–Child Relations during the Twentieth Century in the United States', *Journal of the History of Childhood and Youth*, 1, 1 (2008), pp.95–105.

Lee, J.J., *Ireland 1912–1985: Politics and Society* (Cambridge: Cambridge University Press, 1989).

Lindquist Dorr, L., 'The Perils of the Back Seat: Date Rape, Race and

Gender in 1950s America', *Gender and History*, 20, 1 (2008), pp.27–47.

Lord, Rev. D.A., *M is for Marriage and More* (Dublin: Catholic Truth Society, 1962).

Lupton, D., *The Emotional Self* (London: Sage, 1998).

Macnamara, A., *How to Choose a Wife* (Dublin: Redemptorist Publications, 1967).

Macnamara, A., *When to Give Sex Instruction* (Dublin: Redemptorist Publications, 1968).

Macnamara, A., *Living and Loving* (Dublin: Veritas, 1969).

Macnamara, A., *Ready, Steady, Grow!* (Dublin: Veritas, 1996).

Macnamara, A., *Will Our Children Build Healthy Relationships?* (Dublin: Veritas, 1999).

Macnamara, A., *Yours Sincerely* (Dublin: Veritas, 2003).

Macnamara, A., *Reflections for the Golden Years* (Dublin, Veritas, 2005).

Mangan, J.A. and Walvin, J., *Manliness and Morality: Middle Class Masculinity in Britain and America 1800–1940* (Manchester: Manchester University Press, 1987).

Mansfield, P. and Collard, J., *The Beginning of the Rest of your Life? A Portrait of Newly-Wed Marriage* (Basingstoke: Macmillan, 1988).

McCourt, H., *Oh How We Danced* (Derry: Guildhall Press, 1992).

McElhone, P., *When the Honeymoon is Over* (Dublin: Veritas, 1977).

McEwan, I., *On Chesil Beach* (London: Jonathan Cape, 2007).

McRobbie, A., *Postmodernism and Popular Culture* (London: Routledge, 1994).

Melucci, A., *Challenging Codes: Collective Action in the Information Age* (Cambridge: Cambridge University Press, 1996).

Messenger, J.C., *Inis Beag: Isle of Ireland* (Prospect Heights, IL: Waveland Press, 1969).

Miley, J., *A Voice for the Country: 50 years of Macra na Feirme* (Dublin: Macra na Feirme, 1994).

Mills, C.W., *The Sociological Imagination* (New York: Oxford University Press, 1959).

Nardi, P.M., Sanders, D. and Marmor, J. (eds), *Growing Up Before Stonewall: Life Stories of Some Gay Men* (London: Routledge, 1994).

Nic Ghiolla Phádraig, M., 'Religion in Ireland: Preliminary Analysis', *Social Studies*, 5, 2 (1976), pp.113–80.

O'Brien, G., *Coming Out: Irish Gay Experiences* (Dublin: Curragh Press, 2003).

O'Brien, M., *De Valera, Fianna Fáil and the Irish Press* (Dublin: Irish Academic Press, 2001).

O'Dea, P., *Dear Frankie* (Dublin: Mentor Press, 1998).

O'Kelly, E., *The Permissive Society in Ireland?* (Cork: Mercier Press, 1974).

O'Suilleabhain, S., *Storytelling in Irish Tradition* (Cork: Mercier Press, 1973).

Plummer, K., *Telling Sexual Stories: Power, Change and Social Worlds* (London: Routledge, 1995).

Porter, K. and Weeks, J., *Between the Acts: Lives of Homosexual Men 1885–1967* (London: Routledge, 1991).

Posner, P.A., *Sex and Reason* (Cambridge, MA: Harvard University Press, 1992).

Power, V., *Send 'em home sweatin': The Showbands' Story* (Dublin: Kildanore Press, 1990).

Preston, J.P., *Hometowns: Gay Men Write About Where They Belong* (New York: Dutton, 1991).

Prior, P., 'The Appeal to Madness in Ireland', in D. Tomlinson and J. Carrier (eds), *Asylum in the Community* (London: Routledge, 1996, pp.67–89.

Radway, J., *Reading the Romance: Women, Patriarchy and Popular Literature* (Chapel Hill, NC: University of North Carolina Press, 1984).

Rogers, A., 'Chaos to Control: Men's Magazines and the Mastering of Intimacy', *Men and Masculinities*, 8, 2 (2005), pp.175–94.

Rohan, D., *Marriage Irish Style* (Cork: Mercier Press, 1969).

Rose, K., 'The Tenderness of the Peoples', in I. O'Carroll and E. Collins (eds), *Lesbian and Gay Visions of Ireland* (London: Cassell, 1995), pp.71–85.

Ryan, L., 'Faith Under Survey', *The Furrow*, 34, 1 (1983), pp.3–15.

Ryan, J. and Ryan, M., *Love and Sexuality* (Dublin: M.H. Gill & Son, 1968).

Ryan, P., 'Coming Out, Staying In: The Personal Narratives of Some Irish Gay Men', *Irish Journal of Sociology*, 12, 2 (2003), pp.68–85.

Ryan, P., *Strangers In Their Own Land: The Everyday Lives of Irish Gay Men and Irish Society* (unpublished doctoral thesis, University College Dublin, 2005).

Ryan, P., 'Coming Out of the Dark: A Decade of Gay Mobilisation in Ireland, 1970–80', in L. Connolly and N. Hourigan (eds), *Social Movements and Ireland* (Manchester: Manchester University Press, 2006), pp.86–105.

Ryan, P., 'Researching Irish Gay Male Lives: Reflections on Disclosure and Intellectual Autobiography in the Production of Personal Narratives', *Qualitative Research*, 6, 2 (2006), pp.151–68.

Sacred Congregation for the Doctrine of the Faith, Persona Humana: Declarations on Certain Questions Concerning Sexual Ethics (Vatican City: Tipografia Poliglotta Vaticana, 1975).

Savage, Jr, R.J., *Irish Television: The Political and Social Origins* (Cork: Cork University Press, 1996).

Scheper-Hughes, N., *Saints, Scholars and Schizophrenics: Mental Illness in Rural Ireland* (Berkeley, CA: University of California Press, 1979).

Scott, SJ, M.J., *Courtship and Marriage: Practical Talks to Young Men and Women* (Dublin: Office of the Irish Messenger, 1934).

Seidman, S., 'Constructing Sex as a Domain of Pleasure and Self-Expression: Sexual Ideology in the Sixties', *Theory, Culture & Society*, 6, 2 (1989), pp.293–315.

Seidman, S., *Romantic Longings: Love in America 1830–1980* (London: Routledge, 1991).

Seidman, S., *Embattled Eros: Sexual Politics and Ethics in Contemporary America* (New York: Routledge, 1992).

Smith, J.M., The Politics of Sexual Knowledge: The Origins of Ireland's Containment Culture and the Carrigan Report (1931)', *Journal of the History of Sexuality*, 13, 2 (2004), pp.208–33.

Smyth, E., 'Labour Market Structures and Women's Employment in the Republic of Ireland', in A. Byrne and M. Leonard (eds), *Women and Irish Society: A Sociological Reader* (Belfast: Beyond the Pale Publications, 1997), pp.67–80.

Solomon, Y., Warin, J., Lewis, C. and Langford, W., 'Intimate Talk between Parents and their Teenage Children: Democratic Openness or Covert Control?', *Sociology*, 36, 4 (2002), pp.965–83.

Southgate, W., *That's The Way It Was: A Working Class Autobiography 1890–1950* (London: New Clarion, 1982).

Stearns, P.N., 'Fatherhood in Historical Perspective: The Role of Social Change', in F.W. Bozett and S.M.H. Hanson (eds), *Fatherhood and Families in Cultural Context* (New York: Springer, 1991), pp.2–23.

Swidler, A., *Talk of Love: How Culture Matters* (Chicago, IL: University of Chicago Press, 2001).

Tobin, F., *The Best of Decades: Ireland in the Nineteen Sixties* (Dublin: Gill & Macmillan, 1984).

Touraine, A., *The Voice and the Eye: An Analysis of Social Movements* (Cambridge: Cambridge University Press, 1981).

Travers, P., *Eamon de Valera* (Dundalk: Dundalgan Press, 1994).

Ussher, J., *Women's Madness: Misogyny or Mental Illness?* (London: Harvester Wheatsheaf, 1991).

Warren, A., 'Popular Manliness: Baden Powell, Scouting and the Development of Manly Character', in J.A. Mangan and J. Walvin (eds), *Manliness and Morality: Middle Class Masculinity in Britain and America, 1800–1940* (Manchester: Manchester University Press, 1987), pp.198–217.

Weeks, J., *Coming Out: Homosexual Politics in Britain from the Nineteenth Century to the Present* (London: Quartet, 1977).

Weeks, J., *Sexuality and its Discontents: Meanings, Myths and Modern Sexualities* (London: Routledge, 1985).

Weeks, J., 'Capitalism and the Organisation of Sex', in Gay Left Collective (ed.), *Homosexuality: Power and Politics* (London: Allison & Busby, 1988), pp.11–20.

Weeks, J., *Sex, Politics and Society: The Regulation of Sexuality since 1800* (London: Longman, 1989).

Weeks, J., 'The Construction of Homosexuality', in S. Seidman (ed.), *Queer Theory/Sociology* (Cambridge: Blackwell, 1996), pp.41–63.

Wouters, C., 'Balancing Sex and Love since the 1960s Sexual Revolution', *Theory, Culture & Society*, 15, 3–4 (1998), pp.187–214.

Wouters, C., *Sex and Manners: Female Emancipation in the West 1890–2000* (London: Sage, 2004).

Wouters, C., *Informalization: Manners and Emotions since 1890* (London: Sage, 2007).

Yeates, N., 'Gender and the Development of the Irish Social Welfare System', in B. Byrne and M. Leonard (eds), *Women and Irish Society* (Belfast: Beyond the Pale Publications, 1997), pp.145–69.

Zeegers, W., *De Zonnige zijde van seks: De nawerking van positef beleedfde seksualiteit* (Leiden: DSWO Press, 1994).

Zelizer, V., *Pricing the Priceless Child* (Princeton, NJ: Princeton University Press, 1985).

Index